To Charles,
with best wishes

The God Secret

Greg Rigby

Eloquent Books
New York, New York

Strategic Book Publishing
An imprint of AEG Publishing Group
845 Third Avenue, 6th Floor – 6016
New York, NY 10022
www.eloquentbooks.com

ISBN: 978-1-60693-828-7   1-60693-828-2

Printed in the United States of America

Book Design: Arlinda Van, Dedicated Business Solutions, Inc.

Acknowledgements

The author is grateful for the help he has received from family and friends during the period in which this book was researched and compiled. In particular, the work that was carried out decoding the Book of Revelation by Merrilye Ganemyr and the support and encouragement by Sarah, my wife, and by John and Joy Miller, architect-planners of the Saunière Society.

Contents

Introduction

During the recent past, the proliferation of new web sites has given access to information to an ever-wider audience. Unfortunately, much of this data is a replication of biased historical text that perpetuates the status quo. New ideas are sometimes presented on blog pages, but they are frequently limited by their author's existing knowledge of the subject and by any belief system to which he or she subscribes.

This book attempts to transcend these limitations and therefore requires the reader to examine the evidence presented with an open mind.

Questioning the origins and foundations of the world's great religions is generally considered taboo by the believers within each particular religion. So much so is this the case that authors and researchers must be careful not to offend or confront them for fear of reprisal.

Here we seek to understand the motivation of the constructors of one of the world's greatest ancient and historical monuments. In doing so, we are forced to examine the compelling pattern found in this construction and to link it with other similar patterns from ancient times.

Ancient monuments of whatever kind were usually connected to reverence of a deity and, more often than not, are constructed to acknowledge celestial coincidences. Often, their location and orientation give clues to the belief system that underpinned their existence. This is the case with the construction that you will read about here. Its location and its shape provide a link to the origins of the Judeo-Christian religions in Egypt and provoke questions that have never previously been aired. In particular, the evidence presented suggests a conspiracy of silence concerning the stories told about God in his many and varied forms and an ancient link between these stories and other myths and legends that have provoked the human psyche.

Since the beginning, the human race has been at the mercy of those propounding "belief in God." Ordinary people did not have first-hand experience of any divine entity. Instead, they latched onto a mechanism of belief that was propounded by priests, kings, and mystics. It can now be seen that named deities, theatrical stories, and threats of reward and punishment were most likely born in surmise and the misinterpretation of scientific facts as the "wise men" concocted stories from pictures they drew in the stars.

These same belief systems are perpetuated today by those who dare to speak for "the Lord" and they are supported by a hidden conclave that, for reasons we could only imagine, seems to have a vested interested in retaining the status quo.

Yet an enormous intellectual achievement is presumed in this organization of Heaven, in naming the constellations and in tracing the paths of the planets. Lofty and intricate theories grew to account for the motions of the Cosmos. One would wonder about the obsessive concern with the stars and their motion, were it not the case that those earthly thinkers thought they had located the gods which ruled the universe and with it also the destiny of the soul down here and after death.

—Hamlet's Mill; Giorgio de Santallina
and Hertha Von Dechend

Chapter One

The Discovery

The most well-known and easily discernible star constellation in the Northern Hemisphere is Ursa Major. It is also known as the Plough, the Chariot, and the Big Dipper (Fig 1).

In 1997, the book *On Earth as it is in Heaven* detailed the incredible discovery that the constellation of Ursa Major had at one time been duplicated across 302.4 miles of Northern Europe (Fig 2).

Four of the seven points of the ground pattern lie at the center point of the four prominent French cathedrals in Chartres, Reims, St. Quentin, and Verdun. Another of the points lies on an ancient Celtic Fort at Donnersberg in West

Fig 1 Ursa Major, known popularly as the Plough, Chariot, or Big Dipper

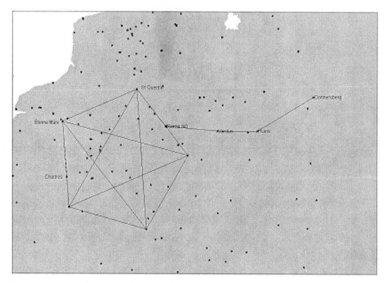

Fig 2 the ground pattern in Northern France

Germany. The remaining two points have no evidence of any edifice, religious or otherwise, albeit that one of the sites is located in a village with the evocative name of Bonne Mare (Good Mother), a title not that far removed from the "Notre Dame" designation enjoyed by many of the cathedrals. The arduous task of locating these seven points is described in detail in *On Earth as it is in Heaven* and will remove much of the skepticism that any new recruit to the subject would quite naturally evince. Suffice it to say that if one draws a line from the center of every cathedral in what was Gaul to the center of every other cathedral, there are seven points where more of the lines intersect than they do anywhere else. These seven points form a shape that copies the shape of the constellation of Ursa Major.

The cathedrals were constructed on the sites of the first Christian churches. These same early churches were deliberately and methodically constructed on ancient Celtic religious sites. Because of this and because one of the locations is an acknowledged Celtic site, it is not difficult to conclude that the ground pattern was put down in pre-Christian times. The infamous Druids have yet another extraordinary construction to answer for.

An examination of this enormous seven-point pattern produced some extraordinary facts:

- The interior angles of the cup are both 108°.
- The overall length is 302.4 miles, which equals 1,050,000 Greek cubits, 2,520 Greek furlongs, 1,386,000 Egyptian feet, and 924,000 Egyptian cubits. 2,520 Greek furlongs is significant because in *Timaeus,* Plato defines the world number as 114048, which John Michell analyses to show the diameter of the world soul to be 252 platonic units[1].

The interior angles of 108° invite the construction of a regular pentagon and its interior pentagram inside the cup. When this is done, a series of additional geometric co-incidences emerge (Fig 3).

- The line from the cathedral in St. Quentin to the opposite corner of the pentagon goes through the center of Notre Dame in Paris (Fig 3).
- The line from the cathedral in Verdun to the cathedral at Chartres goes through the center of the pentagon (Fig 3).
- Three circles made around the same center point go through all seven of the points of the pattern of the constellation (Fig 3).

Perhaps more remarkably, the ancient Paris meridian precisely and accurately bisects the base of the cup (Fig 46). The coordinates of the seven points were plotted with care and this intersection is accurate to the foot, a precision that it is almost beyond belief.

The ancient Paris meridian was delineated in the seventeenth century and preceded the current zero meridian

[1] John Michell, The Dimensions of Paradise (Thames and Hudson 1988) Chapter 4

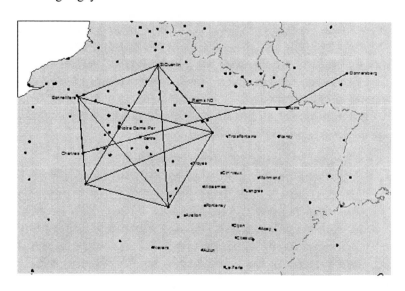

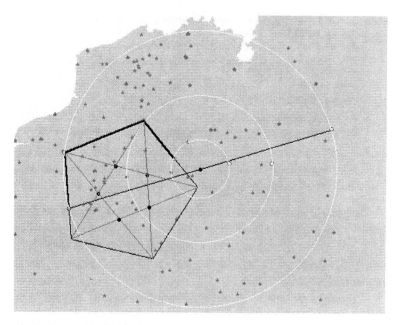

Fig 3 The ground pattern with its geometric additions

through Greenwich. If its position was chosen at that time, it would mean that someone from then knew of the ground pattern and arranged that it cut the base of the pattern. Such an unlikely enterprise, involving the deception of Louis XVI, the king of France, could only have been undertaken for esoteric reasons and it is unlikely that it could have remained a closely guarded secret for so long. The other and more likely possibility was that the meridian was constructed on a line that had been specified many centuries previously, that the seventeenth century architects somehow had access to its precise location and they did not realize its significance in relation to the ground pattern. Again we are forced to conclude that this is an ancient pattern.

Another clue to the ancient origins of the ground pattern might be its orientation. If we look into the northern sky, at the constellation of Ursa Major, then we see the picture in Fig 4.

If we are located anywhere in the northern hemisphere and we lie on the ground with our heads pointing north,

Fig 4 Ursa Major as we see it when standing up looking northwards

the picture we see is different. This is the pattern that corresponds to the ground pattern in Northern France.

In other words, the ground pattern could only have originated in a time when its designers studied the northern sky this way (lying down on the ground)—and that can only have been in the most ancient of times.

An alternative view of Ursa Major can be obtained in northern latitudes where there is limited sunlight/daylight in mid-winter. During the dark winter months, inhabitants of these northern latitudes see the constellation in the daytime, when it has rotated around the pole, until its appearance (to the observer) is similar to that in Fig 5. For this second explanation to be the reason for the orientation of the ground plan, it would mean that the pattern was designed by architects that originated from latitudes of 67° and upwards (inside the Arctic Circle), a possibility we will return to examine in a later chapter.

When the ground pattern was examined, it was found that a connection could be made with the Temple of Isis at Philae by extrapolating lines that connect the seven points. An-

Fig 5 Ursa Major as seen lying on the ground with head facing North

other line runs from the stone circle at Avebury in Southern England, through the Cathedrals in St. Quentin and Verdun, through Ephesus in Turkey and on to Mount Sion in Jerusalem. These connections imply a universal pattern that links the ancient religions of Northern Europe to the religions of Egypt and the Middle East.

An interesting connection to Ancient Greece was discovered linked to the subject of Gematria, Isopsephia, or numerology. In ancient times, each Hebrew and Greek letter was attributed a numerical value. Accordingly, each word had a value, which was the sum of the values of the letters it contained.

Chapter one of the Book of Revelation contains the phrase "The mystery of the Seven Stars." The numerical value of this phrase is 4,540 and equals the numerical value of Kallisto (Ursa Major) plus Son of the Cosmos (the pentagram) plus the outer pentagon plus the inner pentagon. It also equals the values of the phrases "Amen behold he comes with the clouds" and "Naked he walks and they see the shame."

There is an abundance of additional mathematical and geometric information that can be extracted from the pattern and from the numerical value of sacred names and phrases that relate to it. All of this data creates a mountain of evidence to indicate that the construction represents something that had a deep and comprehensive religious significance to its creators.

When examining some of the evidence that was compiled when writing *On Earth as it is in Heaven*, a series of strange discoveries was unearthed related to the foundations of the Cistercians in the eleventh and twelfth centuries. The first Abbey of the Cistercians was constructed at Citeaux in AD 1098. Three years later in AD 1101, the Abbey was moved "half a league" further south and oriented in a slightly different direction. The new location created a precise and direct line from Cluny (the founding Abbey of the Benedictines) through the new Abbey of Citeaux to the sixth point of the ground pattern at Landonvillers (Fig 6). In later years, two

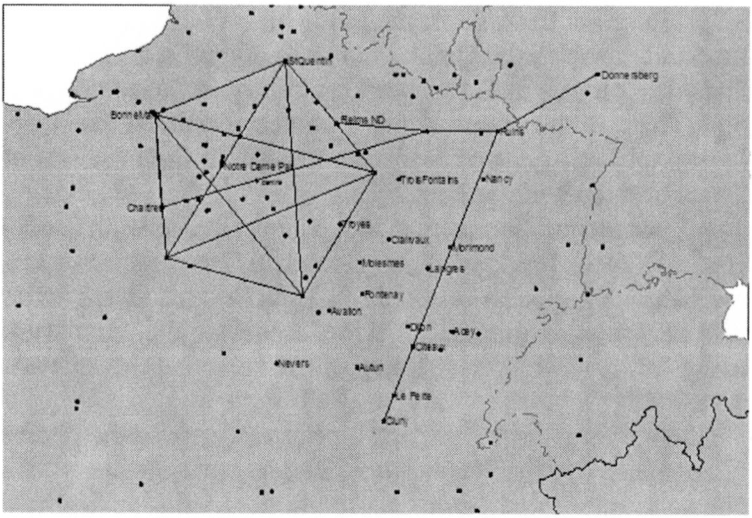

Fig 6 the connections made by moving the abbey at Citeaux

additional Cistercian Abbeys were to be constructed on this same line, at La Férté and Morimond.

The orientation of the new Abbey at Citeaux was directly towards one of the corners of the Pentagon held by the ground plan.

In AD 1115, three years after he joined the Cistercians, St. Bernard established an Abbey at Clairvaux. Twenty years later, this Abbey, too, was reconstructed. This time, the Abbey was moved a mere 500 meters. The new position created a series of alignments so accurate that they are beyond the bounds of coincidence (Fig 7):

- The line from Citeaux II through the cathedral at Dijon and through the center of the Abbey at Clairvaux II goes directly to the bottom corner of the pentagram.
- The line from Clairvaux II to the center of Notre Dame Cathedral in Reims goes through the centre of Abbey St. Remi.

• The line from the center of the Abbey at Mont St. Michel to the center of Clairvaux II goes through the center of Chartres cathedral and extends on to the Abbey at Morimond.

The precise alignments, created by the movement of two of the earliest and most prominent Cistercian Abbeys, are evidence beyond doubt that someone involved in choosing the position of those early Abbeys was aware of the ground copy of Ursa Major. More than that, this same person or persons had access to the same kind of accurate positioning techniques used to pinpoint the ground positions of the seven points that constitute the image of the constellation.

All of this information has remained a secret until now. The fact that the secret has stayed hidden for so long means that its guardians were confident that the information they possessed was worth the efforts that they made to keep it concealed. Thus we have prima-facie evidence of a conspiracy of silence by a group of Cistercians and possibly by

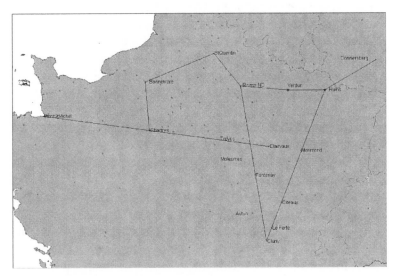

Fig 7 the connections made by Clairvaux II

the founding members of the Knights Templar who were so closely associated with them.

There has been much speculation about the enigmatic warrior monks who made up *The Order of the Poor Knights of the Temple of Solomon*, later called *The Knights Templar*. Intriguingly, it is suggested by many devotes that The Knights Templar discovered some cache of information whilst tunneling under the Dome of the Rock in Jerusalem in search of the Ark of the Covenant. Whilst there is no direct proof of this, there is strong circumstantial evidence that they did bring knowledge back to France that provoked the sudden appearance of Gothic architecture in AD 1130. Thereafter, they are known to have acquired enormous power and influence throughout Europe. Many of the castle and strongholds they constructed are still in existence.

A veritable industry of Templar enthusiasts is still at work, trying to uncover the secrets of an organization that was so violently put down in the early fourteenth century. Its proponents claim that a Templar treasure still exists and that, in all probability, it is hidden under the foundations of Rosslyn Chapel near Edinburgh. Others maintain that a group of Templars, who fled to Scotland to avoid certain death, included the originators of the Freemasonry movement, the Freemasons being another organization of people who are reputed to have information that they endeavor to keep concealed. Whatever the current truth, these things are certain:

- The constellation of Ursa Major has been duplicated on the ground in Northern France.
- People using Greek units of measure laid down the construction in pre-Christian times.
- The base or cup of the construction incorporates the shape of a regular pentagon.
- The ancient French meridian bisects the base of the pattern.
- Three circles drawn through the same center point can intersect the seven points.

- There is a link, via Gematria to the Book of Revelation (discussed in more detail in a later chapter).

The only question left to be answered is "why." Why was this massive construction undertaken? What were the architects trying to achieve? To have remained such a closely guarded secret for so long implies that its originators constructed something that they wished to remain invisible to the common eye. Because of that, it is unlike all other massive structures such as Stonehenge and the Pyramids. The most enormous project of all time remains undiscerned. It was completed in ancient times and its existence was known only to its creators.

The secret was carefully guarded through the ages so that the pattern's existence was only known to a privileged few. The architects and builders used their knowledge and efforts to ensure that Druid religious centers in Northern Europe were precisely located to fit a massive pattern that duplicated a constellation that was in plain view to anyone who cared to look up into the northern sky. At the same time, they neglected to make their achievements common knowledge. The ground pattern that has now been uncovered must have been the most closely guarded secret of the Druids and, until now, it has probably been the secret of secrets through all the ages.

Chapter Two

The Horned God

There are two logically possible reasons why this wonderful, precise, and yet mysterious ground pattern was so painstakingly traced across 302.4 miles of northern Europe. Either its designers wanted to construct a monument (out of reverence) to something or someone or they did it to leave some kind of permanent message for the future. Either way, the structure is so grand and so painstakingly located on the ground that it must have reflected something that the designers perceived as awesome.

If the pattern was constructed out of reverence, there must be additional evidence that in ancient times, the constellation of Ursa Major was looked upon with wonderment and that it attracted some form of veneration. It is not possible that a conception requiring such resources and attention could be based on convictions that did not manifest themselves in other parts of the belief systems of its constructors. For this reason, an examination of the records of gods and religious practices in pre-Christian Gaul was undertaken to search for evidence of the constellation and/or its distinctive pattern.

Ursa Major is most often associated with its seven principal stars. The complete constellation has twenty-three significant stars in addition to the basic seven. The thirty stars (including the double star Alcor in The Plough itself) are illustrated in Fig 8.

Above the base or cup of the traditional "Plough" or "Big Dipper," there are two appendages that look like a stag's horns. To the sides of the cup are two further appendages that are more like the horns of a ram. So striking are these appendages that they provoked a search for references to "horns" in the lit-

Fig 8 Ursa Major with its horns

erature concerning the Celts and their religious practices. Not surprisingly, such references were not difficult to find. Horned entities have been revered from the most ancient of times and, in some dates, they predate the Celts.

Cave drawings and carvings have been located in Europe that indicate that an entity with antlers was revered from the earliest of times. The earliest of these is the painted image made fifteen thousand years ago and found at Les Trois Frères in the Pyrenees (Fig 9). Over one hundred and forty thousand paintings and carvings were located at Valcamonica in Northern Italy. They date from circa 8000 BC and include carvings and engravings of animals and human shaped entities sporting horns or antlers (Fig 10).

This ancient reverence for horned beings grew into a well-documented tradition of horned gods in Celtic/Druidic Gaul.

Fig 9 the image found at Les Trois Fréres

The name given to the Gallic/Celtic horned God that has been located on most of the Celtic carvings, coins, and pottery in Europe is Cernunnus. With little evidence, he has been variously described as "Lord of the Beasts" and "Patron of Commercial Prosperity,"[2] "Lord of the Animals,"[3] "Lord of the Living Beings,"[4] and "Lord of Beasts and Fecundity."[5] These modern researchers have no way of knowing his ac-

[2] *Anne Ross, Pagan Celtic Britain, Hutchinson Radius (January 1997)*
[3] *Proinsias MacCana, Celtic Mythology, Hamlyn (1970)*
[4] *David Rankin, Celts and the Classical World, Routledge (1996)*
[5] *Miranda Green, Symbol and Image in Celtic Religious Art, Routledge, (1992)*

Fig 10 engravings found at Valcamonica

tual area of jurisdiction. Suffice it to say that these various claims seem to coincide well with a similar spread of influence attributed to both Dionysius in Greece and Osiris in Egypt. Two famous engravings are believed to illustrate him (other than the picture found at Valcamonica). In AD 1891,

Fig 11 Cernunnus on the Gundestrop Cauldron

the remains of a Cauldron were found in a dry section of a peat bog at Gundestrop in Himmerland, Denmark. It was made of ninety-seven percent pure silver and engraved with various motifs of animals, plants, and pagan deities. Central amongst the engravings is a figure seated amongst animals (Fig 11), who researchers believe to be Cernunnus.[2]

It is possible that Cernunnus and the various animals is a stylized depiction of the northern star constellations (Draco, Leo Minor, Leo Major, Lynx, Canis etc . . .) that are adjacent to Ursa Major and rotate around the Northern Pole position.

The second famous monument was found in Paris. It is located under Notre Dame and features a carving that is believed to be a depiction of the same god. Discernible on the block is the relief of a bust of a balding man with antlers on which are hung torcs. As well as antlers, he has the ears of a deer. Over his head is the inscription generally read as "Cernunnus" (Fig 12).

When Julius Caesar conquered Gaul, he kept a record of his experiences. In these records he states that the Celts used

---

[2] *Anne Ross, Pagan Celtic Britain, Hutchinson Radius (January 1997)*

Fig 12 the Paris carving, believed to be Cernunnus

Greek letters, and that the representations of their gods were the same or similar to the Roman gods Jupiter and Mercury, gods which were a Romanization of the Greek gods Zeus and Hermes. In addition, there is evidence that Cernunnus was connected with the Greek gods Hercules and Apollo. Cernunnus is shown with Hercules, once on the back of a statuary group from Saintes and again on a lost altar from Le Chatelet.[6] He is joined by Apollo three times, twice on carvings from Reims (Fig 13) and once from Vendeuvres. In these pictures, Apollo is depicted on Cernunnus's right and Mercury/Hermes on his left.

Another interesting depiction was found on an ancient coin in Hertfordshire, England (Fig 14). The picture on this coin has been the source of considerable debate. What we

---

[6] Bober, Phyllis Pray, *Cernunnos: Origin and Transformation of a Celtic Divinity*, American Journal of Archaeology 55 (1951) 13–51.

Fig 13 the Reims carving of Cernunnus, Apollo, and Hermes

Fig 14 coin depicting the head of Cernunnus

know is that it depicts a horned figure with a provocative pattern held in a circle between the horns.

Horned gods (and some horned goddesses) are also found, though more rarely, across all of southern England, from Kent to Somerset and from Suffolk to Staffordshire. In some instances, they are attributed to Herne the Hunter, the entity who inherited the Cernunnus crown.

Outside the British Isles, there are records of ancient horned gods in Mesopotamia, Greece, Egypt, and Italy.

We have archaeological evidence that in 3000 BC, the Sumerians could create carvings that had a three dimensional effect. Fig 15 shows an angel or a winged being following a horned God. In 2000 BC, we see engravings of a winged creature in Assyria and Babylonia (Fig 16). One thousand years later, these winged creatures have matured into the Lamassu. These strange creatures were a mixture of bull and lion and had a human head. They had wings and horns decorating their ornamental caps. The five legs allowed them to appear to be striding forward from the side and standing firmly when viewed from the front (Fig 17). Not long afterward we see evidence of Mithra in Persia. Mithras (Fig 18) was a light-bringer god, whose cult flourished between 1500 BC and the time of Christ, in lands as far apart as India and Great Britain, with a basis in what was then known as Persia.

Fig 15 Sumerian winged being following a horned god

Fig 16 Winged Babylonian
entity

Fig 17 The Lamassu

Fig 18 Mithras wearing his Phrygian cap

The details of this religion are a mystery but it is proposed by researchers to have been based on worship of the cosmos and the various constellations it contains.[7]

Mithraism was the most prevalent religion in Persia when Zoroaster was alive. In the Zoroastrian religion Mithras was considered to be an angel (Fig 19) who mediated between

---

[7] David Ulansey, The Origins of the Mithraic Mysteries, Oxford University Press, USA (1991)

Fig 19 Mithras with wings

heaven and earth and who later becoming judge and pre-
server of the created world.

Zoroaster was living in Persia around 650 BC. He spread
a monotheistic religious message that became the religion of
the Persian Empire. Zoroastrianism identifies six archangels
along with at least forty lesser angels called "adorable ones."
All of them were considered to be aspects or manifestations
of the "Lord of Light."

In the Greek pantheon there are an abundance of gods and
goddesses sporting horns or wings; Pan or Faunus (Fig 22),
Apollo (as Karnean), Dionysus, Hermes, Io (Fig 21), and
Zeus.

Fig 20 a Zoroastrian angel

Dis or Dis Pater was the one all-mighty God of the Druids, responsible for and progenitor of humanity in the same way that Jehovah was the "One God" of the Jews.

The Roman god Jupiter (Fig 23) was the Greek god Zeus. He was the supreme deity of classical antiquity and was akin

Fig 21 Io the consort of Zeus

Fig 22 Pan or Faunus

Fig 23 Jupiter

Fig 24 Jupiter-Amon

to the Egyptian god Amon as Jupiter Amon (Fig 24). He was the father of mankind.

Anne Ross, the acknowledged authority on Cernunnus tells us that the horned god was "associated with Jupiter." At the same time, Ward Rutherford tells us that the names "Jupiter" and "Dis Pater" have the same Indo-European origin and are one and the same.[8] "Another Indo-European root, dyeus peter, interpreted as 'father God' yields Jupiter as well as Dispater whom Caesar declares to have been the most important of all the Celtic gods."[9] This idea fits well with the varied claims that Cernunnus was Dis Pater on the one hand and Jupiter on the other.

---

[8] *Ward Rutherford, Celtic Lore, Thorsons Publishers (May 1993)*
[9] *Rutherford. Celtic Lore*

This simple and attractive idea of the two names for the same divinity would seem to have been contradicted by Julius Caesar:

> Besides this they (the Druids) have many discussions as touching the stars and their movement, the size of the universe, and of the earth, the order of nature, the strength and the powers of the immortal gods, and hand down their power to the young men.
>
> Among the gods, they most worship Mercury. There are numerous images of him; they declare him the inventor of the arts, the guide for every road and journey, and they deem him to have the greatest influence for all money making and traffic. After him they set Apollo, Mars, Jupiter and Minerva. Of these deities, they have almost the same idea as all other nations: Apollo drives away diseases, Minerva supplies the first principles of arts and crafts, Jupiter holds the empire of Heaven and Mars controls wars.
>
> The Gauls affirm that they are all descended from a common father, Dis, and say that this is the tradition of the Druids. For that reason they determine all periods of time by the number, not of days, but of nights, and in their observance of birthdays and in the beginnings of months and years day follows night.[10]

The contradiction lies in his claims that "Among the Gods they most worship Mercury," "Jupiter holds the empire of Heaven," and "The Gauls affirm that they are all descended from a common father, Dis."

The idea that "Above all other gods they worship Mercury" is confirmed by Tacitus.[11]

These conflicting statements invite us to resolve how the Celts could have revered Dis Pater above all else and, at the same time, have relegated Jupiter to second place behind Mercury. Such an idea would not seem to be consistent if Dis Pater (revered above all things) and Jupiter (revered second to Mercury) were one and the same.

[10] *Julius Caesar, The Gallic War, Oxford University Press USA (March 1999)*
[11] *Tacitus, The Agricola, Penguin Classics (1971)*

By way of explanation, we can look at analogous Christian practice. To an outsider, it might seem as though Christians put Jesus before God the Father. Christ, the Son, is the active principal of the godhead whilst the less outspoken Father retains the power. Christ is the messenger whilst his heavenly father is "the word."

In the Roman framework, Jupiter achieved his dominant position by usurping his own father, Saturn (Cronos). Jupiter, with his brothers Neptune and Pluto (Dis), then divided the dominions so that Jupiter took control of the Heavens, Neptune the oceans, and Pluto the realm of the dead. Earth was common property and all three divine principals had an equal claim. On earth, they were different aspects of the same divinity. Mercury or Hermes was the son of Jupiter and was his messenger. He was the link between Heaven and Earth, between God and man. As such, he was a Gallo-Roman version of the Christ figure.

Perhaps significantly, Mercury was believed to preside over science and commerce, wrestling, and thieving, and was patron of travelers and rogues, vagabonds and thieves. The fact that Caesar tells us of Mercury being ". . . the inventor of all arts, the guide for every road and journey, and they deem him to have the greatest influence for all money-making and traffic" might in reality be a clue to the type of activities that were prevalent among the Celts in AD 50 and it might say nothing of Caesar's view of the divine hierarchy.

The solution, however, lies in Caesar's statement, "There are numerous images of him." Since the names of the Roman and Gallic god(s) must have been different, Caesar must have made his deductions from the images he saw. He is telling us that (to him) the images were similar to those he was used to seeing that represented the Roman god Mercury. It is noteworthy, therefore, that the wings on Mercury's helmet (Fig 25) bear a very strong resemblance to the antlers of Ursa Major.

Fig 25 Mercury with his winged helmet

Horned gods and some horned goddesses are also found, though more rarely, across all of southern England, from Kent to Somerset and from Suffolk to Staffordshire. They are indeed, common across northern Europe in both Celtic and Germanic areas and found in the Mediterranean in the form of Pan and (in some incarnations) Faunus. Pagan iconography would hardly miss such an obvious symbol of power and pride. Those in Britain may all have been negative personalities. But some may have been images of Roman deities such as Mars, upon whom horns were put by local artists used to conceiving gods in this way. Some of the icons of Mercury in Britain made his winged helmet into something uncommonly like a horned head.[12]

One thing is certain: the previously little know god Cernunnus (Dis Pater) was in reality a personification of the most

[12] *Ronald Hutton, The Pagan Religions of the Ancient British Isles, Wiley-Blackwell (1993)*

Fig 26 a relief of Osiris with ram's horns

powerful and all encompassing deities known to mankind. He was the equivalent of the Jewish Jehovah. "The British Dis, in fact, was no mere Pluto but a universal God corresponding closely with the Jehovah of the Hebrew prophets. The Lord of the Seven-Day-Week was Dis, the transcendental God of the Hyperboreans, whose secret name was betrayed to Gwydion. The connection between the early myths of the Hebrews, Greeks and the Celts is that all three races were civilized by the same Aegean people whom they conquered and absorbed. The Bran cult seems also to have been imported from the Aegean."[13]

Cernunnus was the same deity as the Roman Jupiter and the Greek Zeus. In other aspects he was also seen as Mercury, Apollo, Pluto, Typhon, and even Cronos.[14]

The one place left of significance where one can readily demonstrate the existence of horned and winged gods and goddesses is Egypt. There, the study of the Heavens was integral to the Egyptian's religion and to the identity of the gods in the Egyptian pantheon. Amongst the principal deities, Osiris (Fig 26) was normally portrayed as horned, and Anubis (Fig 27) was portrayed with ears that could just as

[13] Robert Graves, The White Goddess, Faber and Faber (1999)
[14] Caitlin & John Matthews, The Encyclopedia of Celtic Wisdom, (paperback) Element Books Ltd (2000)

Fig 27 the god Anubis

easily be horns. The goddesses Hathor (Fig 28) and Isis were portrayed with cows' horns and Isis (Fig 29) and Maat with wings.

The other principal gods who have been identified with Celtic times are Esus (Silvanus in the Latinized version), Smertullus, Sucellus, Hu, Teutates, The Daghda (in Ireland), Culchulainn, and Ceridwen. All of these deities have in com-

Fig 28 the goddess Hathor with horns

Fig 29 the goddess Isis with horns and wings

mon that they were associated with a hammer or club and, at the same time, with some form of cup or cauldron. Is it just a coincidence that these attachments can so easily be located in the constellation of Ursa Major?

At a purely visual level, it is easy to see how the pattern made by the seven principal stars could have been thought to encompass both of these items. Viewed vertically (Fig 30), we can see a club, hammer, or axe.

Viewed in a different position on the constellation's apparent journey (second part of Fig 30), we have the key part of the same constellation that can be perceived as a cauldron or cup. By observing the stars during different hours in the earth's rotational cycle, the constellation of Ursa Major can therefore be viewed as horns, club, ladle, or cup.

Dis-Pater is the same god as Jupiter who was and who emanated from the same source as the Hebrew Jehovah, the Greek Zeus, and the Egyptian Amon-Ra. At the same time, Dis is closely associated with Pluto, god of the underworld, the realm of Lucifer, the horned one.

The greatest of divine mysteries from our past seem to come together as we peel the layers of understanding from a pattern that has been duplicated on the landscape of Northern Europe. Does Ursa Major, the most prominent constellation in

Fig 30 Ursa Major in its aspect of club or hammer (left) and cup or ladle (right)

the northern sky, the constellation most easily recognized by every person in the street, contain the secrets of the ancients? Is its apparent rotation about the Pole Star a parody, mocking our feeble attempts to locate the divine? Could it be that, since the most ancient times, it was believed to contain the creator of time and the father of mankind?

On Earth as it is in Heaven suggests a possible connection between the ground pattern and the Grail myths. While it will be necessary to return to the question of *"the grail"* in a later chapter, this proposition missed the truth that is so glaringly obvious, now that it has been pointed out. The complex pattern that duplicates the constellation of Ursa Major in Northern Europe is more likely to be a reverential acknowledgement of and statement about the supreme godhead. It incorporates the story of the gods and could demonstrate how there can be one all-powerful God who has, at the same time, a number of different, separate, and living aspects of his self. The pattern's measurements and geometry are so carefully measured and so exactingly precise that analysis of the geometry it contains may open the Pandora's Box that shows us the ancient knowledge that so-called initiates or illuminati have kept hidden for so long.

As well as attempting to uncover the significance of the pattern, it behooves the searcher for truth to understand the motivation of those who successfully concealed the greatest temple on Earth from mankind. What was it that provoked the powers-that-be to keep this extraordinary construction secret from all but the initiated? Perhaps more importantly, how have they managed to keep this knowledge hidden for so long?

There is, of course, a possibility that it was never hidden or even lost. It is conceivable that historians and analysts of ancient customs and myths got caught up in the names and imagery of the many gods and were unable to understand the underlying principals without the benefit of being steeped in the culture of the temple's creators, so much so that they treated the designations as self-defining and did not link them back to their divine (and therefore hidden) origins.

MacCulloch tells us that Irish and Welsh cognates of Mercury are "Arthur" and "Ploughed land."

> Three divinities have claims to be the God whom Caesar calls Dispater—a God with a hammer, a crouching God called Cernunnus, and a God called Esus or Silvanus. The native names of the gods assimilated with Mercury are many in number: in some instances they are epithets derived from the names of places where a local "Mercury" was worshipped, in others they are derived from some function of the gods. One of these titles is Artaios, perhaps cognate with Irish art, "God" or connected with artos "bear." Professor Rhys however finds its cognate in Welsh dr, "ploughed land," as if one of the god's functions connected him with agriculture.[15]

Perhaps our ancestors simply lost interest in the winged messenger god Mercury and picked up and remembered the Plough or Bear designation as the old and powerful gods were replaced by a more fashionable (and more heavily prosecuted) Christian ethos.

We know that from ancient times there has been a consistent belief in "One God" and that different civilizations have succeeded in portraying different aspects of that "One God" by a variety of forms, personalities, and titles. What we have not seen anywhere (until now) is an ancient portrayal of Almighty God himself. He has been hidden behind his many aspects and the only true representation (if that is what it is) has remained a closely guarded secret. In the coming chapters, we will examine the possibility that the pattern that has been duplicated in Northern France is a representation of the "One-Great-God" of the heavens in his many aspects.

---

[15] J A MacCulloch, The Religion of the Ancient Celts,.Constable (1991)

Chapter Three

The Ancient "God-Protector"
Hidden by His Many Disguises

The current designations of the constellation of the Ursa Major around the world are Big Dipper (USA), Great Bear (universal), Plough and "butcher's Cleaver" (UK), Chariot, Great Wagon, Men's Wagon, Casserole, Salmon Net (Europe), and Seven Sages, The Ladle, and The Seven Stars of the Northern Dipper (India and the Far East).

Many of the European appellations are based in antiquity. Their origins stem from an inevitable evolution of words and titles as Celts, Greeks, Norsemen, Romans, Huns, and Visigoths marched their culture, language, and influence into Northern Europe. The Greek Hermes or Roman Mercury was closely associated with a Bear, Plough, and Ploughman.

> If the earlier form of his name was Artor, "a ploughman," but perhaps with a wider significance, and having an equivalent in Artaius, a Gaelic god equated with Mercury.
>
> An old bear cult gave place to the cult of a bear-goddess and probably a god. At Berne—an old Celtic place name, meaning "bear"—was found a bronze group of a goddess holding a patera with fruit and a bear approaching her as if to be fed
>
> From an old Celtic Artos, fem Arta, "bear" were derived various divine names. Of these, Dea Artio (n) means "bear goddess" and Artaios equated with Mercury, is perhaps a bear god. Another bear goddess, Andarta, was honored at Die (Drome), the word perhaps meaning "strong bear"—and being an augmentive. Numerous place names derived from Artos perhaps bear witness to a wide spread cult of the bear, and the word also occurs in Welsh and Irish personal names—Arthmael, Arthbiu and possibly Arthur, and the

numerous Arts of Irish texts. Descent from the divine bear is also signified in names like Welsh Arthgen, Irish Artigen, from Artigenos, "son of bear." Another Celtic name for bear was the Gaulish matu, Irish math, found in Matugenos, "son of bear," and in Mac-Mahon, which is the corrupt form of Mac-Math-ghamhain "son of the bear's son" or "of the bear."[16]

Names such as Plough, Bear, and Arthur created their own imagery, which successive generations embellished. As a consequence, and helped by the uncontrollable power of human imagination, these initial designations soon had to share their existence with exciting mythological ideas of King Arthur, the knights of the round table, the cup or cauldron, the grail, the hammer, an axe or club, the tree of knowledge, the sword, and the throne of the god-king.

There is now strong reason to believe that these latter designations can each trace their separate existences in religious mythology and popular folklore to the same intrusive group of seven stars. Perhaps of more concern for those who have been encouraged to put their trust in one all-powerful God, it is possible that all the great religions of the Western World owe their origins to a catalogue of fanciful deductions that have been made concerning the constellation of Ursa Major.

Caesar informed us that the Druids "used Greek letters," implying that the use of Greek was a general state of affairs, rather than the particular activity of one isolated Druid. To obtain such a universal situation, there must have been considerable interplay between the Druids and their counterparts among Greek poets and philosophers over a prolonged period.

Alternatively, Greek letters (or what looked to the Romans like Greek letters) may have an ancient Celtic derivation:

Plato refers to the Hyperborean letters, and the Celtae or Druids were the Hyperboreans to the ancient Greek. Strabo says of the Turditani who lived in Spain: "These are the wisest amongst the

---

[16] *J A MacCulloch, The Religion of the Ancient Celt, Constable (1991) Chapter XIV Animal Worships: (www.gutenberg.org/files/14672/14672-h/14672-h.htm)*

Iberians. They have letters, and written histories of ancient trans-
actions, and poems, and laws in verse, as they assert, six thousand
years old." Mela, a learned Spaniard, who had special facilities for
ascertaining the origin of the Turditani, affirmed they were part of
the Celtae. According to Xenophon, those letters, which were supposed to have been brought out of Phoenicia into Greece, resem-
bled Gaulish rather than Phoenician characters. This must mean
that the Celtae or Gauls were known to have possessed far back in
the remote past, letters of their own.[17]

All of this would perhaps help to explain why so many
Celtic words and their modern day equivalents had their origins in Greek. Today, when all authors have the opportunity
for entomological research, there are an abundance of texts
claiming widely different derivations for the Greek word for
"bear." These include Artion, Arctos, Arcturus, Arcos, and
Artos. It is no wonder therefore that in a time when communication was more basic, bastardizations of this word grew
into the name Arthur.

The Greek words meaning bear and ploughman, "Artos"
and "Artor," were very similar to one another. Either word
could be an original for Arthur and, because of that, it is possible that Arthur became the word that implied both "bear"
and "ploughman." In a later chapter, we will examine how Arthur became the catalyst for a series of anecdotal tales that incorporated the now famous Grail and we will show how these
"Arthurian Romances" were deeply rooted in the geometry of
the intricate ground pattern put down in Northern France.

The current official appellation of the constellation is Ursa
Major, a Latin expression meaning "Great Bear." In order
to substantiate this "bear" appellation, great effort has been
made to somehow fit a picture of a bear to the star pattern
(Fig 31). Most observers would agree that these pictures are
unsatisfactory.

There are those who believe that the title "bear" was preceded by the "boar" and that the word Hyperborean was used

---

[17] *John Daniel, Philosophy of Ancient Britain: Kennikat Press (1970)*

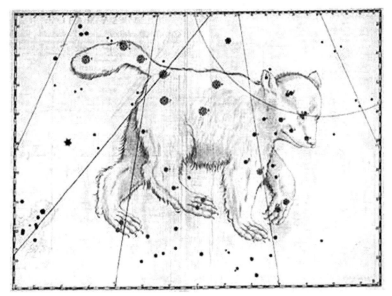

Fig 31 picture of The Great Bear

by the Greeks to describe those northerners who lived under the constellation.

In René Guénon's fascinating study on "The Boar and the Bear," one reads, "The boar formally represented the constellation that later became the Great Bear. This substitution of names is a manifestation of what the Celts symbolized by the conflict of the boar and the bear, that is, the representatives of temporal power against the supremacy of spiritual authority."

In his note Le Roi du Monde, R. Guénon wrote, "The name Arthur has a very remarkable meaning which is related to 'polar' symbolism, which I may explain on another occasion. This name is in fact equivalent to Arcturus. (In Celtic languages, "bear" is Arth.) King Arthur is thus the guardian of the Bear, in other words, the depository of the Hyperborean tradition."[18]

---

[18] *Jean Richer. The Sacred Geography of the Ancient Greeks, State University of New York Press (1994)*

The tradition of the boar was probably stronger among the Irish and the Welsh. In the Irish pantheon, Tuan mac Carill, who is great-grandson of the invader Partholon, is said to have related:

> Then there grew upon my head
> Two antlers with three score points
> So that I am rough and grey in shape
> After my age has changed from feebleness
> After this and from the time that I (Tuan) was in the
> shape of a stag,
> I was the leader of the herds of Ireland, and wherever
> I went there was a large herd of stags about me. . .
> Then I passed into the shape of a wild boar.
> 'Tis then I said:
> A boar am I today among the herds
> A mighty lord I am with great triumphs
> He has put me in wonderful grief,
> The King of all, in many shapes.[19]

The implication of this poem is that there came a time when the antlers or upper protuberances in the constellation became less important and focus narrowed upon the more boar-like shape of the seven stars and the two lower horns where the incumbent was "the King of all." As we have already seen, this evolution continued in Egypt where the gods were endowed with the horns of a ram.

Welsh folklore tells of the magic boar, the Twrch Trwyth, hunted by Arthur, who was captured by a god with the unlikely name of Manawyddan. (This is the same god as the Irish Manannan.) Interestingly, the story of a boar hunt was the first recorded story in which Arthur appeared:

> For the Arthur-as-God hypothesis there is a scintilla of evidence. In
> several parts of the West Country and Wales he is associated with
> a phantom boar-hunt, and a boar-hunt is the main subject of the

---

[19] Matthews, *The Encyclopedia of Celtic Wisdom,*.

earliest story in which Arthur appears—"How Kulhwch won Olwen." However, mythical Celtic boar-hunts predate both Kulhwch and the time in which Arthur was supposed to have reigned. They may even predate the Celts themselves for a famous one occurs in the Greek Adonis myth, suggesting that the theme may once have been the common heritage of a whole group of ethnically related peoples.[20]

It is perhaps significant that the Bear, Boar, and Plough attributions became prevalent following the introduction of Christianity into the lands of the Celts. The Church would not have wanted to admit any affiliation between the Godhead and a prominent group of northern stars. They would therefore have encouraged designations for the constellation that were related to its secular appearance and would have sought to condemn any reference to a horned god. Echoes of this strategy are still evident in the Church's enduring threat of Hell fire and eternal damnation for anyone found consorting with the devil (The Horned One).

In the Middle Ages, when myths re-surfaced concerning Arthur and the cup that became the Grail, the Cistercians cleverly diverted the curiosity of the faithful by having the stories rewritten. The Grail became the cup that Christ drank from at the Last Supper and Arthur and his knights, a luckless band of naive but chivalrous protagonists, got caught up in tales that would have been as provocative and exciting then as Star Trek is today.

Despite this, there is an abundance of evidence that links the seven stars to the Grail Cup or to a chalice that contains abundance in the form of a self reproducing and never ending link to God in one of his most potent forms.

A connection between the cup or cauldron and the pattern of the constellation is easy to make because of the obvious cup-like shape made by four of the seven stars in the constellation (Fig 32).

---

[20] *Rutherford, Celtic Mythology*

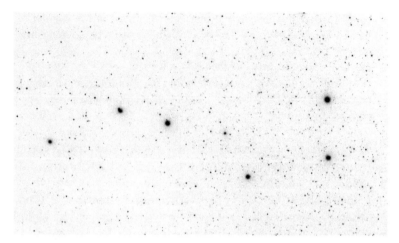

Fig 32 the cup held by the constellation of Ursa Major

An abundance of references to the cup exist in ancient Celtic literature but direct connections to the Ursa Major constellation can only be inferred. These references do give us six prototypes for the now more famous Grail:

1. The pearl-rimmed cauldron of the Head of Annwyn, otherwise known as the cauldron of the Diwrnach or the cauldron of Tyrnoc (the same as the cauldron of Ceridwen according to Lewis Spence).[21]
2. The Cauldron of Britain, of which Manawyd was perpetual guardian.
3. The Cauldron of Bran, (who was practically the double of Manawyd) most often known as the Cauldron of Ceridwen,
4. Manannan's cup of truth.
5. The Cup of Sovereignty in the palace of Lug, which may be synonymous with the Cauldron of Dagda from which no company ever went unthankful.
6. The Cauldron of Blathnat.

---

[21] *Lewis Spence, The Mysteries of Celtic Britain, Siena Publishers Association (1998)*

A link between the ancient cauldron and Arthur (the Great Bear) is nowhere better found than in the now famous poem from the Taliesin entitled "Preiddeu Annwm" (The Spoils of Annwm).[22]

Praise to the Lord, Supreme Ruler of the Heavens,
Who hath extended his dominion to the shore of the world.
Complete was the prison of Gwair in Caer Sidi
Through the spite of Pwyll and Pryderi.
No one before him went into it;
A heavy blue chain firmly held the youth,
And for the spoils of Annwm gloomily he sings,
And till doom shall he continue his lay.
Thrice the fullness of Prydwen we went into it;
Except seven, none returned from Caer Sidi.
Am I not a candidate for fame, to be heard in the song?
In Caer Pedryvan four times revolving,
The first word from the cauldron, when it was spoken?
By the breath of nine damsels is it gently warmed.
It is not the cauldron of the chief of Annwm, in its fashion
With a ridge around its edge of pearls?
It will not boil the food of a coward or of one forsworn,
A sword bright flashing to him will be brought,
And left in the hand of Lleminawg,
And before the portals of the cold place the horns of light shall be
    burning
And when we went with Arthur in his splendid labors,
Except seven, none returned from Caer Vediwid.
Am I not a candidate for fame, to be heard in the song?
In the four-cornered enclosure, in the island of the strong door,
Where the twilight and the black of night move together,
Bright wine was the beverage of the host.
Three times the fullness of Prydwen, we went to sea,
Except seven, none returned to Caer Rigor.
I will not allow praise to the lords of literature.
Beyond Caer Wydr they behold not the prowess of Arthur.
Three times twenty hundred men stood on the wall. (6000)

---

[22] *Graves, The White Goddess*

It was difficult to converse with their sentinel.
Three times the fullness of Prydwen, we went with Arthur.
Except seven none returned to Caer Colur.
I will not allow praise to the men with trailing shields
They know not on what day, or who caused it,
Or at what hour of the splendid day Cwy was born,
Or who prevented him from going to the dales of Devwy.
They know not the bridled ox, with his thick head band,
And seven score knobs on his collar. (140)
And when we went with Arthur of mournful memory
Except seven, none returned from Vaer Vandwy
I will not allow praise to men of drooping courage
They know not on what day the chief arose
Or at what hour in the splendid day the owner was born;
Or what animal they keep of silver head.
When we went with Arthur of mournful contention,
Except seven, none returned from Caer Ochren.

Annwm is the Celtic title of Elysium, the Greek paradise to which heroes on whom the gods conferred immortality were sent. The recurring reference to "seven" relates to the seven principal stars of the constellation of Ursa Major. Robert Graves describes Caer Sidi (the revolving castle) as "the area around the Pole star in which the constellation appears to circulate" and "Prydwen" as "Arthur's magic ship."

The various cauldrons have in common that they are bountiful and a never-ending source of life and sustenance. This aspect is perhaps most easily appreciated now we are aware that the cup contains a regular pentagon (Fig 33). The five-pointed star contained within the pentagon is commonly associated with the occult. Through the star, the five-sided geometric figure is self-creating (see appendix 1). This reproductive feature suggests an interesting foundation for all the ancient myths concerning the virgin birth.

Arthur equated with Mercury, the Roman derivation of Greek Hermes and Egyptian Toth. In the pictures, vase decorations, and statues that remain today, this "Messenger-God" who sponsored commerce and science is depicted wearing

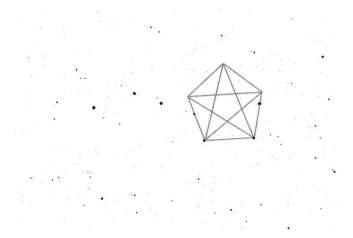

Fig 33 the pentagram within the cup of Ursa Major

a winged cap (Fig 25). In his case, the inverted cup of the constellation became Mercury's cap and the horns became the wings.

Jean Richer makes another interesting connection between this God and the constellation:

> It was quite rightly that pseudo-Hyginus associated Hermes with the constellation of the Charioteer, which is not far from Cyllene in the zodiacal projection. The cult of Hermes seems to have been derived from the religion of the sons of Arcas and the "Pelasgians."
>
> It is clear from Hesiod's Theogony that Hermes was the last-born of the seven great planetary gods.[23]

The sons of Arcas are the Arcadians (the bear people). They are the same people who traveled up the Danube and the Rhine in the first half of the first millennia BC, bringing their customs and culture into Northern France. Since the ground pattern is located largely in this part of France and the pattern's dimensions are plainly Greek, these "noble savages"

---

[23] Richer, *The Sacred Geography of the Ancient Greeks*

lauded by Homer, Pliny, and Xenophon are of considerable interest and a study of them could offer valuable clues to the prosecutors of the God Pattern.

"Zeus united with the bear Callisto, which represents the center and the pole. From this union Arcas was born, who gave his name to Arcadia, the central region of the Peloponnese."[23]

The fact that the French call the constellation "le Chariot" is an indication that they inherited this designation from their multi-colored past. It is based on the similarity of shape between the two-wheeled chariot and horse combination introduced into Egypt by the Hyksos, its later Greek and Roman versions, and the shape of the constellation. As the ground pattern is located in the home of "the Chariot" designation, we might reasonably expect that French custom and culture would give us clues that would help us to convert ancient allegory into direct statements about the pentagonal passenger in the chariot in the sky. In fact, there is a dearth of literature that could help to establish this French attribution, so much so that one is forced to speculate that, at some time in the past, the information was suppressed.

Ancient allusions that could refer to "the Chariot" occur in the Old Testament where Ezekiel in a vision is shown the divine throne-chariot and Elijah is taken up into heaven in a chariot of fire.[24] These are supplemented by references in other ancient writings:

> And that male descendent of the gods that came from the chariot and was seen by her exactly after him, with him as a model, she formed and built the first man. And after that female-formed descendant of the Gods (i.e. the Maiden of Light) that came from the chariot and was seen by the Az, so she had formed and built the first woman.[25]

[24] Bible, Old Testament, 2 Kings 2 - 11
[25] Willis Barnstone, The Other Bible; Manichaean Creation myths (from the speech on Gehmurd and Murdiyanag) Harper One (2005)

Interestingly, the Book of Ezekiel and the Hebrew and Gnostic apocryphal texts quoted above refer to the chariot as the 'throne-chariot'. It is the royal seat of a divine power that surveys the Northern Hemisphere and circulates continually around the Pole. At the same time, these texts point us to a pattern and to male and female shapes coming from the chariot that specifically refer to the quasi human shape in the form of a pentagram that it was known to contain.

Other mythological references to the throne-chariot are many. In all of these references, the chariot has wings (sometimes of fire) or is drawn by winged creatures (cherubim, fiery horses, or swans) or antlered creatures (deer). By including such pictorial description in their texts, the authors ensure that we cannot be mistaken when we attribute the chariot to the Ursa Major constellation. The horn/fire/wing-like projection above the seven stars is easily recognizable and unique in its proximity to a group of stars that was thought to represent a chariot.

Occasionally, attempts to screen the true identity of God are alluded to in the text. These attempts by definition admit to the very thing that they try to conceal:

> The master of the Pole enthroned upon the constellation of the Chariot . . . The most ancient form of the Jewish mysticism was nourished upon the vision of the divine Throne: Here, the revolving spheres are palaces; they are the Hekhaloth, and in the seventh of them (the highest) is the chariot celebrated in the visions of Ezechiel and Daniel, that is, the Throne—Merkaba, the primal image of the Pleroma which contains all the forms of creation. Among the most characteristic elements around this Throne is the curtain, the cosmic veil which screens the glory of their Lord from the hosts of angels, as we find it does in the Book of Enoch.[26]

Chariots were only introduced into Egypt by the Hyksos circa 1720 BC (Fig 34). Prior to this time, all of the Egyptian

[26] *Jean Doresse, The Secret Book of the Egyptian Gnostics, Inner Traditions International (1986)*

Fig 34 the Egyptian Chariot with Ursa Major below

gods were depicted on thrones or barges. This tradition was continued in Greece and Rome so that the earliest Egyptian tomb paintings, Gallic, Greek, and Roman carvings all show their gods enthroned (Fig 35).

An interesting link between the ancient and more recent God-chariot-throne designations is contained in the Book of Revelation. In ancient Greek (the language in which the Book of Revelation was written), the word "horse" (ιππος) also meant chariot. Extracts from Chapter 6 can therefore be read:

> I saw and behold a chariot white/bright and the (one) sitting on it (Rev; 6,2);
> I saw and behold a chariot red and the (one) sitting on it (Rev; 6,4);

Fig 35 Toth, Osiris, and
Jupiter enthroned

I saw and behold a chariot black and the (one) sitting on it (Rev; 6,5);
I saw and behold a chariot green and the (one) sitting on it (Rev; 6,8).

If the chariot refers to our enigmatic constellation, the changes in color can be readily explained by viewings of the sky at different times of the day and night. It might also point to viewings from latitudes much further north than those of Greece and, in that context, would point us once again to possible Hyperborean origins. We will return to the links between Ursa Major and the Book of Revelation in a later chapter.

So important was the throne that it was (and still is today) common to speak of "the king or queen ascending to The Throne." "The Throne" in this context means "the monarchy" and the complete phrase implies "to assume absolute power of the monarch/God-king." The constant always is "The Throne." It is where the power lies. It is where any pretender must be in order to be recognized as God or King.

The horned Egyptian God Khnemu, one aspect of the God of God's, had a sevenfold nature. In one of them, "the Creator" is depicted enthroned. Thus, he creates humankind on his equivalent of a potters-wheel (Fig 36).

The thrones that we have seen have in common that they appear to be square. As there are no obviously square shapes amongst the seven principal stars of the constellation, we would have to look for assistance from other stars in and around the constellation if this shape of a throne is to be found amongst the northern stars as portrayed. In relation to the throne/chariot and its occupant(s), the preponderance of circumstantial evidence implies that it might be possible to combine myth with geometry in an attempt to locate the hidden or unspoken God Amon or the hidden name of God in the Hebrew tradition. First, however, it is necessary to look for other disguises that were meant to conceal God from the uninitiated.

The protrusions that emanate from the seven principal stars of the constellation might have been interpreted as wings

Fig 36 Khnemu enthroned as he creates mankind

(Figs 15-29). Apart from the winged gods and goddesses, the best known winged beings with a quasi-human form are the angels and the devils. These elusive personalities are most easily identified when we realize that, in ancient times, they were thought to be stars. There is an abundance of literature informing us that angels were associated with stars, not the least of which relates to "Lucifer," the archangel who became "the Fallen One." Origen was one of the prominent Christian philosophers in the second and third centuries AD. He was based in Alexandria and, along with Clement, competed for influence of the faithful with Rome. He suggests that Satan is a fallen star and that "the redeemed" will take his place "among the stars of Heaven." Commenting on Revelation 12; 7-9, which says that Michael and his angels cast down the dragon and his angels from heaven, Origin writes:

> Do you not see that the dragon fought with the angels, and when he was hard pressed he was thrown down from Heaven. As he fell he drew with him a third of the stars. It is likely that these stars were

divine powers which had revolted with him, and they were borne down with the dragon, as Isaiah said, "How the morning star fell from Heaven." [27]

This interpretation conjures a picture of stars falling below the horizon and hangs well with the idea that the seven archangels were the seven principal stars of the constellation of Ursa Major, guarding the throne of God:

> . . . a carefully graded hierarchy crowned by the divine septet of the seven archangels who have entry to the presence of the glory of the Lord (Tobit 12:15). Three of the seven archangels, Michael, Gabriel and Raphael, formed the group of "the angels of the divine presence" together with Phanuel (later Uriel, one of the septet) and came to be envisaged as situated at the four sides of God's throne. [28]

One possible explanation of how Satan came to be "the Fallen One" is detailed in chapter ten. The first encounter we have with Satan (in the Hebrew/Christian tradition) is in the Book of Genesis. There he persuades Eve to eat of the fruit of the tree of knowledge of good and evil. The story of "the tree of knowledge" is integral to the story of the fall of Adam and Eve. In a later chapter we will explain the 25,920-year rotation of the Pole of the Ecliptic. This rotation and the dominance of the constellations containing the stars that take Pole position will offer a simple explanation for the Adam and Eve story. It will show how their eating of the fruit of the tree of knowledge resulted in these "first created" being removed from the Garden of Eden. The location of the Tree of Life is confirmed in the Book of Revelation, which tells us: "To the (one) overcoming I will give to him to eat/consume of/from the tree of the life which is in the Paradise of the (one) God" (Rev 2,7).

It is not surprising therefore that Celtic, Egyptian, and Greek god myths have a tree at the center of their theosophy.

---

[27] Alan Scott , Origin and the Life of the Stars Clarendon Press (1994)
[28] Yuri Stoyanov, The Hidden Tradition of Europe, Penguin (1995)

In Celtic tradition, the "cup of truth" is reported as being "in a house near a golden tree."[29] The Irish God Curoi, the forerunner of the "hung-up naked man" is suspended from the branch of a tree.[30] Such specific incidents only supplement the general importance given to the oak tree by the Druids, who "chose oak woods for their sacred groves and performed no sacred rites without oak trees."[32] A special importance was attributed to "the oak" by the Greeks. Oak trees were sacred to Zeus (as well as many other gods and goddesses) and the famous oak grove at Dordona was where the rustling of the leaves gave voice to whatever prophesies or divination was sought from the Gods. We are even told that, "the Celtic image of Zeus was a lofty oak."[33]

The Greco-Egyptian theosophy proposed several significant tree connections. The name Adonis meant "Lord" and was attributed to the Babylonian God Tammuz. The mysteries of Adonis were celebrated in Greece and in many parts of Egypt. After an incestuous relationship with her father, his mother, Smyrna, was turned into a tree by the gods and a little time later, on the twenty-fourth of December, the bark of the tree was burst open by a boar and Adonis, the infant savior, issued forth. [34] In an alternative tradition, Osiris, who is probably the single most important of the Egyptian gods and the Egyptian form of Adonis, is referred to in inscriptions as "the (one) in the tree" and "the solitary one in the Acacia." His is reputed to have been "a tree God."[35]

The representation of a tree can be located within the boundaries of the constellation of Ursa Major (Fig 37). Thus, as we have seen, whilst Ursa Major can be viewed as a cup, chariot, stag, swan, plough, throne, etc., there is strong evidence to

---

[29] Alwyn & Brinley Rees, Celtic Heritage Thames and Hudson (1961)
[30] R S Loomis Celtic Myth and Arthurian Romances, Constable: London, 1993 p21;
[32] MacCulloch, The Religion of the Ancient Celts
[33] Ibid
[34] Manly P Hall, The Secret Teachings of all Ages, Philosophical Research Society, (October 1998)
[35] John G Jackson, Man, God and Civilization Citadel (2001)

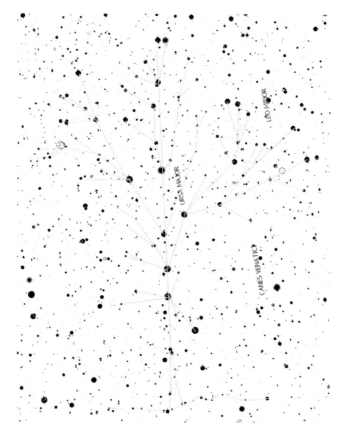

Fig 37 the constellation of Ursa Major viewed as a tree

support the view that the full pattern of the constellation could also be perceived as "the tree" (Fig 37).

On the basis of everything we have discovered thus far, this tree is located in "the house of God" and could actually be regarded as a representation of God himself. Since (apart from the base of the trunk) the tree in Fig 37 does not fall outside the boundaries of the constellation, this could imply that Ursa Major in its entirety is the location of Paradise. If the constellation of Ursa Major is synonymous with "the tree of knowledge," then the tree is associated with The

Horned One, Pluto, and the Serpent that tempted Eve. At the same time, it holds within its branches a selection of benevolent and divine personalities such as Adonis and Osiris. The Garden of Eden becomes, therefore, a place where good and evil, God and the devil, and Adonis and Beelzebub co-exist in a prolonged cycle of alternating dominance.

The only significant disguise of the Ursa Major constellation that we have not yet mentioned is the one that was used and embellished by the priests of Egypt. In common with American Indians and with modern day Arabs, the Egyptian priest-astronomers taught that the seven principal stars of Ursa Major represented a coffin or ark. In particular, they postulated that it was the coffin of the god Osiris. This designation will be discussed later in an analysis of the Egyptian pantheon and the mysteries it contained.

Ursa Major was also described by the Egyptians as "the thigh" and is depicted as such in the famous astrological zodiac on the ceiling of the Dendera Temple (Fig 38). Significantly, the thigh is depicted very close to the center of the picture and must relate to the period when the Pole position was directly "under" the tail or handle of Ursa Major, i.e. between 3500 and 2800 BC (see Fig 48).

Fig 38 the Dendera Zodiac

The thigh is the thigh of the Bull and in the pyramid texts we are told that "Unas is the Bull of Heaven" and that "he taketh his seat/throne and his back is towards Seb." Pyramid text number 276 says:

> The Great (Uraeus) fumigates the Bull of Nekhen (Hierakonpolis).
> The heat of the fiery breath is against you, you who are about the shrine (kAr)!
> O Great God whose name is unknown, (bring) at once a meal of the Unique Lord.
> O lord of the Horizon (Ax.t), make place for Unas.
> If you fail to make place for Unas, Unas will pronounce a curse against his father Geb: the earth shall not speak any more;
> Geb shall not be able to defend himself.
> (He) whom Unas finds on his way, he will eat him piecemeal.
> The hnt-pelican announces (sr), the ennead(psD.t)-pelican comes out.
> The Great One rises. The enneads speak: completely dammed-off shall be the land.[36]

Again we are led to the conclusion that the constellation of Ursa Major, whatever its form or designation, is associated with the Great God of Heaven.

Current popular belief is that the western religions had their origins in the Middle East. Egyptian, Mesopotamian (Babylonian), and Persian beliefs are known to have contributed to the birth of the Hebrew, Moslem, and Christian traditions that were prosecuted so violently on peoples with long-standing Ammonistic, Mithraic, or Druidic beliefs and practices. It has recently been proposed, however, that the Middle Eastern tradition had a precursor in Northern Europe and that the forerunners of the Druids could well have been the forerunners of Sumerian and Egyptian high religions.

> We believe that the influx of newcomers who brought civilization to Sumer might have been the Grooved Ware traders who settled in an environment they found attractive whilst keeping links with the other groups possibly in places like Gebel in Lebanon.

---

[36] *West Wall Hieroglyphs, Utterance 254, verse 276*

We believe that the Sumerians and the "incomers" to the Levant were Grooved Ware migrants, and both groups show similarities beyond their Venus based theology.

Sun worship is central to many ancient religions, but Venus is also important to the cultures that we believe are connected to the Grooved Ware people. Venus was highly important to megalithic Britons, and it is the light of the rising Venus that illuminates the "darkness of death" for a third degree Masonic candidate. We discovered Venus associations amongst the Sumerians, the Caanites, the Egyptians, and the Jews.

The founders of Egypt at this time also brought with them the skills of building, navigation, and astronomy that kick-started one of the greatest civilization of all time. We noted that the main feature of Newgrange is its spectacular white quartz wall; and the first city of Egypt was called Memphis, meaning White Wall. We now believe that there is a strong case to be made that the dispersion of the Grooved Ware people seeded the later civilizations in the Middle East."[37]

It has been further suggested that this ancient astronomical observatory (until recently thought to have been a burial mound) at Newgrange in Ireland, constructed circa 3000 BC, could be the mysterious place with "walls of crystal" shown by Uriel to Enoch and described so graphically in Chapter 14 of the Book of Enoch.[38]

Thigh, coffin, tree, wings, throne, chariot, cauldron, hammer, boar or bear, the Ursa Major constellation in all these forms is simultaneously linked to the God of Gods in one or other of his many manifestations. A large section of ancient mythology seems to have been a by-product of observation of one particular section of "the Heavens." Druids, priests, and astronomers conjured myths around their observations and simultaneously kept secret the true basis for the God stories they created. They shared their secrets with initiates and potentates who used the information to their own advantage. Here, perhaps for the first time, this information

[37] Christopher Knight & Robert Lomas, The Book of Hiram. Element Books Ltd (2004)
[38] Christopher Knight & Robert Lomas, Uriel's Machine, Element Books Ltd (2000)

is made available to everyone and it will no doubt attract attacks from those who have come to fervently believe the myths.

The constellation of Ursa Major is visible and known to everyone in the Northern Hemisphere. At the same time, it is at the source of most, if not all, the myths and allegories that have shaped our lives. Once natural skepticism to this fact has been overcome and the weight of evidence has been accepted, the interested searcher can delve further to look for the answer to other fundamental questions that have previously denied informed analysis.

In order to find the answer to such questions, it is necessary to go back to the beginning. In the earliest days, the ancient beliefs provoked the construction of an extraordinary and massive earthly temple. At the same time, these same beliefs were protected to ensure that the temple's very existence was only known to a select and limited few.

Chapter Four

Osiris, Horus, and Isis found

The Egyptians revered the omnipresent divinity Amon-Ra. At the same time, they recognized a large number of gods and goddesses as aspects or kindred of Amon. In the Karnac Temple in Thebes dedicated to Amon, the deity is depicted as a curly horned god[39] providing a direct link with the horned god discussed in the previous chapters. A variety of other male and female deities and Kings are depicted in carvings, paintings, and statues as horned, notably Osiris, Horus, Khnum, Hathor, and Isis. Amon's sacred animal was the ram.

The picture of the beginning of the world (Fig 39) shows Nut assisted by various ram-headed gods with curly horns. In addition and perhaps as significantly, the shape of Nut as she spans creation is the same shape as the cup of Ursa Major (inset) with interior angles of 108°.

An intriguing possibility, therefore, is that Nut (as well as representing the Heavens) is the cup of Ursa Major. She is given the names "Tomb" and "Sarcophagus" and the Pyramid texts confirm that she could be another name for this sacred constellation:

> In the Pyramid Texts, Nut performs a pivotal role in restoring the dead king Osiris to life. She spreads herself over him, conceals and protects him; she reassembles his limbs; she brings his heart and places it in his body; she cleanses and purifies him; she embraces and unfolds him; she gives birth to him (on one occasion in *Ament*, "the hidden land"); she bears him as 'a great one, the son of a great one' and a spirit *(akh)*; she takes his hand, or lays her hands on him,

---

[39] *J S Gordon, Land of the Fallen Star Gods, Orpheus (1998)*

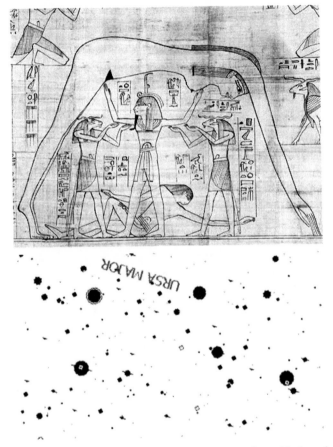

Fig 39 Nut assisted by various curly horned ram gods and below the upturned cup of Ursa Major

and gives him a road to the *akhet*; she carries him to the sky; she receives him in the sky; she makes him an imperishable star in her body; and she bears him alive every day like Re, as he circuits with the sun-God from the west to the east.[40]

The name Amon is variously written as Amen or Amun and means "hidden," "the hidden one," or "the one who con-

---

[40] *Alan F Alford, The Midnight Sun, Eridu (2004)*

ceals himself": "Unknown is his name in Heaven. Whose
name is hidden from his creatures. His name which is Amen
(hidden)."[41] "The designation Amun only means Arcane or
concealed, implying that it was not regarded as the real name
of the divinity."[42]

Ra is the principle of life itself, the principal of existence.
He was the one defining God that created everything. Amon-
Ra was the hidden principal of existence. The Egyptian belief
in Amon-Ra as a single all-embracing deity who manifested
himself in a variety of forms and personalities paved the way
for the monotheistic doctrines of Christianity, Islam, and Ju-
daism.

The Egyptians saw all phenomenal effects in Nature as
the bodily functions of one defining universal life force. At
the same time, Amon-Ra was one of three aspects of the
same god. The other two were Aten-Ra, the objectively en-
souling function of Ra or, more specifically, the Elohim soul
of our solar system and Ra-Tem the actively creative function. With this threesome, the Egyptians anticipated a fundamental tenant of Christianity, the doctrine of "The Trinity."
(The Elohim of the Jews were supposedly seven in number.
They were the Spirits of the dawn, more commonly known
as Archangels controlling the planets)[43]

> "The androgynous or bisexual Atum (Tem) (one of the three aspects
> of the godhead) who is the principal of primordial unity, generates
> duality from himself. Shu and Tefnut represent the emergence of
> duality—in the form of sexual polarity—from unity. Not only are
> they two (distinct from each other) but they are Two distinct from
> the original One. In this way the One becomes Three."[44]

The single all-powerful God of Gods is represented in
the following terms: "Atum precedes the divine hierarchy.

---

[41] *The Ritual of the Dead, Ancient papyrus in the British Museum*
[42] *Iamblichos, translated by Alexander Wilder, Theurgia or the Egyptian Mysteries , Kes-
    singer 1942*
[43] *Hall, The Secret Teachings of all the Ages*
[44] *Jeremy Naydler, Temple of the Cosmos, Bear and Company (1996)*

Described in metaphysical terms, he is the divine entity from which All sprang: his name might be Beginning-and-End. He is thus the Presence and the secret Counsel whom one feels tempted to equate with the starry sky itself. His decree must be of immutable perfection. But here it seems that there are forces, which have worked iniquity (gross injustice) in secret."[45]

"Atum, whose name means 'The Complete One,' was one of the great creator gods, possibly the oldest deity to be worshipped at Iunu, where, coalesced with Re (Ra) to form Re-Atum, he became a Sun God."[46]

From a single and universal principal, represented as a trinity of functions, emanates a family of nine gods. According to the Egyptian tradition, the world began as a watery chaos called Nun, from which the Sun Atum came out. He then begat the deities Shu (Air) and Tefnut (Moisture), who in turn produced Geb (Earth) and Nut (Sky). Geb and Nut then produced Osiris, Isis, Set, and Nephthys. The nine *neterw* (gods) formed the divine Ennead. In later texts, the Ennead (company of nine) was often regarded as a single divine entity.[47]

Our ability to fully comprehend the originally prescribed meaning of each of the names of the Egyptian gods is limited. Translators of hieroglyphics are able to replace the pictograms with letters from the modern alphabet. However, they have no way of transmitting the meaning held within each hieroglyphic picture. Wallis Budge tells us that the common hieroglyph for God is neter, which he then says "can be depicted by either of two pictograms."

It does not take a great deal of imagination to see that the actual meaning of Neter 1 (above) to the ancient Egyptians must have been different from that of Neter 2.

[45] *Georgio de Santillana & Hertha Von Dechend, Hamlets Mill, Macmillan (1970)*
[46] *Barbara Watterson, The Gods of Ancient Egypt, Sutton (1999)*
[47] *Mustaffa Gadalla, Historical Deception, The untold story of Ancient Egypt , Bastet (1996)*

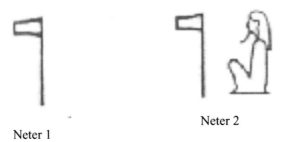

Neter 2

Neter 1

In addition to our limited ability to understand the hieroglyphics, we are also presented with a variety of spellings for the name of each god, as well as being presented with different names for what appears to be the same god or goddess. If one is to believe that the Egyptians were monotheistic, it is essential to assume, therefore, that many of these gods must represent different aspects of the same universal entity:

Nun is Atum; Atum is Rā; Atum-Rā is Nun; and yet Nun and Atum are evidently distinguishable. Indeed it is the very fact of their implicit difference, one from the other, that causes Atum to differentiate himself from Nun. But in this act of self-differentiation, Atum moves on, and becomes Kheprer—a movement whose completion is in Kheprer "becoming" Rā. Rā, we could say, is the end of the process: the fourth hypostasis of the One Godhead. But Rā has in reality been present and active in the process of his own self-unfolding. In the following passage, the beautifully enigmatic relationship of the four to each other is expressed:

> *I am Atum rising up*
> *I am the only One.*
> *I came into existence (Kheprer-na) in Nun*
> *I am Rā in his rising in the beginning . . .*
> *I am the Great God who came into existence*
> *By himself (Kheprer t'esef)*

Nun, that is, who created his name
"Substance (or Father) of the Gods," as God."[48]

The confusion of names and aspects becomes even more complicated when we examine the names of the Egyptian goddesses, their principal names being Neith, Mut, Annu, Hathor, Sekhet, and Isis.

"The God Tem (Atem or Atum) was the Father-God, and the lord of heaven, and the begetter of the gods, therefore Neith, the goddess associated with him, became; the great lady, the mother-goddess, the lady of heaven and the queen of the gods."[49]

"Neith was a primeval bisexual goddess who was said to have created the world and to be the virgin mother of the sun."[50]

"Mut is another personification of the one Great God whose other forms include Hathor, Sekhet, Isis, Nut . . . She is usually depicted wearing a vulture head-dress . . . Legends told that the vulture had no male species. The female vulture impregnated herself by exposing herself to the winds (i.e. the gods). The vulture is therefore a symbol of the virgin birth."[51]

The Mother Goddess is represented as Isis in the modern day Iconography. Isis is the Greek name for the Egyptian Goddess As-t, sometimes written Aset. She, in turn, is but one aspect of the goddess known as Hathor (Figs 28 and 40).

Hathor was certainly a cosmic goddess, and was associated with the sun God Rā, of whom she was the principal female counterpart.

[48] *Naydler, Temple of the Cosmos*
[49] *E A Wallis Budge, Gods of the Egyptians,Kessinger (2003)*
[50] *The Rev. George Oliver, D.D., (1782–1867) was one of the most distinguished and learned of English Freemasons, and a copious Masonic author. The History of Initiation in twelve lectures, comprising a detailed account of the Rites and Ceremonies, Doctrines and Discipline, of all the Secret and Mysterious Institutions of the Ancient World, published in 1840*
[51] *Gadalla , Historical Deception; The untold story of Ancient Egypt*

In comparatively late dynastic times Sekhet and Bast were identified with forms of Hathor, and were regarded as the goddesses of
the West and East respectively. [52]

Dr E A Wallis Budge was one of the foremost Egyptologists of the twentieth century. He claims that Hathor is
identified with Nu or Nu-t, the sky, the place in which she
brought forth and suckled Horus. She is the female power
of nature, and has some attributes of Isis, Nu-t, and Maāt.
Dr Wallis Budge's book compiles a list of the names and
forms she (Hathor) took in all the large cities in Upper and
Lower Egypt and shows that she was identified with Amen-
thet, Anqet, Anthat, Ashet, Bast (goddess of the East), Be-
hutet, Hatmehit, Heqet, Hert, Isis, Iusaset, Khekhsit, Khent
Abtet, Khersekhet, Khuit, Maat, Mehit-Tefnut-Khut-Menhit,
Mehurt, Mehenit, Menat, Menhit, Mersekhent, Mut, Nebt-
Hetep, Nebuarekht-Aat, Nebuut, Nehemauait, Nehemauait,
Net Nit or Neith (the lady of the West), Nekhebet (goddess
of the South), Nephthys, Nubt, Pakhth, Rat-Tauit, Renpit,
Repit, Satet, Sefkhet-Aabut, Sekhet (goddess of the West),
Sekhet-Bast-Rā (represented the gentle fructifying heat of
the sun), Tait, Tatet, Tefnut, Tep-Ahet, Tetet, Thenenet,
Uatchet (goddess of the north), Urt-Apset, and Usert-Heqet.
   J Norman Lockyer, an equally eminent authority on the
subject of ancient Egypt, claims that Hathor and therefore Isis
was worshipped under different names in every nome (area of
Egypt).[53] He claims that she was Sekhet of Memphis, Neith of
Sais, Saosis of Heliopolis, Nehem-an of Hermopolis, Bast or
Bes-t of Bubastis, Anub-et of Lycopolis, Amen-t of Thebes,
Bouto of Unas, Sothis of Elephantine, Apet, Mena-t, Horus
(female) of Edfu, and Isis-Sati of Philae.
   Such a regional variation might imply that the different
names were simply attributes of the different areas and temples in which the goddess was worshipped. However, just as
the Virgin Mary is known to Christians as The Immaculate

[52] Budge, Gods of the Egyptians
[53] J Norman Lockyer, The Dawn of Astronomy, Kessinger (1997)

Fig 40 the goddess Hathor
(with horns), accompanied by
the Pharaoh Mycerinus and a
local goddess

Conception, The Mother of God, etc., there is a strong probability that the many names of the Egyptian goddess related
to different aspects of a single Mother Goddess. To promote
this possibility, Wallis Budge points us to an interesting text
in the Ptolemaïc temple at Dêr al-Medina, on the Western
bank of the Nile opposite Thebes:

> ". . . we find that Hathor is called Nubt i.e., the 'Golden One' and
> that she is addressed as the 'queen of the gods' and her adorer says;
> 'thou standest high in the south as the lady of Teka (Eileithyiaspo-
> lis) and thou illuminest the West as the lady of Saïs. Thou appear-
> est and thou art commemorated in festivals as Hathor, the great
> lady, the beloved of Rā in (thy) seven forms.'"

Since, at first glance, the number seven in this inscription could indicate a link between the goddess and the seven principal stars of constellation of Ursa Major, this reference to Hathor or Isis having seven forms is provocative. However, Rev. George Oliver in his *History of Initiation* may have inadvertently provided an explanation that negates such a connection:

> The inviolable oath of Jupiter, by Styx, was referred to in the initiations, and is thought by Mr. Faber to bear reference to the oath of God, at the Deluge, that he would no more drown the world; "for which reason, Isis, the rainbow, the daughter of Thaumas, is represented by Hesiod as hovering over the broad surface of the ocean when this oath of Jupiter was taken." Now that such a phenomenon appeared immediately after the Deluge, we are expressly informed by Moses; and it is observable moreover, that it was made a special sign of God's oath to Noah."[54]

If the seven colors of the rainbow were the "seven forms" referred to in the temple text, then the arc of all seven spectral colors would be an interesting link between the Mother Goddess and the sun God Atum (as the source of light).

An additional and fundamental link between the pattern of the constellation of Ursa Major and the Egyptian Pantheon (represented by a myriad of names and aspects) is perhaps to be found in the mythology emanating from Egyptian pre-history, which became known as "The Mysteries." No one has been able to identify what these mysteries were, but we do know that, each year, a series of rituals were played out to celebrate/venerate "The Mysteries." The most enduring allegory is the one concerning Osiris, Set, and Isis and Horus. Plutarch tells us that once Osiris had become ruler of Egypt and had given the people the full advantage of intellectual light, he continued his path through the heavens, visiting the people of other nations and conversing with those whom he

---

[54] *Oliver, The History of initiation*

came into contact. While he was away, his brother, Typhon Set, with seventy-two others, plotted against him. Set had a box, coffin, or arc made the same size as the body of Osiris, which he then brought into the banqueting hall where the gods and goddesses were eating together. Everyone admired it and Set promised to give the box to the one whose body fit it most perfectly. Everyone was disappointed except Osiris, who fit it exactly. The moment he was in the box, Set and his accomplices nailed down the lid and sealed it with molten lead. They then cast the box into the Nile. Plutarch is specific and tells us that this happened on the seventeenth day of the month of Athyr, when the sun was in the constellation of Scorpio. (The sun was in Scorpio between 17380 and 15220 BC or earlier between 43300 and 41140 BC.) The Pans and Satyrs made the alarm. When Isis received the news of her husband's murder she set off in search of him. She eventually recovered the box and the body of Osiris from under a Tamarind tree only to have it stolen from her by Set who found the coffer as he was hunting a boar. He cut the body into fourteen pieces, which he scattered all over the earth. In despair, Isis gathered up the parts of her husband but could only find thirteen. The phallus had been thrown into the Nile and eaten by a fish. Isis refashioned the phallus from gold, reassembled the body, and revived Osiris. It was Osiris' son Horus who later avenged his father's death by slaying the monster Typhon Set. Osiris was placed on a lion-headed bier and conveyed to the underworld (the darkness). There he disputed his fate by appealing to the great God Atum/Aten, saying, "Oh Atum, what is this desolate place into which I have come? It is without water; it is without air; its depth is unfathomable; its darkness is black as night. Must I wander hopelessly here where one cannot live in peace of heart or satisfy the longings of love?" [55]

Atum told him that contentment and peace would make air, water, and love unnecessary. When Osiris asked him if

---

[55] *Plutarch, Of Isis and Osiris, Loeb Classical (1936)*

he would see the light of day again, Atum told him that he would remain in the underworld, ruling as king, but seeing no other God, while his son Horus took his place on the throne of Egypt. In ancient times, "the underworld" was a common designation of the night sky. It was the place where there was no daylight. It is possible therefore that Osiris' destination was the night sky, where he continues to abide.

"For these men (Egyptian priests) perceived that the things which were said respecting the Sun-God as the Demiurgos, or Creator of the Universe, and concerning Osiris and Isis, and all the sacred legends, may be interpreted as relating to the stars, their phases, occultation, and revolutions in their orbits."[56]

We already know that the cup of Ursa Major is a perfect receptacle for a regular pentagon. The idea of Osiris being a perfect fit for the coffin manufactured by Set implies a tempting metaphor for this same concept. In chapter three, we saw that Osiris was acknowledged as "the one in the tree."

Given the proposition that "the tree" represents the conglomeration of stars in Ursa Major, these references could point to Osiris, found under the Tamarind tree, amidst the stars that circumnavigate the pole. Such a link, when coupled with the fact that Ursa Major was regarded symbolically by the Egyptians as a coffin[57], makes attractive the idea that the story of Osiris somehow relates to the constellation of Ursa Major and to the geometric pattern it holds. This tentative proposition is supported by an abundance of additional circumstantial evidence:

- A lament for Osiris, which has the lines "Within the court divine, the sevenfold sacred shrine."[58]
- The fact that the Temple of Osiris at Abydos has seven sanctuaries.

[56] *Theurgia or the Egyptian Mysteries – Iamblichos, translated by Alexander Wilder*
[57] *Gordon, Land of the Fallen Star Gods*
[58] *Gadalla, Historical Deception; The Untold Story of Ancient Egypt*

- The fact that Osiris was called "Child of Kronos" and accepted as "Men's Heavenly Horn" and the equivalent of Dionysus[59], Attis (The Most high God who holds the Universe together)[60], Adonis, Bacchus, and Pluto[61], who (we have already seen) can be readily identified with the pattern of the constellation.
- Osiris and Dionysus (his Greek equivalent) were both represented as "horned."
- "It is Osiris who is Lord of the Dwat (sometimes translated as "Lord of the House"—Greek οικορεσηοτηζ, Hebrew *Baal Zebul*) and who governs the cycles of generation and destruction, of coming into being and passing away to which all creatures are subject."[62] In Beelzebub (a derivation of Baal Zebul), we are provided with a link between Osiris and "The Horned One."
- The comments of Norman Lockyer: If we return for a moment to the zodiac at Denderah, we find that the constellations which I indicated—the Thigh, the Hippopotamus and the Jackal—represent our present constellations of the Great Bear, Draco and the Little Bear . . . It seems very probable that the circumpolar stars were very early regarded as representing the powers of darkness (the Dwat or Tuat) because they were there, visible in the dark, always disappearing and never appearing at sunrise. The "seven stars" are held by many to mean the Pleiades, and not the Great Bear; but this I think is very improbable. Hymn to Osiris: "O Osiris! Thou art the youth *at the horizon* of heaven daily, and thine old age at the beginning of all seasons . . ." "The *ever-moving* stars are under obedience to him, and so are *the stars which set.*"[63]
- "It is Osiris who is the Lord of the Dwat (underworld) and who governs the cycles of generation and destruction, of coming into being, and passing away to which all creatures are subject."

[59] Herodotus, The Histories, Penguin Classics (1996)
[60] Graves, The White Goddess
[61] Hippolytus commentary on the Nassene chant.
[62] Naydler, Temple of the Cosmos
[63] Lockyer, The Dawn of Astronomy;

Fig 41 the hieroglyph of Osiris   Fig 42 the hieroglyph of the Tuat

- "The writers of the religious texts were not all agreed as to the exact position of this place, but from first to last, whatever might be the conceptions entertained about it, it was called TUAT (Dwat). In the nineteenth dynasty we know that the TUAT was believed to be situated not below the earth, but away beyond the earth, probably in the sky, and certainly near the heaven wherein the gods dwelt; it was the realm of Osiris."[64]
- The hieroglyphic symbols that depict the Osiris name (Fig 41) include a seat or throne, a kneeling and bearded individual (slightly different from the figure in Neter 2), and an eye.

The hieroglyph of Taut (Fig 42) shows a star in the form of a pentagram, a bird facing the star, an arc that may be the sun rising, and a box with an opening in the side that is furthest from the rising (or setting) sun.

This hieroglyph contains many obvious connections to the sacred pattern hidden inside the Ursa Major constellation: a throne, a five-pointed star, a bird (with wings), and a container.

The word hieroglyph has its origins in Greek and means "holy script."[65] This holy script hid the secrets of "The Mysteries." The entire Egyptian metaphysical system, like a biblical parable, was meant to be interpreted at various levels according to the insight of the listener. "The most esoteric secrets thus remained concealed by their obviousness."[66]

[64] Budge, Gods of the Egyptians
[65] Gadalla, Historical Deception; The untold story of Ancient Egypt
[66] Gordon, Land of the Fallen Star Gods

The jealousy of the hierophants or dispensers of "The Mysteries" became at length so strongly excited, that trembling for their secret, they invented a new hieroglyphic or sacred symbolical character and language, which was exclusively appropriated to the highest "Degree" of their order. It is probable that the same symbolical characters were made use of, but the hidden meaning attached to each was entirely changed. So effectively was the higher meaning of the hieroglyphics hidden from all but a distinguished few, that in the process of time the interpretation of the symbols was entirely lost. Thus, in the common hieroglyphic, a hawk signified the *human soul,* in the sacred hieroglyphic it would stand for *Expedition*; and thus would the signification of every particular emblem be altered.[67]

Given the double significance of this ancient form of communication, it does not seem unreasonable that we look for hidden meanings in the pictograms that make up each hieroglyph. Unfortunately, we have no way of knowing the concealed or secret meanings and, like so much of ancient history, we are left to surmise.

A considerable library of information and scientific interpretation exists concerning the god Osiris. In *Land of the Fallen Star Gods* by J S Gordon, we read:

Osiris on his funeral bier is shown in a variety of different positions and poses. Sometimes he is face up, sometimes face down; sometimes with his head at one end, sometimes at the other; sometimes in funeral wrappings, sometimes not; sometimes bearded, sometimes not; sometimes wearing a Horus mask or crown, sometimes nothing. The general inference therefore taking into account a probable sequence or progression is that the symbolism refers to the axial rotation and orbit of our solar system, relative to the plane of its parent star, or even the galaxy itself.

The author goes on to illustrate that Egypt was laid out as a duplicate of the circum-polar stars and shows Osiris riding

---

[67] *Oliver, The History of Initiation*

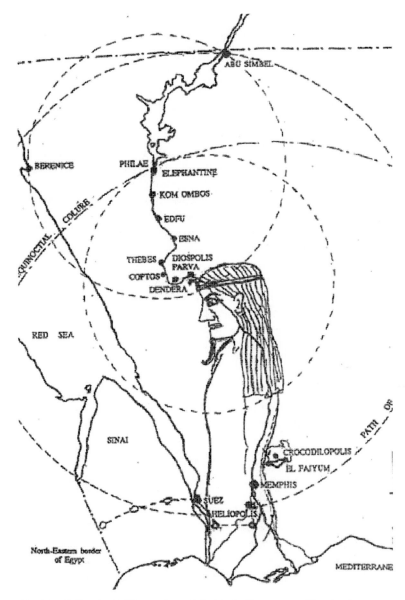

Fig 43 J S Gordon's illustration of Osiris in Egypt, standing in the cup of Ursa Major

in the cup of Ursa Major with the handle as the replacement phallus (Fig 43). In an attempt to encourage the feeling of mystery, he goes on to say:

> The expression "The Children of Israel" seems originally intended to signify mankind in general —but in a spiritual sense, as "As-r-El" ("As-r" being the Egyptian form of the name Osiris)—the semi-divine progeny of the Demi-Urgos—the "El" being the Elohim already mentioned in the Old Testament. Thus the name "Israel" (given to the metaphorical Jacob after he had fought the angel at Beth-el) signified a semi-divine or celestial state; the "Promised Land" to which the offspring of his twelve sons (a purely zodiacal metaphor) would return at "God's own appointed time."
>
> The name Osiris is the Greek form of the Egyptian "As-r" which we anglicize as AUSAR. It appears to coincide rather interestingly with the verbal root of the Sanskrit "As" (meaning "to be") and is otherwise to be found as ASHER in the Hebrew kabalistic expression "Ehyeh Asher Ehyeh" (I am that I am). Thus the original meaning of the name Osiris seems to have been THAT—the imponderable, self created (i.e. immaculately conceived) divinity in Man—by virtue of man's origin as the emanation and offspring of the great God Ra."

Set, the other male God protagonist, in the myth of Isis and Osiris is acknowledged by most Egyptologists to have been associated with Draconis, the snake-like constellation that wraps itself between Ursa Major and Ursa Minor (Fig 44) and by some authors with the entirety of the circumpolar stars.

> "Set" seems to have been a generic name applied to the northern (circumpolar) constellations, perhaps because Set equates with darkness, and these stars, being always visible in the night, may have in time typified it. Taurt the Hippopotamus was the wife of Set. The Thigh was the thigh of Set, etc. The star γ (gamma) Draconis was associated therefore with Set, and the symbolism for Set-Hathor was the Hippopotamus with the horns and disc.[68]

---

[68] *Lockyer, The Dawn of Astronomy*

Fig 44 the constellations of Ursa Major, Ursa Minor, and Draco

Another interpretation was that (as well as being the thigh of the bull Unas as seen in the previous chapter) Ursa Major was the thigh of Set: "From the earliest of times, the Egyptians worshipped God in the form of a bull whose dismembered body parts had been spiritualized in the sky. In particular, it was believed that the northern stars formed the pattern of two forelegs or two thighs which were held to be the limbs of Seth. These stars are known today as Ursa Minor and Ursa Major."[69]

A piece of iron called an *adze* was used in all the sacred ceremonies. This implement was shaped like Ursa Major (Fig 45).

"The *adze* that opens the king's mouth is made of 'the iron which issues from Seth[.]'. . . . [T]he designated king Horus performs the ritual on the mummy of his father Osiris, in re-enactment of the original resurrection of the God. He uses an *adze* that is modeled in the shape of the northern stars, in anticipation of the result of

[69] *Alford, The Midnight Sun*

Fig 45 Alan F Alford's illustration of the seven stars of Ursa Major pictured as an *adze* (left) and a bull's foreleg or thigh (right)

> the ritual, i.e. the spiritualization of the gods. . . . [S]ince the *adze* was modeled on the northern stars and since Seth was dwelling in those stars, the iron of the *adze* would have been viewed as the metal of Seth."[69]

In chapter one, we found a regular pentagon holding a regular pentagram in the earth-based duplication of the constellation of Ursa Major (see Fig 46 below).

If these geometrical shapes were thought by the Egyptians to have existed as an unseen or hidden pattern in the constellation in the heavens, there must to be a link between the story of Osiris (and his murder by Typhon Set) and their existence. In other words, like the body of Osiris, there must be a way in which the pattern in the cup of the constellation can become cut into fourteen parts. Interestingly, when one examines the pattern and imagines that it is sitting in the constellation itself, there is a way in which the pattern *can* be cut into the fourteen pieces:

The pattern sitting in the plough, coffin, throne, or chariot consists of eleven pieces, ten triangles, and one central pentagon.

In the ground pattern, any line that falls between (a) an extended line from Reims to the point of intersection of the meridian and the base of the cup (BB) and (b) the East most point of the pentagram and the same point of intersection of the meridian and the base line of the cup (AA) cuts each of three of the triangles into two separate shapes and makes the resulting number of pieces in the overall pattern equal to fourteen. Thus, the original pattern is dissected into a total

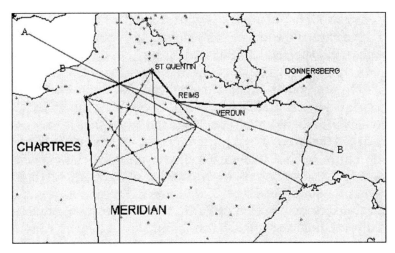

Fig 46 the lines that create 14 pieces within the pattern

of fourteen pieces by any such a line. Given that the intersection of such a line is the method by which the body is cut
up, it is only necessary that we locate the link between the
ground-pattern, the constellations of Ursa Major and Draconis (assuming we believe Typhon-Set to have been Draconis)
and the Egyptian allegory of Isis and Osiris. If there is such
a link, it will be possible to determine how such a dissec-
tion of the pattern could have occurred in reality. In other
words, it is necessary to identify the line in the heavens that
cut through the geometric shape in the hidden pattern. If and
when this is established, the final step will be to determine
how this event came to be interpreted by Egyptian priests
and the kings and queens they served as a divine parody.

The constellation of Draconis sits adjacent to the constellation of Ursa Major (Figs 44 and 48). The name Draconis has
the same Greek root as the English word "draconian" meaning monstrous and points us to this constellation being viewed
as "the monster" in ancient times. It seems self-evident, therefore, that we should look closer at this constellation for evidence of Typhon Set, the Egyptian monster, and from there try

to discover what line from Draconis could be the one bisecting the base of the cup of Ursa Major and cutting the invisible pattern it contained into fourteen pieces.

In compiling his famous star catalogue (circa 129 BC), the Greek astronomer Hipparchus noticed that the positions of the stars were shifted in a systematic way from earlier Babylonian (Chaldean) measures. This indicated that it was not the stars that were moving but rather the observing platform, the Earth. Such a motion is called precession and consists of a cyclic wobbling in the orientation of the Earth's axis of rotation with a period of 25,920 years. Precession was the third-discovered motion of Earth, after the far more obvious daily rotation and annual revolution. Precession is caused by the gravitational influence of the sun and the moon acting on Earth's equatorial bulge. At the same time and to a much lesser extent, the planets exert influence. The projection onto the sky of the Earth's axis of rotation results in two notable points at opposite directions: the north and south celestial poles (Fig 47). Because of precession, the extensions of Earth's axis trace out circles on the sky, one in the north and one in the south. Today, the north celestial pole points

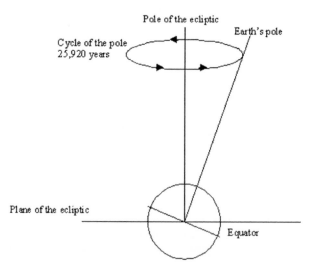

Fig 47 the movement of the pole position in the heavens

to within just 2° of the arc of Polaris. It will point closest to Polaris between AD 2100 and AD 2115.

The star Thuban is the principal star in the constellation of Draconis. It takes the position of "Pole Star" every 25,920 years, and it is the star nearest to the invisible point in the heavens about which everything appears to revolve. In that same period, as the sky revolves around the pole of the ecliptic, the constellations of Draconis (holding Thuban), Ursa Major, Draconis, Ursa Minor (holding Polaris), Cepheus, Cygnus, Lyra holding Vega, and Boots holding Arcturus are nearest to the "pole position" in their turn.

Fig 48 illustrates the arc of the circular path that "the pole" takes through the constellations of Ursa Major, Draconis, and Ursa Minor. When the lines "AA" and "BB" (which are duplications of the lines in Fig 46) are imposed on the constellation of Ursa Major, the line AA intersects the circle of the "pole" positions at approximately 3300 BC. The line BB falls outside the circle. Thus, at about 3400 BC, when "the pole" was about to move into Ursa Major, a line from the

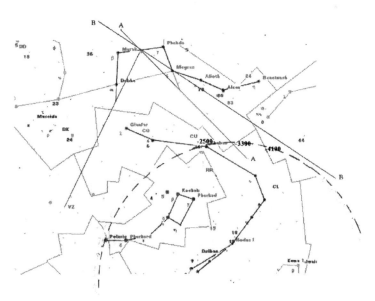

Fig 48 lines AA and BB from Ursa Major to the circle of "the pole"

"the pole" to the center of the cup of Ursa Major would have cut the hidden pattern inside the cup into fourteen pieces. Between 4100 BC and 3400 BC, "the pole" had been located in Draconis, assuming that the boundaries of the constellations were the same as they are now. In other words, Typhon-Set had occupied the place around which all else revolved. In 3400 BC, Ursa Major took over "the pole," which meant that Osiris would assume the dominant role. It was at this time of transition that a line from "the pole" would have dissected the pattern to make the eleven pieces into fourteen. It is our proposition that this is the way that the monster Typhon-Set would have cut the body of Osiris into fourteen pieces. Associated confirmation of this hypothesis can be obtained from the Cambridge star atlas, which shows that the number of visible stars (magnitude five or above) in the constellation of Draconis is seventy-two. It seems hardly a coincidence that seventy-two is the number of Seth's coconspirators.

> We have no way of knowing that the hypothetical lines that divide one constellation from another are the same today as they were in 3400 BC However: "The science in which the Egyptian priesthood was most proficient, and which they most jealously guarded, was that of astronomy . . . Pythagoras, who introduced the true system of the universe into Greece, received it from the Egyptians."[70]

Modern star charts are known to accurately reproduce those of the Greek astronomer Hipparchus (albeit they now contain more detail). Hipparchus was an "initiate" and follower of Pythagoras. To such a man the science of the stars was sacred and it was not something that he would have cavalierly changed. Therefore, we can reasonably assume that current definitions of the constellations are similar to those of the early Egyptians. Thus, if the constellation of Draconis was Typhon-Set and the constellation holds seventy-two major stars, it may not be unreasonable to assume that these

---

[70] *Robert Hewitt Brown, Stellar Theology and Masonic Astronomy, Book Tree (2002)*

seventy-two stars represent the seventy-two individual con-
spirators that helped Set in his treacherous deed.

In Fig 48 we can see that "the pole" moves back into
Draconis and stays there from 2800 BC to 1750 BC at which
date it moves into the constellation of Ursa Minor. In Ursa
Minor, therefore, we have the usurper of Draconis and a
strong candidate for the role of Horus.

The drama resulting in the removal of Draconis from his
grip on the pole position by Ursa Minor leads us to look for
Horus (the slayer of Seth) in Ursa Minor and for Isis (the
rescuer of Osiris, her husband and Mother of Horus) as the
link between the cup in Ursa Major and the constellation of
Ursa Minor. This picture becomes clearer when we make the
somewhat obvious assumption that the Horus child is within
the Ursa Minor constellation. From that premise, it is but
a small leap to see his mother Isis as the line that links the
God pattern in Ursa Major with the child held in its mother's
arms (Fig 51). This proposition is possible and the slaying of
the monster completed because and when the constellation
of Ursa Minor usurps the Dragon and moves to take its peri-
odic position at the crown of the heavens (i.e. holding on to
"the pole"). The picture of the usurping of Draconis is best
described in Revelation 12, 1-5:

> And a great sign appeared in heaven; A woman clothed with the
> sun, and the moon under her feet, and on her head a crown of
> twelve stars: 2. And being with child, she cried travailing in birth,
> and was in pain to be delivered. 3. And there was seen another sign
> in heaven: and behold a great red dragon, having seven heads, and
> ten horns: and on his heads seven diadems: 4. And his tail drew the
> third part of the stars of heaven, and cast them to the earth: and the
> dragon stood before the woman who was ready to be delivered;
> that when she should be delivered, he might devour her son. 5. And
> she brought forth a man-child, who was to rule all nations with an
> iron rod: and her son was taken up to God and to his throne.

An intriguing question that grows out of this hypothesis relates to the timeline. The story of Isis and Osiris was sacred

and underpinned the ancient and hidden teachings of "The Mysteries." Does the story relate to the single set of observations made by Egyptian priests between, say, 5000 BC and 1000 BC or did records of the complete precessional cycle exist in the early dynasties of Ancient Egypt, implying that the priests were aware of the 25,920-year period between successive "pole" positions?

Herodotus was one of the foremost of the Roman historians. He tells us that the first king of Egypt was Minos. He spells out dates and timelines and claims that Egypt was ruled by gods prior to the first king. In relation to his stipulation of fifteen thousand years as the length of time between Heracles and Amasis (526 BC), he states that, "They claim to be certain of these dates because they have kept a careful written record of the passage of time."[71]

Cicero in his treatise on Divination declares that the Chaldeans had records of the stars for the space of three hundred and seventy thousand years, and Diodoros the Sicilian asserts that their observation comprehended four hundred and seventy thousand years. Kallisthenes, when in Babylon, sent the computations of the Chaldeans to his Uncle Aristotle.

Simplicius (sixth century AD) tells us that he had always heard that the Egyptians had kept astronomical observations and records for the last six hundred and thirty thousand years.

Diogenes Laertius carried back the astronomical calculations of the Egyptians to 48,863 years before Alexander the Great. Martianus Copella corroborates the same by telling posterity that the Egyptians had secretly studied astronomy for over forty thousand years before they imparted their knowledge to the world.

It is a current-day and popular surmise that an advanced human civilization existed before the flood and that the equatorial region, including Egypt, was the region where it was possible for man to have dwelled throughout the last

---

[71] *Herodotus, The Histories*

ice age (80,000–7,000 BC, peaking between 24,000 BC and 14,000 BC). Evidence for this idea that has been put forward by the small but vociferous number of proponents is the erosion of the Sphinx. They claim that the erosion could only have been caused by prolonged rainfall and that (according to various climatic experts) such rainfall could only have occurred around 40,000 BC or (more likely) between 8000 BC and 4500 BC.

If it was true that the Egyptians held records of the complete precessional cycle, then the story of Isis and Osiris could presumably refer to an excerpt from its entire 25,920 years. However, the story is limited in the context of such a complete cycle and starts with Osiris and Set. It then moves on to include Isis and Horus. In other words, assuming that the allegory of Osiris, Set, Isis, and Horus represents the story of the precessional movements of the northern constellations around the "pole," it only includes those circumpolar stars in the arc of the precessional cycle that includes Ursa Major, Draconis, and Ursa Minor. Thus, it can be concluded that the allegory either relates to a period starting after 4100 BC or to a period between 27020 BC and 12580 BC.

An alternative interpretation of the usurping of Set in Draco relates to the rotation of the constellations around "the pole." When observing the stars from Egypt, the "pole" lies close to the northern horizon. Because of that, only a small number of stars were circumpolar. i.e., they are seen to revolve around "the pole" and were always visible. Stars that are not circumpolar appeared and disappeared as they rose and set (Fig 49).

The stars in Draco were circumpolar, and could, therefore, have been destroyed (or rendered invisible) as the hippopotami were destroyed in the myth (the slaying of Set by Horus) by the rising sun about 5000 BC, and be it noted that at that time there was only one star in the Great Bear (or The Thigh) which was circumpolar. But at 2000 BC the stars in Ursa Major were the circumpolar ones and the chief stars in the constellation Draco, which formed the ancient constellation of the Hippopotamus, rose and set; so that, if there is anything at all in the explanation of the myth which I have given, and if there is anything at all in the idea that the myth is very ancient and refers to the time when the constellation of the Hippopotamus was really circumpolar—a time 7,000 years ago—we ought to find that, as the myth existed in more recent times, we should no longer be dealing with Draco or the Hippo because Draco was no longer circumpolar. As a matter of fact, in later times we get Horus destroying no longer the hippopotamus or the crocodile, but the Thigh of Set; and as I have said, 2000 years BC the Thigh occupied exactly the same position in the heavens with regard to the pole as the Hippopotamus or Crocodile did 3,000 years before. Thus, I think, we may claim that this myth is astronomical from top to bottom; it is as old as, and probably older than Neville thought, because it must certainly have originated in a period somewhere about 5000 years BC otherwise the constellation of the Hippopotamus would not have figured it in."[72]

It is most likely that the real solution to the story lies in a combination of these concepts. At the start of the story, Horus was not there, i.e. "the pole" was in Draconis, and Ursa Minor was not amongst the circumpolar stars. However, the myth was (presumably) created in its entirety and included Horus, i.e. the story came into being after Ursa Minor (Polaris) had joined the circumpolar stars.

If this reasoning is valid, the inception of "The Mysteries" would have occurred circa 3500 BC (or 26,592 years prior to that), provided that the viewing point was at Heliopolis. If the story originated further south, it would have taken longer for Ursa Minor to become circumpolar and the story would have been devised at a later date, which may explain why the cult of Horus originated in the Delta and moved south.[73] Alternatively, if the Isis, Osiris, Horus myth was in no way based upon the timing of any parts of the constellations being circumpolar and it came into being when "the pole" entered the constellation of Ursa Minor, then it would have to

---

[72] *Lockyer, The Dawn of Astronomy*
[73] *Watterson, The Gods of Ancient Egypt*

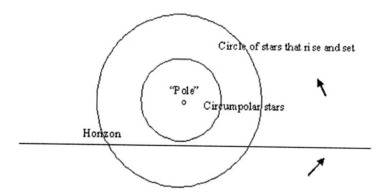

Fig 49 the nearer stars are to the current pole position and the further
north the observer, the more likely they are to stay above the horizon
and be "circumpolar"

have been dated much later circa 1500 BC (or 26,592 years
prior to that).

Plutarch tells us that "this (Osiris's coffin being dumped
in the Nile with Osiris inside) happened on the seventeenth
day of the month of Athyr (Hathor = August), when the Sun
was in the constellation of Scorpio." The period when the
sun rose in Scorpio was from 17423 BC to 15263 BC and
the period when the sun set in Scorpio was from 4463 BC to
2303 BC. The period when midsummer's day occurred with
"the sun in Scorpio" represented the midpoint between these
two periods, i.e. 10943 BC to 8783 BC.

Without more information, therefore, it is impossible to
know which of these three periods Plutarch was attempting
to catalog. It does, however, imply that it was no later than
2303 BC, which, given that Ursa Minor only took over "the
pole" four hundred and fifty hundred years later, is the stron-
gest evidence we have that the Egyptian priests were aware
of the complete precessional cycle, i.e. they were aware that
"the pole" would move into Ursa Minor and that the whole
allegory had been formed much earlier.

Plutarch's statement itself seems to point to a precise day of the year, implying that some aspect of "The Mystery" is related to the day in the year that "it" took place.

We know that "the ancient Egyptians used three calendars: a lunar calendar of alternating twenty-nine and thirty months, a civil calendar of 360 days plus five additional days (on which the *neteroo* were said to be born) and a calendar of 365.25 days based on the heliacal return of the star Sirius."[74] Unfortunately, we do not know which of these three calendars Plutarch might have been referring to. Plutarch's date does, however, suggest that the phenomenon (whatever it was) related to a specific day of the year, inviting us to surmise that some element of "The Mystery" occurs annually. An interesting observation of Plutarch is related to us by J Norman Lockyer and may provide a clue.

"Since the observations of alpha Draconis might be used to herald the sunrise almost all the year round; and since the modern constellation Draco is the old Hippopotamus, we can readily understand Plutarch's statement that 'Tuart presides over the birth of the sun,' and why Tuart and Mut should be called 'The Mistress of Darkness.'"[75]

If the growing evidence is correct and the allegory behind "The Mysteries" relates to the precessional movement of the Draconis and Ursa Minor constellations as they relate to the position of Ursa Major and "the pole," the final piece of the jigsaw must be the determination of the exact identity of Isis, distinguished by Locker thus: "Isis represents the Dawn and the Twilight; she prepares the way for the Sun-God. The rising sun between Isis and Nephthys = morning. Nephthys is the Dawn and the Twilight, sometimes sunset."[76]

This view of the goddess is confirmed by her hieroglyph (Fig 50) depicting two beams of light at sunrise and/or sunset. Additionally, there is the reference to her seven forms,

---

[74] *Moustaffa Gadalla, Egyptian Cosmology, Bastet (1997)*
[75] *Lockyer, The Dawn of Astronomy*

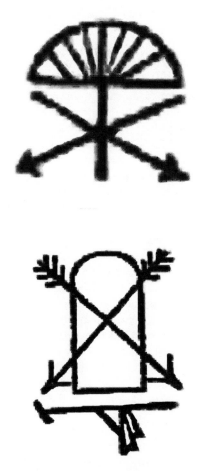

Fig 50 the pre-dynastic and dynastic hieroglyphs for the Goddess

suggesting that (sometimes) she manifests herself as a rainbow or spectrum.

In order to fully complete the picture, these concepts need
to be congruent with the hypothesis that we have already

presented that Isis can represent a link between Ursa Minor and the center of the cup of Ursa Major.

According to Erman-Grapow the word *mnj.t.* is used as (1) symbolical expression for the king; (2) symbolical expression for Isis and Nephthys who fetched Osiris from the water. It is a constellation, the instrument for impaling, the post to which a person to be punished is bound. This *mnj.t wr.t*—Mercer writes it *min. t*—the "great landing stick" is said "to mourn" for the soul of the dead in the Pyramid Texts, and Mercer comments that "the great stake". . . is personified as a "mourning woman" in reference here to Isis. The constellation occurs in two categories of astronomical monuments namely (1) in the Ramesside Star Clocks and (2) in the ceiling pictures of royal tombs, in the zodiacs of Dendera, etc. In every case the peg or post resting the hands of Isis disguised as a hippopotamus; fastened to the mooring post is a rope or chain, to the other end of which is tied *Maskheti*, the bull's thigh, i.e., the Big Dipper, and in one of the texts it is stated that "it is the office of Isis-Hippopotamus to guard this chain." According to the Ramesside Star Clocks *mnj.t* included six different parts, and only after these six parts follow *rrt* "female hippopotamus" comprising eight positions. Boll remarks that this constellation must be thought of as being parallel to either the equator or zodiac, and as being rather long because otherwise it could not need more than four hours of ascending.

Most of the scholars dealing with the Egyptian astronomical ceilings took it for granted that the main scenery represented the northern circumpolar constellations, because the Big Dipper, Maskheti, holds the determinant position upon the stage, and they tried their hardest to identify Isis-Hippopotamus holding the mooring post, and carrying upon her back a crocodile, with a constellation very near the pole.

Now we do not mean to go into details of the Egyptian sphere as represented in these ceiling decorations, which is an extremely difficult task, and nothing has been gained in the past by the different efforts to settle the affair by simply looking at the sky (worse, at sky maps) trying to imitate Zeus by "catasterizing" on one's own account, and giving keen verdicts. Let us say only this much: (1) as yet no single proposition concerning the Hippopotamus holding the mooring-post is satisfying; (2) that the determinative group of the ceiling pictures show decisive factors of the frame; Leo, Scorpius, Taurus, serving thus a kind of key of the whole presentation. In some Egyptian texts, we have the "double *mnj.t*." We do not yet know why."[77]

Here we have the chain or rope representing the line from "the pole." Since all lines from "the pole" are meridians, the chain or rope represents a very specific meridian, it being the one that connects with Mskheti, The Thigh, or Ursa Major. It has already been shown that the constellation of Ursa Major was variously seen as a coffin or a throne and therefore this link to Ursa Major also fits with the conventional picture of Isis sitting on her throne.

"Isis is the Greek translation of the Egyptian 'As-t' or Aset. Aset in Egyptian means throne. She is portrayed wearing the vulture head-dress, the crescent and the disc, with a pair of horns surrounding the disk. She is equated in Greek mythology with Persephone, Ceres and Athene."[78]

The famous figure of Isis is depicted in Fig 51. She is sitting on a throne, nursing her child (Horus) and with two significant appendages spreading upward from a base that lies flat on her head. These two extensions can only represent horns or a cup. Between these two protrusions is an orb, conventionally believed to represent the sun. As throne, horns, and cup are all aspects of Ursa Major, the head-dress could therefore suggest "the sun in Ursa Major."

In a carving on the Temple at Denderah (Fig 52) she is depicted with a hieroglyphic "throne of the north" sign on her head, the two horns or cup containing the orb of the sun and two curly horns normally attributed to aspects of male gods such as Osiris.

[76] *Lockyer, The Dawn of Astronomy*
[77] *Santillana & Dechend, Hamlets Mill*
[78] *Gadalla, Historical Deception, The Untold Story of Ancient Egypt*

Fig 51 Isis and Horus

The same hieroglyphic throne sign is also the first syllable
of the hieroglyphic name of Osiris and is variously translated
as "*as-r*" or "*ws-ir*" and pronounced Osiris by the Greeks.
Thus, if we accept the hypothesis that Isis is the line from
"the pole" that bisects the base of Ursa Major, we have confirmation that Osiris is sitting in the constellation and may
therefore be the pentagram and five-pointed star it contains.

This picture of Isis/Hathor in Fig 52 provides the link between all of the ingredients that make up this goddess. Isis
must represent the line that travels from the sun at dawn or

Fig 52 Isis/Hathor with curly horns, the sun in a horn cup, and the throne of the north on her head

sunset; she must go through "the pole" and she must bisect the cup of Ursa Major. Isis, therefore, is simultaneously a beam of light from the sun (made up of the seven colors of the rainbow) and the meridian (line through "the pole") emanating from or going through the midpoint of the cup of Ursa Major that holds the body of her husband Osiris.

Alignment of Sun, Pole, and Ursa Major occurs at sunrise and sunset four times per year, twice at sunrise and twice at sunset. A table of dates at Heliopolis from 4000 BC to 1000 BC is given below.

Year	Sun rise		Sun set	
4000 BC	2/2	14/7	9/4	18/9
3000 BC	17/2	31/7	30/4	7/10
2000 BC	11/3	21/8	22/5	4/11
1000 BC	30/3	20/9	11/6	25/11

The chart indicates that the dates of the conjunction change each year and that there is no linear pattern to this change of date. The early-year date of the sunrise conjunction changed its date by fifty-seven days in three thousand years. The summer sunrise conjunction changed by sixty-nine days in the same period. During the same three thousand years, the spring sunset conjunction changed by sixty-three days and the winter sunset conjunction by sixty-eight days.

The twentieth of June was the most important day in the Egyptian calendar. It simultaneously represented the Egyptian new-year's day and the summer solstice. The star Sirius rose at dawn on this day and the Egyptians read this to signal the rising of the Nile. Because of the importance of this day, we studied the conjunction patterns to find the year when a line from the sun rising would go through "the pole" to the midpoint of the Ursa Major constellation on twentieth June. Such a conjunction occurred circa 6750 BC. There was no January sunrise conjunction in that year because, at that time of year, Ursa Major was below the horizon when viewed from Heliopolis. Interestingly, and perhaps significantly, in that same year, a sunset conjunction of sun, pole, and the mid-point of the cup of Ursa Major occurred at the time of the spring solstice. In other words, the conjunction of sun rising, "pole," and the mid-point of the cup of Ursa Major occurred on the two most important astronomical days of the year in the same year, 6750 BC. Could this be the year when the conjunction of sun, pole, and constellation was given its importance? If so, it would be interesting to know the earthly events that led the priests to give the concurrent astronomical events their significance. The date of the mid-year sunset conjunction in 6750 BC was August twenty-fourth.

Speculation aside, it seems reasonable to assume (given the weight of evidence) that the ancient priest astronomers determined that Isis had appeared in her guise as the wife of Osiris at the conjunction of sunrise, the pole, and the mid-point of the cup of Ursa Major and such a determination was first made circa 6750 BC. She was the beam of light from the sun that created the conjunction. In all her other aspects, she must also have been considered as a beam of light. She always emanated from the sun but she took different paths and illuminated different places.

This revelation of the true identity of Isis explains why the Temples dedicated to "The Goddess" at Annu, Edfu, and Denderah are oriented to allow a single beam of sunlight to travel down the central axis of the temple and illuminate the inner sanctum at sunrise on particular days. At these times, The Goddess herself entered the temple to bring her divine message from Atum-Ra.

The pre-dynastic hieroglyph for the ancient goddess (Fig 50) shows crossed arrows emanating from a rising or setting sun.

> "Esoterically, the symbolism of the arrow refers to the shaft of light, which, when woven with others, produces the form of the "light-body," or Ka—the double, of which Nut is the cosmic counterpart".[79]

The pictograms in Fig 50 would seem to confirm that the goddess was represented as the sun's rays and in her aspect of As-t she was a ray from the sun at sunrise and sunset. In

---

[79] Gordon, *Land of the fallen Star Gods*

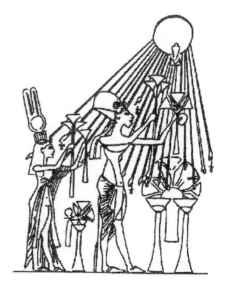

Fig 53 part of a limestone
relief in the Cairo museum,
taken from the temple at
Armana. Life from the Aten
brought by the goddesses to
Akhenaton and Nefertiti

dynastic times, the hieroglyph changed to show the rays going through an aperture to meet a strange horizontal shape
at the bottom of the picture. Given the rest of the hypothesis,
it is possible that this hieroglyph might represent a ray from
the sun going through an imaginary orifice around "the pole"
to meet the base of the cup in the Ursa Major constellation.

J Norman Lockyer provides additional and tangible links
between the goddess and Ursa Major. Discussing the alignment of the temple dedicated to Horus (the child of Isis and
consort of Hathor) at Edfu, he says:

> The king is represented as speaking thus: "I have grasped the
> wooden peg and the handle of the club; I hold the rope with Ses-
> heta; my glance follows the course of the stars; my eye is on Mes(et
> (that is the 'Bull's Thigh constellation,' or Great Bear); (mine is
> the part of time of the number of the hour-clock); I establish the
> corners of thy house of God.
>
> And in another place: 'I have grasped the wooden peg; I hold
> the handle of the club; I grasp the cord with Sesheta; I cast my
> face towards the course of the rising constellations; I let my glance
> enter the constellation of the Great Bear (the part of my time stands

in the place of his hour-clock); I establish the four corners of thy temple."[76]

In relation to the alignment of the great Temple of Hathor at Denderah, he quotes the temple hieroglyphic inscriptions:

The inscriptions state that the king while stretching the cord had his glance directed to the *ãk* of the constellation of The Thigh—the old name of the constellation which we now recognize as the Great Bear—and on this line was built the new temple, "as had been done there before."

The actual inscription has been translated as follows: "The living God, the magnificent son of Asti (a name of Toth), nourished by the sublime goddess in the temple, the sovereign of the country, stretches the rope in joy. With his glance towards the *ãk* (the middle?) of the Bull's Thigh constellation, he establishes the temple house of the mistress of Denderah, as took place there before."

At another place the king says, "Looking to the sky at the course of the rising stars (and) recognizing the *ãk* of the Bull's Thigh constellation, I establish the corners of the Temple of Her Majesty.

. . .[I]t may be suggested that the word *ãk* used in relation to the king's observation, more probably referred to the brightest star Dubhe (alpha Ursa Majoris) in the asterism, or the "middle point" of the constellation, which would be about represented by the star (delta) Ursa Major, which lies nearly at the center of the seven stars of the Great Bear.[76]

We agree with Norman Lockyer that the word *ãk* is likely to represent "the middle point" of the constellation and that this could point to δ (delta) Ursa Major . However, given the evidence we have brought forward to link the middle of the cup of the constellation to "the pole" and the rising sun, we propose that the word *ãk* could equally direct us to the center of the cup. If this suggestion is valid, the inscription is the nearest thing to written proof of the link between Hathor/Isis and the "middle point" of the constellation of Ursa Major that exists.

In the same temple there is an inscription that says:

THE PLACE OF THE BIRTH OF ISIS IS TO THE NORTH-WEST OF THE TEMPLE OF HATHOR, ITS PORTAL IS TURNED TO THE EAST, AND THE SUN RISES ON ITS PORTAL WHEN IT RISES TO ILLUMINATE THE WORLD.

This orientation of the temple towards Ursa Major and of the adjacent Iseum towards the sunrise implies a geometric relationship between the three positions and therefore implies a particular day of the year.

As can be seen in Fig 54, the great temple is orientated 20° east of north and the Iseum 22° south of east. There has never been a date when the sun rose at 22° south of east and

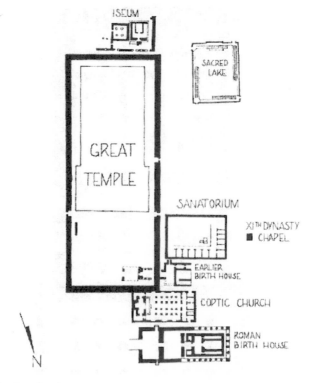

Fig 54 the Denderah complex

simultaneously the sun, pole, and constellation alignment took place. However, it is probably significant that sunrise on the Spring Equinox in the year 6750 BC occurred 22° south of ast and at that same moment δ Ursa Major (the star at the center of the Ursa Major constellation and mentioned by Norman Locker) was facing 20° east of north.

The oldest temple location in Egypt is the Temple of Annu in Heliopolis. Annu is the name of the goddess brought from Babylon in pre-dynastic times. Norman Locker describes the orientation of this temple as:

> The north and south faces (at Annu) bear 13° north of west, 13° south of east. I have elsewhere shown that there is good reason for believing that the original foundation for the temple at Annu dates from a time when the north-pointing member of such a double system was directed to α Ursæ Majoris. This was somewhat earlier than 5000 BC . . . at Annu in the old days, and at Tell el-Armana afterwards, the sun was worshipped on the same day of the year. At both places the sunlight at sunset would enter the temple on April 18 and August 24 of the Gregorian year; hence both temples were probably built really to observe the sunset on a special day.[76]

The date of August 24th has already shown to be significant because it was the date of the second sunset conjunction with "the pole" and Ursa Major in the year 6750 BC However, the angle of the sun from the East West line varies, depending on date and location. Despite that, at no time in history could sunset on April 18th have fallen on the line 13° south of east, 13° north of west. It is, however, true that on April 18th 6750 BC the sun *rose* 13° south of east (Fig 55) at Heliopolis and on that day it would have created a beam of light that would have traversed the center of the temple of Annu.

We have therefore located all the players, the goddess in her various forms of Nut, Annu, Hathor, Taurt, and Isis, Aten in the Sun, Osiris and Amon in Ursa Major, Set in Draconis and Ursa Major and Horus in Ursa Minor. By extrapolation,

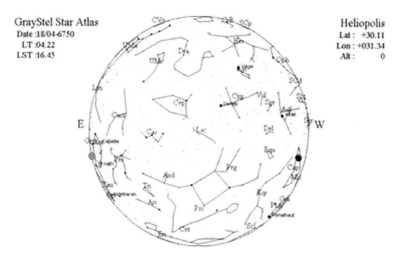

GrayStel Star Atlas
Date :18/04-6750
LT :04.22
LST :16.45

Heliopolis
Lat : +30.11
Lon : +031.34
Alt :   0

Fig 55 the sun rising 13° south of east on 18ᵗʰ April 6750 BC at Heliopolis

we may also have discovered the year of the birth of Osiris to
be 6750 BC (or 25,920 years earlier).

The birth concept could relate to two possibilities:

1. The year in which the angle of the cup of Ursa Major first
   looked (to the ground observer) to be 108°.
2. The first year that the constellation did not set below the
   horizon.

Both of these possibilities would tell us the latitude of the
observer (on the earth) from which the heavenly observations were made.

The Osiris Isis mystery has been one of the world's most
enduring mysteries. Now, for the first time since it was hidden by the priests of Egypt, its secret meaning and illusion
has been disclosed.

Today, the reader of this explanation might reasonably say
"so what?" Then, it could only have been hidden for one of
two reasons. Either the priests and kings of Egypt believed

that the science was too complex a subject for the ordinary citizen to understand (and because of that, in order to increase and consolidate their power, they created allegories that they thought people could relate to without understanding), or, the priests and kings interpreted science as the manifestation of God and believed their own God stories which they encouraged the citizens to celebrate by elaborate rituals.

The fact that the priests and kings built such enormous and elaborate tombs and went to such great lengths to ensure that they were prepared for their great journey at death is a clear indication that they did believe the stories. They believed that they knew the location of the gods and that, in death, they would join them in the proximity of the northern stars.

Today, we know that all scientific reality is a manifestation of God, only in the sense that we wonder at the magnificence of the Universe and the relationships between its countless elements. Despite that, there is a possibility that the fervent religious beliefs of many of today's world citizens have been passed down in varied forms and therefore inherited from the same stories of these well-meaning priest/kings.

Chapter Five

The Face of God

In 1972 and again (with revisions) in 1985, R. O. Faulkner published translations of the corpus funerary texts of Ancient Egypt known as *The Book of the Dead*. This document gives a large number of clues to the location of the Egyptian Gods among the northern stars and in particular it directs us to "The Face of God."

"As for those gods the Lords of Justice, they are Seth and Isdes, the Lords of the West. As for the tribunal which is behind Osiris, Imsety, Haty, Duamutef, and Qebehsenuef, it is these who are behind the Great Bear in the northern sky."[80]

"I am one whose face is hidden within the Great Mansion, the Upper Place, the shrine of the god, and I have reached there after the purification of Hathor. I am one who creates a multitude, who raises up Truth to Re and who destroys the might of Apep; I am one who opens up the firmament, who drives off the storm, who makes the crew of Re alive, and who raises up offerings to the place where they are. I have caused the sacred Bark to make its fair voyage; a way is prepared for me that I may pass on it. My face is that of a Great One, my hinder parts are the Double Crown. I am a possessor of power, I am content in the horizon, and I am joyful at telling. O you who are awake prepare a path for your Lord Osiris."[81]

"Happy are you O Osiris! You have appeared in glory, you have power, you are spirit; you have made your shape everlasting, and your face is that of Anubis. Re rejoices over

---

[80] *R O Faulkner, Book of the Dead Spell 17, University of Texas Press (2000)*
[81] *Faulkner Book of the Dead, Spell 144*

you and he is well-disposed towards your beauty. You have
seated yourself on your pure throne which Geb, who loves
you, made for you; you receive him in your arms in the West,
you cross the sky daily, you convey him to his mother Nut
when he goes to rest daily in the West in the Bark of Re,
together with Horus who loves you. The protection of Re is
your safeguard, the power of Thoth is behind you, and the
spells of Isis pervade your members.

I have come to you, O Lord of the Sacred Land, Osiris
Foremost of the Westerners, Wennefer who will exist for
ever and ever."[82]

"Hail to you Foremost of the Westerners, who re-fash-
ioned mankind, who comes as one rejuvenated in his time,
better than he was formerly. Your son Horus is your protector, in the function of Atum; your face is potent, O Wennefer.
Raise yourself, O Bull of the West, be firm as you were firm
in the womb of your mother Nut . . . I am Thoth; I have come
today from Kheraha, I have knotted the chord and have put
the ferry-boat in good order, I have fetched East and West, I
am uplifted on my standard higher than any god in this my
name of Him whose face is on high; I have opened those
things which are good in this my name of Wepwawet; I have
given praise and made homage to Osiris Wennefer, who shall
exist forever and ever." [83]

On the West Bank of the Nile at Thebes there exist a series
of tombs. One of these, designated number 1, is the tomb of
Sennedjem, "Servant in the place of Truth." "No tomb has
been reproduced in books on Egyptian art as often as that of
Sennedjem, not only because of the freshness of its paintings but also because of their exquisite quality." [84]

There is controversy regarding the identity of Sennedjem
and the meaning of his title "Servant in The Place of Truth."
The extensive decoration of the tomb and the enigmatic

[82] Faulkner, Book of the Dead, Spell 181
[83] Faulkner, Book of the Dead, Spell 182
[84] R Porter and B Moss, commentary by Sydney Aufrere, Topographical Bibliography of
Ancient Egyptian Hieroglyphic Texts,, Griffith Institute (2004)

nature of this decoration lead us to the conclusion that the paintings found here do in fact depict "the truth" to those initiated in the deeper meanings of the mysteries. They also give many clues to the hidden meanings of many of the other paintings found on scrolls and tomb and temple walls.

The center painting on the North wall is a strange picture of Osiris (Fig 56), strange because the entire picture is a Salvador Dali-like picture of a face. Two eyes dominate the top

Fig 56 the picture of Osiris on the wall of the Sennedjem tomb

of the painting, the two hands of Osiris represent nostrils and an inverted V made by two intersecting wands form the central part of the upper lip. The legs of Osiris create the elongated beard common to the gods.

In addition, a line through the center of the crown of Osiris intersects the patterned border at the top of the painting at the exact point that creates the golden section ratio 1.618. Since this ratio is central to the dimensional characteristics of a regular pentagram (see appendix 2a), the painting was studied more carefully to discover if such a geometric shape could be detected within the painting itself.

Careful and close examination led us to uncover a series of anomalies and points within the painting that invite scrutiny.

The upper arms of Osiris each contain a slight indentation (Fig 58). This phenomenon is only found in pictures of

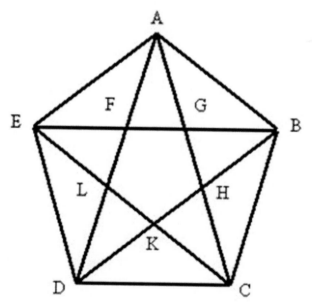

Fig 57 a regular pentagon and the pentagram it holds

Fig 58 the lines from the tip of the beard through an arm indentation
and the 108° angle they create

Osiris, not in the pictures of any other gods and such inden-
tations are not normally as pronounced as they are in this
particular painting.

- A line drawn from the tip of the beard, through the indentation in Osiris' left arm was found to just touch the
  tip of the small spike below one of the large eyes.
- A second line drawn from the tip of the beard through
  the other indentation is parallel to the top of the paint-

ing and, more importantly, creates an angle with the first line of 108°, the interior angle of a regular pentagon (Fig 58).

Intriguingly, this angle is precisely bisected by a line joining the tip of the beard to the point made by the cobra ornamentation at the top of the crown, the point that creates the golden ratio in its division of the upper frieze (Fig 59).

Without doubt, this painting was created by a master in the science of geometry and mathematics. He was able to

Fig 59 the bisection of the 108° angle

create angles accurately and knew the technique for reproducing the golden ratio (see appendix 2b).

The fact that such noticeable anomalies in the painting allow an easy creation of the 108° angle makes it seem highly
likely that this picture holds a regular pentagon (the shape in
Fig 57) and that this five-sided shape surrounds the head of
Osiris.

Such a design would be remarkable and it would neces-
sitate that the complete picture contains other distinctive
features that would help locate the pattern precisely. The ex-
ercise of locating these points and the pentagram they delin-
eate is outlined below.

Assuming that the tip of the beard is one of the five
points, another point would lie on the line we have already
determined from the tip of the beard through the indentation in Osiris's right arm. An examination of the picture
located six lines that intersect precisely at same position
on this line.

On the right of Osiris:

- A line from the iris in the large eye to the center tip of
  the bulrush;
- A line from the tip of the down protrusion from the eye
  to the tip of the differently colored leaf of the ornamental bulrush;
- A line from the center of the curl below the eye to the tip
  of Osiris' left elbow.

On the left of Osiris:

- A line from the tip of the eye to the tip of the first leaf of
  Osiris' fan;
- A line from the iris in the large eye to the tip of the second leaf in Osiris' fan (this has been omitted from Fig
  60 to avoid congestion);
- A line from the nipple on the protrusion beneath the
  large eye to the tip of the third leaf in Osiris's fan and

Fig 60 the intersecting lines

on to the tip of the splay on the end of the suspended animal's tail.

Intriguingly, the point identified by these intersections is the same distance from the tip of the beard as is the distance from tip of the beard to the nipple below the eye on the left of Osiris and which was used to find the 108° angle we saw in Fig 59. It would seem, therefore, that three points of the pentagon have been accurately located, allowing us to draw two sides of the pentagram (Fig 60).

Fig 61 the fourth point located

The three points are:

- The tip of the beard
- The nipple on the protrusion beneath the left eye
- The point of intersection of the lines in Fig 60

The painter/mathematician master craftsman positioned guides to the remaining two points of the pentagon with the same clinical precision.

Significant points in the two large eye-decorations unlock the secret to the location of the fourth point. Joining these points by straight lines created an intersection in precisely the correct location (Fig 61).

On Osiris' right side:

- A line from the tip of the right eyebrow to the tip of Osiris' left elbow;
- A line from the iris in the right eye to the bottom tip of the protrusion beneath the left eye;
- The nipple of the protrusion beneath the right eye to the iris of the left eye;
- The tip of the protrusion beneath the right eye to the tip of the fifth tear in the top border of the painting.

The length of the line between this new point and the point of intersection of the lines in Fig 60 is exactly the same as the length of the two orange lines in Fig 61 and the new interior angle is once again 108° (Fig 62).

With only four points of the five located, there is no doubt that this painting is a complex mathematical and geometrical design, which allows the interested ob-server to locate an accurate pentagram around the face of Osiris.

The finding of the fifth point of the pentagon is again un-demanding. As well as utilizing one of the eyes and the tips of the elbows, the artist made use of the tears in the border at the top of the painting (Fig 63).

- The tip of the first tear to the left of Osiris' crown was joined to the tip of Osiris left elbow.
- The tip of the second tear was joined to the tip of Osiris' right elbow.
- The tip of the third tear was joined to the tip of the pro-trusion beneath the large eye.
- The tip of the forth tear was joined to the nipple on the protrusion beneath the large eye.

Fig 62 three sides of the pentagram

The fifth point allows two more lines to be inserted into the pentagon that are exactly the same length as the other three lines. All the interior angles of the pentagram made by joining the five points are exactly 108° (Fig 64). The pentagram is now complete. Joining key points in the picture has allowed us to reproduce an exact pentagram around the face of Osiris. Unlike the modern claims of difficult to locate codes in the paintings of Maestros, here is a real and intrigu-

Fig 63 locating the fifth point

ing "code" that has been hidden in this painting for almost five thousand years.

The pentagram or five-pointed star that is created by joining each of the five points of the pentagon with every other point produces another smaller pentagon inside the outer one. The inner pentagon lies immediately round the face of Osiris (Fig 64). This combination of five-sided figures gives us clear evidence that the "initiated" believed Osiris

Fig 64 the pentagon around the face of Osiris and the inner pentagram it creates

to be either the pentagon or the pentagram or both. Each of the two geometric shapes is created by, from, and out of the other in a spiral of self-perpetuating endless creation (see appendix 1). No fertilization by an outside source is needed to promote the process of reproduction. However, as we have already seen, the sun's rays at dawn into the cup holding the pentagram in the northern sky had great significance to the propagators of this sacred drama. For that reason, we can deduce that the Ancient Egyptians looked to the sun as the entity holding or hiding the principle of life in the person of Atum-Ra.

The Book of the Dead provides a series of spells and vignettes with pictures of gods and goddesses in boats. In particular, Ra or Re is seen travelling through the netherworld in his solar barque. There, his light arouses the occupants on whom he makes judgments. His declared aim is to unite with his body, which is symbolized by the corpse of Osiris.

Fig 65 the plan of Ursa Major superimposed on the picture, holding the pentagram in its cup

This is achieved in the sacred drama and "resurrection" takes place.

In many spells, Osiris is called "*Akhet* from which Re comes forth," and in one passage of pyramid text, Re is pictured inside the earth "in his fetters" as if he is synonymous with the body of Osiris.[85]

The eye of God, often known as "The Eye of Horus" is most often depicted looking towards the left (as we look at it) and is therefore most likely represented by the eye on the left side of Osiris in the painting in the Tomb of Sennedjem. When a representation of the seven key stars of the constellation of Ursa Major is superimposed on this picture (in such a way that the pentagram sits in the cup) (Fig 65), the link between the constellation and this left eye becomes evident. One of the stars of the constellation lies exactly on the iris of the eye and the total pattern of the eye and eyebrow decorations can be located by means of the seven stars.

Additionally, when we examine the total constellation of Ursa Major, we see that there are protrusions on either

---

[85] *Alford; The Midnight Sun quoting pyramid text 285 Cf CT, VI, 237*

side of the cup holding the pentagram and other protrusions above (Fig 66).

This image of the total constellation invites us to envisage the protrusions (which we have previously seen as wings or horns) as connections to the two eyes on either side of the cup of the constellation and the face of God contained within it. The prominent stars above the four stars that form the cup create protrusions that could equally be links to the crown.

Alternatively, the two lateral protrusions of the constellation are the horns of Osiris. In the many pictures of this god that do not illustrate the Eyes of God (which we see in the painting in the tomb of Sennedjem), the horns are shown protruding from beneath the crown. In Fig 68, for example, the pentagram would surround the face of Osiris and the two horns would then be in the correct place to represent the lateral protrusions from the constellation. Osiris' crown can readily be located amongst the stars protruding upwards above the cup and above the face of God that the cup contains.

The link between the constellation, the eye, and the boat/barque that conveys the gods is perhaps confirmed by the

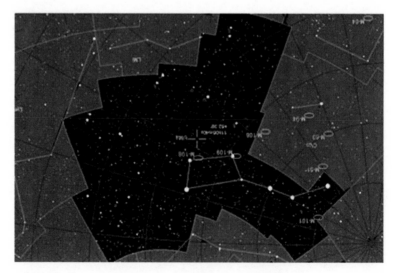

Fig 66 all the stars in the constellation of Ursa Major

Fig 67 the additional protrusions created by the constellation overlaid on the picture

Eye of Horus that is visible on the prow of the Amun's barque painted on the wall of the chapel of Set at Abydos.[86] Bridget McDermott also tells us:

> In mythology Horus, the falcon-headed god, was the symbol of divine kingship. Early myths tell of an eye injury sustained by Horus during battle with his uncle Seth: the goddess Hathor used a potion

---

[86] *Bridgett McDermott; Decoding Egyptian Hieroglyphic, Chronicle Books (2001), Ch 4*

of gazelle milk to restore the eye, which was later revered as a sacred symbol and associated with the healing arts. In hieroglyphic texts the eye of Horus symbol is translated as "whole." In another myth Horus's eye shattered into many pieces when Seth tore it out and hurled it away, but the Ibis headed god Toth collected them and restored them to wholeness.

The pyramid texts tell us that there is a close link between the Ursa Major constellation and the "opening of the mouth" ceremony, which was central to the ritual surrounding the celebration of the Isis, Osiris mystery.

Fig 68 the horns of Osiris are the extensions within Ursa Major

These northern stars (Ursa Major) provided the magical symbolism for the opening of the mouth ceremony. Firstly the *adze* was made in the image of one of Seth's forelegs (either Ursa Minor or the Plough in Ursa Major) and given the stellar name *mskhtiu*, determined by the size of the *adze*. And secondly, the key offering in the ritual was the bull's foreleg *(khpsh)* which was the principal form of the eye of Horus. Hence in utterance 20 the priest says: O Osiris-the-king, I split open the mouth for you with the *khpkh* of the Eye of Horus —one foreleg *(khpsh)*.[87]

Alford goes on to say (in his chapter on the fiery eye):

The uraeus the Eye of Horus has an identity with the king's crowns . . . In its identity of the dual crowns, the Eye of Horus was called the great Magic . . . It is worth mentioning at this juncture that the adze which split open the mouth and the eyes of Osiris is described in the pyramid texts as "the Great of Magic Adze" . . . as if to anticipate the emergence of the Great of Magic Eye and eyes.

The allegory of three eyes has been unexplained by Egyptologists other than by the remote and implausible hypothesis that that "the eyes" represent the moon and sun. In the painting of Osiris at Sennedjem there are three eyes, one in the central small pentagram that surrounds Osiris' face and two larger eyes on either side of Osiris' crown. The secret geometry that we have discovered in this painting is far more compelling and meaningful than any codes that might have been hidden in the paintings of Leonardo De Vinci. The Sennedjem painting is "The Servant in the Place of Truth" and therefore holds the key to the ceremony of the three eyes and the opening of the mouth.

The touching of the body by the *adze* in the shape of the seven stars of Ursa Major is a ceremony behooving the spirit of the dead king to go to the place of the *adze*, the place of the three eyes, which is the home of Osiris within the constellation of Ursa Major in order to join God in Paradise.

---

[87] *Alford, The Midnight Sun Ch8*

The mouth of Osiris lies at the midpoint of the base of the smaller pentagram. It is also the intersection point between this base line and the line from the tip of the beard to the line that makes the base of the cup in the larger pentagram (Fig 69).

An explanation of the opening of the mouth ceremony is clearly linked to the lines, which create the geometric shape inside Ursa Major. When the mouth of the corpse is opened (using the *adze* depicted in figure 45), it is not difficult to envisage that the face of God is being laid on the corpse (or vice versa). The mouth at the key point of the geometric pattern is evidently true in all representations of God, irrespective of how the pattern is superimposed on the face. Nowhere is this better seen than the superimposition of the pentagon on the face of the famous Tutankhamen mask (Fig 70).

Tutankhamen lived in the fourteenth century BC. He took the throne soon after the departure of Akhenaton, who had attempted to reshape Egyptian beliefs and have the Egyptians revere only "one god." This god was to be revered in his guise as the sun disk and no reference was to be made of Amen or Amun (the hidden one). This was the second significant attempt to affect sacred Egyptian beliefs. The first was the attempt by the Semitic Hyksos to similarly influ-

Fig 69 the two key lines intersecting in the mouth of Osiris

Fig 70 the Tutankhamen mask with its particular version of the geometry

ence Egyptian beliefs when they conquered Egypt in the late eighteenth century BC.

The earliest records we have of Egyptian civilization and the Egyptian pantheon is 3500 BC. In the two millennia between the first Pharaoh and Tutankhamen, the secrets held by the priests and initiates stayed intact. As can be seen from Fig 70, however, some artistic license was used in the creation of the mask. The pentagram is rotated in relation to the face and the base of the smaller pentagram encompasses the complete face, including the chin and does not go through the mouth. As was the case in the Osiris painting, however, two lines of the interior pentagon do cross at the mouth.

"The mysteries" were at the heart of the Egyptian religion and later they influenced the beliefs of the Greek initiates and the more esoteric beliefs of the Christian faith. The passage of time allowed sophistication and interpretation, and the underlying principles and definition of "God" and "The Face of God" stayed intact defined by the hidden geometry contained within the cup of Ursa Major.

Chapter Six

Cathedral Clues

There is a popular claim amongst many of the "guides" to the cathedrals in Europe that all the cathedrals face eastwards in "the direction of Jerusalem." This claim is not true. The only cathedral orientated in the direction of Jerusalem is Notre Dame in Paris, which is oriented 114° east of north. Less popularly, it is claimed by some that the gothic cathedral design, which first manifested in Sens in AD 1030, incorporated esoteric and sacred geometry and resulted from secret information retrieved by the Knights Templar in Jerusalem.

The ground pattern of the seven principal stars of Ursa Major includes cathedrals at Chartres, St. Quentin, Reims, and Verdun. None of these four cathedrals face towards Jerusalem. Their geographic orientations are:

Chartres 44° 16′ east of north
St. Quentin 72° 39′ east of north
Reims 58° east of north
Verdun 65° 17′ east of north

There is no obvious connection between these orientations. In fact, without study, they seem to be meaningless and random. The only thing they have in common is that they variously face the northeast quadrant of the compass.

We do know that the ground locations of these cathedrals were precisely chosen, either by Celtic druids when they laid down the original pagan temple sites on which these cathedrals were constructed or by the architects/founders of the cathedrals themselves. The ground pattern, of which the cathedrals are a part, is extremely accurate. And, as we have seen, those who laid down the pattern may have believed that they were doing so in reverence of God. Given what we now know about "The Face of God," the duplication of Ursa Major could even have been thought to be holding a manifestation of God himself.

At the same time, we know that beams of sunlight into the Ursa Major constellation were a link to the Mother Goddess, Isis, and that the cathedrals in question were all dedicated to the mother of God in the person of "Notre Dame."

Given the connections made thus far, one obvious place to look for the answer to the seemingly random orientations of the cathedrals might be to look for direct connections between the cathedrals on the ground, the sun, and the constellation of Ursa Major in the heavens above them.

The constellation of Ursa Major revolves around the pole in the heavens and so, unlike most other stars and constellations, it appears to travel east to west on one half of its rotation and west to east on the other half. When observed from Northern Europe, the constellation does not fall below the horizon. The revolution from the east to the west and back again takes some part of the constellation past the imaginary points made by extending lines out into the sky along the axis of each cathedral. Since the four cathedral edifices are all facing northeast and irrespective of their individual orientations, each cathedral will point towards some part of the constellation at least once and often twice each day. There is nothing special, therefore, about the fact that any of these cathedrals point towards some part of the constellation at some time during a particular day.

What would be significant would be any link between the cathedrals on significant days of the year and/or at key times of the day.

There is good geological evidence that the orientation and layout of ancient Celtic monuments, such as Stonehenge and the function and design of a large number of Egyptian temples, are related to sunrise, sunset, and mid-day. Additionally, there is excellent and observable evidence in these same ancient monuments that the three critical times of the day were considered to be more important on a small number of key days each year.

The earth wobbles backwards and forwards each year. As it does so, each part of the earth moves further away from or nearer to the sun. At the same time, the earth revolves so that each place on the earth moves into the shadow on the side of the earth not illuminated by the sun, a phenomenon we know as night time. The combination of the wobble and the revolution throughout the year creates the seasons and the variation in the time of daylight and night darkness in each twenty-four hour period. In the northern hemisphere, winter nights are long but there is one day in late December when the nighttime is longer than any other day of the year. It is the day when the earth's wobble has reached its limit and the North Pole is furthest away from the sun. This day is called the Winter Solstice.

As we move into spring, the nights get shorter and the days longer until we reach a point when the days start to be longer than the nights. Between the tenth and twenty-fifth days of March there is a day when the time of night darkness is equal to the time of daylight, or, another way of describing it, the time between sunrise and sunset is twelve hours, half of the twenty-four hours of the earth's revolution. This day is called the Spring Equinox or sometimes the Vernal Equinox. Spring moves into summer and the days get longer until we reach a day in June that has the longest time of daylight. This day has been conventionally described as midsummer's day but is known technically as the Summer Solstice. From midsummer's day onwards the days get shorter and the night time gets longer.

About halfway between the summer and the winter solstices there is a day in September when the time of daylight and the time of night darkness is equal. This day is called the Autumn Equinox. After the Autumn Equinox, the nights are longer than the days until we again reach the night of maximum length at the Winter Solstice.

Fig 71 the ancient temple at Newgrange

A 280,000-ton megalithic structure at Newgrange in Ireland (Fig 71) originated in 3500 BC and has been shown to be a precise delineator of the Winter Solstice and of the Summer Equinox, as well as an indicator of the Venus morning star at the Winter Solstice. This edifice is thought by some researchers to have been the chamber represented in *The Book of Enoch*.[88]

This and other ancient monuments such as the Stoney Littleton Long Barrow become illumined internally at sunrise of the Winter Solstice. Other ancient monuments such as Avebury, Stonehenge (Fig 72) and Karnac (Fig 73) have been shown to be precise delineators of all the key astronomical dates and alignments, but the solstices and the equinoxes are of special significance in all the locations. [89]

[88] *Knight and Lomas, Uriel's Machine and The Book of Hiram; Knight and Lomas*
[89] *Terence Meadon, Stonehenge, The Secret of the Solstice and the Secrets of the Avebury Stones, Souvenir Press (1997)*

Fig 72 Stonehenge, the earliest known celestial observatory

In the great temple dedicated to Amun in Karnac in Egypt (Fig 73), the sunrise at the winter solstice and the sunset and the summer solstice sends rays through precisely apertures in pylons and walls that illuminate the sacred rooms deep inside the edifice. [90]

A common theory amongst researchers is that, to the ancient Celts/Druids/Egyptians, the winter solstice represented the time of birth, nine months after fertilization of the goddess at the spring equinox. There is a correspondence between this idea and the fact that the traditional birth dates of many ancient gods such as Mithras, Attis, Osiris, Adonis, Tammuz, and Dionysus, and more recently Jesus Christ, were all on December twenty-fifth, a date close to the Winter Solstice. (It has been claimed that the birth dates of Osiris and Adonis were changed by a Roman emperor in the third century AD possibly to conform to the birth date of Mithra.)

---

[90] *Lockyer, The Dawn of Astronomy*

Fig 73 the temple of Amun in Karnac

In Egypt, the Spring Equinox was the time of the Festival of the restructuring of the heavens, the coming forth of the Great Ones from the House of Ra and the Festival of Aset (Isis). As we have seen, the House of Ra was probably Ursa Major and Isis was connected to the constellation through the sun. In Egypt as in Celtic Europe, the Mother Goddess, and the rays of light that manifested her, was celebrated at this time of fertility and impregnation.

It is no coincidence that dates of the feast of the Annunciation of the Virgin Mary and of the birth of Christ in the Christian calendar are both celebrated on similar dates to their equivalents in the ancient calendar.

The date of the nativity of Christ was first set in 353 AD by Pope Liberius when veneration of Mithras (whose birth date was December 25th) was strong in Rome. To continue this commonality, Christ, like Mithra, Attis, Adonis, and Osiris before him was the product of a virgin birth, was killed and after several days was resurrected.

Mid-summer's day in Egypt represented the beginning of the Egyptian year. In addition to being the day with the most sunlight, it marked the on-set of the Nile floods and the reappearance of Sirius, the star thought by many to represent Isis. Many ceremonies were held at this time including the Wadjet (Ouadjet) ceremony, the Ceremony of the Great Throne and the Rites of the Adoration of Horus. Again, we find a link to the constellation with the "The Great Throne" and a more direct link through the Wadjet ceremony, which included the opening of the mouth with the *adze* in the shape of the constellation (see Fig 45).

For all of these reasons, it would seem pertinent to seek a link between the four cathedrals and the constellation at sunrise, mid-day, or sunset at the spring equinox, the summer solstice, the autumn equinox, and/or the winter solstice.

Star charts were examined for the year 1200 AD (being the era when the four cathedrals were founded) and the solstice and equinox dates were accurate for the individual geographical coordinates of each location. This research was in part disappointing since the only connections involving any of the four cathedrals pointing directly at the cup of the constellation at any of these times were at Chartres (see appendix 3):

- Chartres cathedral points directly at the cup of the constellation at sunset on the spring equinox;
- Chartres cathedral points directly at the cup of the constellation at mid-day on the summer solstice;
- Chartres cathedral points directly at the cup of the constellation at sunrise on the autumn equinox.[91]

Chartres therefore is the only cathedral within the four cathedrals in the pattern, which is oriented directly at the constellation of Ursa Major on three of the key dates and times of the annual celestial cycle. This is disappointing as

---

[91] *The star charts illustrating the connections above are included in appendix 3*

researchers have found that many cathedrals do follow the orientation of the stone circles that preceded them. It is unlikely to be a coincidence that the Chartres orientation is the same as the monument at Stonehenge (See Fig 153).

> Professor Lyle Borst made the discovery that several cathedrals have an east end geometry derived from stone circles. The orientations of these megalithic sites upon various solar and lunar phenomena, having been researched by scholars such as Sir Norman Lockyer and Professor Alex Thom. The geometry of the cathedrals, in overlaying that of multiple orientations of stone circles, must also preserve orientations other than the simple axial one of the patron's day. It may also mean that the patron may have been determined from the major orientation of the pre-existent stone circle.[92]

This remarkable set of coincidences relating to Chartres make up for the lack of any alignment found from the other three cathedrals since there can be no doubt that Notre Dame de Chartres was carefully aligned towards Ursa Major and the God-figure it contains on three of the four most important days in the calendar. Four additional sunrise and four additional sunset connections were found from the four cathedrals, all involving a direct line from the sun through the cathedral and along the arms of the constellation. Since these connections did not involve the orientation of a cathedral itself, they were excluded from this analysis. The star charts illustrating these alignments are included in appendices 3a to 3h.

The cathedral at Chartres represents *dubhe* or alpha Ursa Majoris in the ground pattern in Northern France, and its orientation towards the Ursa Major constellation on these three key dates is dramatic proof that it is a vital key. This cathedral and its orientation provide a tangible and meaningful link between the ground pattern and the constellation itself.

---

[92] *Nigel Pennick , Sacred Geometry Capall Bann (2001)*

The current edifice (Fig 74) was consecrated in 1260 AD and is known to have overlaid the position of the building that has preceded it. This had, in turn, been constructed on a site known to have housed an ancient druidic temple. Whether the orientation of the current construction is unique

Fig 74 Chartres Cathedral

or followed an orientation set by much older religious con-
structions is not known. If it did, then we must assume that
the orientation of the other three cathedrals became altered
over time, so that they no longer perform their greater celestial tasks.

The grand design of gothic cathedrals was first seen in
1130 AD at Sens, thirty-one years after Jerusalem was taken
by the first crusade and the first of the groups that were to
become the Knights Templar returned to France. The design
was fundamentally different to that of any religious sanctuary that had been seen previously. One of the best examples
of this new gothic architecture can be seen in Notre Dame in
Paris (Fig 75).

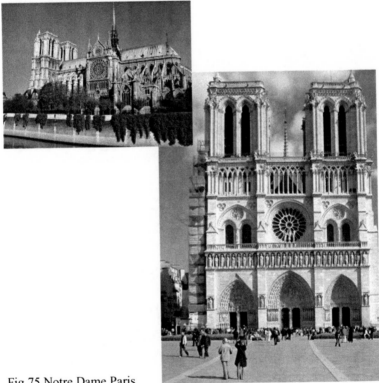

Fig 75 Notre Dame Paris

Founded in 1163 AD, it incorporates all the classical elements of the gothic design and (perhaps not surprisingly) incorporates a pentagon in the northeast transept window. Located close to the center of the cup of the ground plan, it is of major significance, incorporating:

Two towers
A rose window between the towers
Flying buttresses
Transepts
A round sanctuary

This design is a representation of the female body, lying on its back with knees raised, in which:

the towers are the knees;
the rose window is the vagina;
the buttresses the ribs;
the transepts represent the arms;
the Sanctuary is the head.

Once this picture is revealed, it takes little imagination to see that a ray of light through the rose window carries the divine force that fertilizes the womb of the goddess and initiates the "Immaculate Conception." In Chartres, we can presume that this happens at the time of sunset on the spring equinox, the traditional date of fertilization, and a day and time when we know that the cathedral is pointing directly at the constellation. It is possible in this scenario that Isis, rather than being ray of light herself, is the receptacle for a ray of light, the light from the sun being the tool of the divine impregnator and the cathedral (and the cup of the constellation towards which it is oriented) being the womb of the goddess.

The gothic design is an updated and more sophisticated version of the design of ancient Egyptian temples (Fig 76). They, too, had two towers and were known to direct sunlight to inner chambers on key days on the annual calendar.

Fig 76 a side view of the Temple of Isis at Philae

The underlying philosophy of the ancient Egyptian religion was resurrected in the twelfth century under the influence of the Knights Templar and the Cistercians. One cannot be sure from this evidence if they were aware of this similarity or of the underlying philosophy. However, other links to the theosophy of ancient Egypt and to the northern constellations do indicate that a small inner sanctum did have this knowledge. Had they made the information public, it is not difficult to imagine they would have become persecuted as extreme heretics, blasphemers, and enemies of both church and state.

Chapter Seven

The Circle of the Poles

Chapter four gave a description of the "Precession of the Equinoxes" created by the 25,920-year rotational wobble of the earth.

The earth spins on an imaginary axle. The slow movement created by the rotational wobble means that if we extended this imaginary axle up into the heavens, the faraway end of the axle would appear to move slowly in a large circle (Fig 77).

The viewer on Earth sees the pole in the heavens as stationary. In reality, the pole position is moving on the rim of a giant circle, a journey that takes 25,920 years to complete.

This circle in the heavens is a celestial clock. Because we know the date now and we also know the location of the pole on the circle, we can accurately deduce the date in the past or the date in the future when the pole was at a particular past point or a point it will be at on some future point on the same circle. Currently, the pole position appears close to Polaris in the constellation of Ursa Minor (The Little Bear). It will closest to Polaris between 2100 and 2115 AD.

In any one day, the pole position is the point that appears to be fixed. It seems not to move and as the earth rotates, everything else in the heavens appears to rotate around it.

At particular dates in the past, the pole position as seen from Earth has moved through the constellations of Cepheus, Cygnus, Draconis, and Ursa Major (Fig 78). In each of those times, observers from Earth have regarded the star nearest to the pole position with even greater importance than that we attribute to Polaris today. When man navigated using the stars at night, the fixed star positions (the ones that were always

131

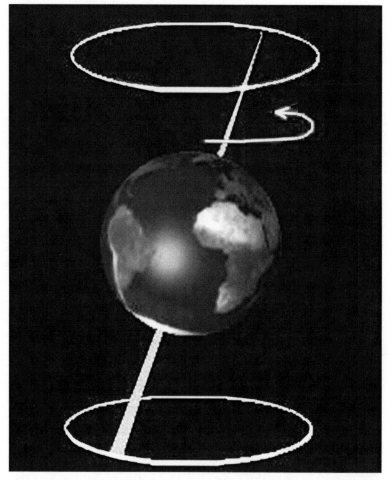

Fig 77 the celestial circles caused by the earth's 25,920-year wobble

visible) were paramount in the business of self-location. The fixed pole position, together with the stars in the immediate vicinity that did not fall below the horizon, represented to the ancients many of the aspects and guises of God.

We are taught in our science classes that the pointer stars in Ursa Major point to "the Pole Star." This is not in fact the case. The two "pointer" stars in Ursa Major are *Dubhe*

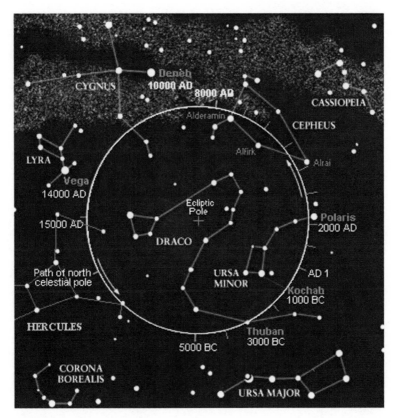

Fig 78 the circle of the Pole of the Ecliptic and the Northern Constellations it traverses

furthest from the pole position and *Merak* nearest to the pole position. When a line is drawn through these stars, it misses Polaris by what seems to be a whisker. Currently, the line from these pointer stars is between 1° and 2° away from the line which goes directly to Polaris.

In reality, the line from the pointer stars in the constellation of Ursa Major *will* point to a pole position in the future but it does not point to *Polaris*.

In fact, if we track the line from the "pointers," we find that it is tangential to the circle of the poles and that the point at which this line touches the circle will be the Pole position in the year AD 2737 (Fig 79).

We have therefore a unique and precise astronomic event involving Ursa Major, which determines an exact date some seven hundred plus years from now.

During the period when this book was being researched and prepared, the author had dinner with Michael Crossley, his cousin by marriage. The concept of the pointer line from Ursa Major being tangential to the circle of the poles and the date that it indicated was discussed. When the date of AD 2737 was mentioned, Michael's reaction was immediate, "That's a million days from the birth of Christ!"

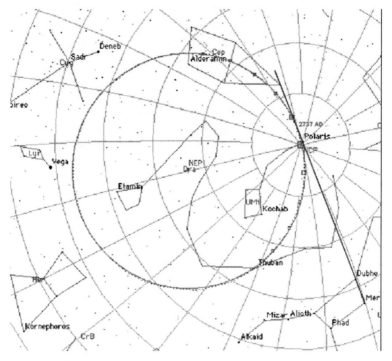

Fig 79 the line from the pointer stars in Ursa Major tangential to the circle of the poles

His outburst produced a look of surprised skepticism from the author. Michael explained that when he was a school boy, his mathematics teacher had asked the class to calculate the date a million days from the twenty fifth of December immediately preceding the year zero. (The date would actually be the twenty fifth of December in 1 BC since there is no year zero in the current calendar.) Apparently, he did this in order to impress upon the class how large and extensive the number "one million" is. The class calculated the date to be the first of November AD 2737. For some reason he found hard to explain, Michael had never forgotten this date and had transferred it from diary to diary ever since that fateful mathematics lesson.

Needless to say, Michael Crossley's date was found to be accurate when using the conventional year length of 365 and one quarters days. If the more accurate vernal year of 365.242374 days is used to make the calculation, the date one million days from the date currently claimed as the birthday of Christ would be the twenty second of November in the same year.

Is it just a coincidence that one million days from the supposed birth of Christ, the line from the pointer stars in Ursa Major point to a single and unique point on the heavens that occurs in only one year every 25,920 years? If it is not a coincidence, what does this conjunction of line and point represent?

Was the supposed date of the birth of Jesus Christ calculated by initiates in the early church choosing a date one million days before the future celestial conjunction of pointer line and Pole? If it was, what significance did they attribute to that forthcoming conjunction?

The Julian calendar came into force in 45 BC. It was chosen after consultation with the astronomer Sosigenes of Alexandria and was probably designed to approximate the tropical year, known at least since Hipparchus. It has a regular year of 365 days divided into twelve months, and a leap day is added to February every four years. Hence, the Julian year is on average 365¼ days long.

The current calendar was established in February AD 1582 by Pope Gregory XIII after being proposed by Alysius Lilius. It was a variation on the Julian calendar that had been in existence since 45 BC and was devised because the lunar (Julian) calendar had become inaccurate. The vernal equinox had slowly drifted backwards through Julian calendar years, causing problems in computing the date of Easter. The Gregorian calendar dealt with these problems by dropping a certain number of days to bring the calendar back into synchronization with the seasons, and then slightly shortening the average number of days in a calendar year, by omitting three Julian leap-days every four hundred years. The days omitted are in the century years, i.e. the twenty ninth of February 1700, 1800, 1900, 2100, 2200, 2300, 2500, 2600, 2700, 2900, etc.

Sosigenes of Alexandria was named by Pliny the Elder as the astronomer consulted by Julius Caesar for the design of the Julian calendar. It appears that little or nothing is known about him apart from two references in Pliny's Natural History. Some web sources say that the calendar was designed by Aristarchus about two hundred years earlier. It is not clear where this idea originates, although a similar reform of the previous Egyptian calendar was decreed by Ptolemy III Euergetes in 238 BC, but never implemented.

Most of the research into the date of the birth of Christ agrees that the date of the twenty fifth of December in the year 1 BC could not be correct. In about AD 523, the papal chancellor, Bonifatius, asked a monk by the name of Dionysius Exiguus to devise a way to implement the rules from the Nicean council (the so-called "Alexandrine Rules") for general use. Dionysius Exiguus (in English known as Denis the Little) was a monk from Scythia. He was a canon in the Roman curia, and his assignment was to prepare calculations of the dates of Easter. This assignment indicates that he had knowledge of astronomy and was sufficiently well-reputed and versed in the subject to have been delegated such an important task.

At that time, it was customary to count years since the reign of Emperor Diocletian, but in his calculations, Dionysius chose to number the years since the birth of Christ, rather than honor the persecutor Diocletian. When he devised his table, Julian calendar years were identified by naming the consuls who held office that year; he himself stated that the "present year" was "the consulship of Probus Junior [Flavius Probus]" which he also stated was five hundred and twenty-five years "since the incarnation [conception] of our Lord Jesus Christ." How he arrived at that number is unknown. He invented a new system of numbering years to replace the Diocletian years that had been used in an old Easter table because he did not wish to continue the memory of a tyrant who persecuted Christians. The Anno Domini era became dominant in Western Europe only after it was used by the Venerable Bede to date the events in his Ecclesiastical History of the English People, which he completed in AD 731 Dionysius (wrongly) fixed Jesus' birth with respect to Diocletian's reign in such a manner that it falls on the twenty fifth of December 753 A.U.C. (ab urbe condita, i.e. since the founding of Rome), thus making the current era start with 1 AD on the first of January 754 A.U.C. The Luke gospel claims that the census that took place at the time of Jesus' birth occurred when "Quirinius was governor of Syria," which means that the earliest date of the census could have been AD 6. The Star of Bethlehem mentioned in the Matthew gospel has been variously claimed to be a conjunction of Saturn and Jupiter in AD 7,[93] a fly past by Hally's comet in 12 BC, a nova or exploding star in 5 BC,[94] and a conjunction of Venus and Mercury in 7 BC, claimed to be the Shekinah.[95]

For all of these reasons, it is a strange and interesting coincidence that the date of the Nativity chosen by Dionysius so conveniently falls one million days before the precise date

---

[93] Santillana & Dechend, Hamlet's Hill
[94] Ian Wilson, Jesus the Evidence, HarperCollins (1985)
[95] Knight & Lomas, The Book of Hiram

established by the tangent of the pointer line from Ursa Major and the circle made by the Pole position in the heavens in AD 2737.

In *On Earth as it is in Heaven* we mentioned the enigmatic village of Rennes le Château in the southwest of France that has been the cause of so much controversy since the publication of *The Holy Blood and the Holy Grail* in 1982[96] and since the BBC documentaries featuring Henry Lincoln, one of the authors. In the last fifteen years of the nineteenth century, the then new parish priest Bèrenger Saunière discovered secret parchments while renovating the church. These documents are reputed to have contained coded information that brought the priest great wealth and gave him access to some of the most prominent people of the time. Prior to his death, it is claimed that his bishop is reputed to have refused him absolution, leading to speculation that the priest had been meddling in things that were unforgivable. Recently, they have given rise to a modern legend concerning a blood line from Jesus Christ and Mary Magdalene, which has been protected by a secret organization known as *Le Prioré de Sion*.

Much speculation continues concerning the information in the *Rennes le Chateau* documents and various serious minded persons have allocated an assortment of ground-pentagrams, a terrestrial zodiac and hidden tombs/chambers to the village and its surrounding terrain. People still arrive there with metal detectors, x-ray machines, topographical maps, and listening devices looking for some remnants of the treasure that they believe Bèrenger Saunière discovered and which he then buried somewhere within his parish. No one really knows what Saunière discovered and it is feasible that published copies of the so-called parchments are forgeries designed to lead people away from any real truth. Perhaps the only fortune is the one made by the numerous authors and film creators who continue to perpetuate the myth.

---

[96] H Lincoln, R Leigh & M Baigent, The Holy Blood and the Holy Grail, Dell (1983)

   Despite the exciting but unlikely stories of treasure and
secret organizations, the truth is that there *is* something very
special about the village of Rennes le Chateau.
   Firstly, the line from the pointer stars in the ground plan
(Bonne Mare and Chartres) goes directly through the church
in the small village. More importantly, it falls precisely at
the point made where the line from the pointer stars (Chartres and Bonne Mare) would touch the terrestrial duplication of the circle of the poles (Fig 81). In other words, the

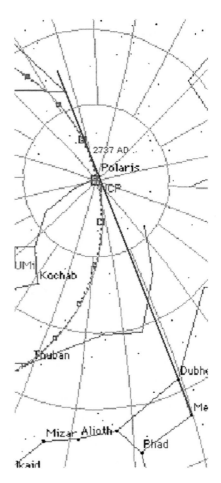

Fig 80 the line from *Merak* and
Dubhe to the tangent point

distance between Chartres and Rennes le Château relative
to the distance between Chartres and Bonne Mare is dimen-
sionally correct. It corresponds (on the ground) to the distance between the tangent point and *Dubhe* (the alpha star
of Ursa Major) relative to the distance between *Dubhe* and
Merak (the beta star of Ursa Major) (Fig 80). Because of

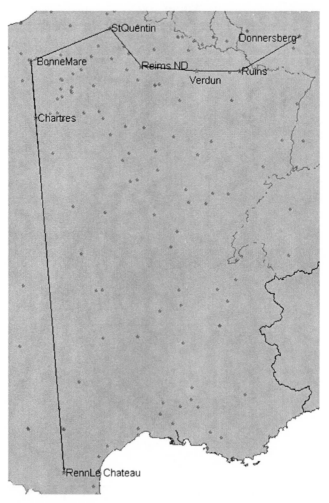

Fig 81 the line from Bonne Mare and Chartres to Rennes le Château

that, it could be argued that the village of Rennes le Château lies at the point that represents a day in the future, a day in November AD 2737.

From this simple yet extraordinary coincidence one can extrapolate from the earthly representation of the Ursa Major constellation and its connection to the village of Rennes le Château that it would be possible to plot the position of the imaginary circle of poles, relative to the location of the ground plan of Ursa Major, on the ground (Fig 82).

Such a circle falls through the Abbey at Cluny which we have already seen is central to the links between the ground pattern and key abbeys and cathedrals. Perhaps more importantly, the circle goes through the Basilica of St. Peter in Rome. This coincidence, in conjunction with all the other precise choice of locations and very accurate dimensions of the ground plan, provides an excess of evidence that a grand map of the heavens has been imprinted in the earth. Additionally, we can deduce with certainty that, at various stages in history, the location of key religious edifices were chosen to complement the pattern.

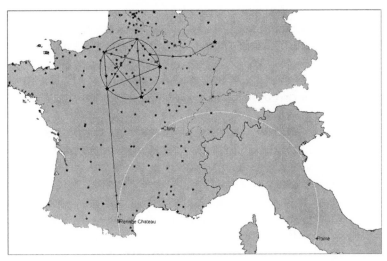

Fig 82 the terrestrial duplication of the precessional circle of the Poles

The Abbey of Cluny was the center of a major monastic reform movement in the Middle Ages. Its church was the largest Christian building in the world until the new St. Peter's Basilica was constructed in Rome in the sixteenth century. Founded in AD 910, the abbey was built on a forested hunting preserve donated by William I the Pious, Duke of Aquitaine and count of Auvergne, and no information is available about the previous history of the site.

The Abbey was occupied by Benedictine monks who wished to observe closer adherence to the Benedictine rule, which had existing since the sixth century.

Construction of the current St. Peter's Basilica was commenced in AD 1506 in the same era that saw the works of Leonardo and which resulted in the new Gregorian calendar. Ancient tradition tells us that the St. Peter's Basilica was constructed over the tomb of St. Peter. Though this myth may not be accurate, the suggestion was sufficiently compelling to persuade Constantine to construct a church dedicated to St. Peter on this site in AD 326.

The Italian peninsula had originally been settled during the Neolithic age by tribes from the north. From the beginning of the second millennium BC, new and more organized tribes from the northern heart of Europe overran the country. Amongst these people were Celtic tribesmen known as the Latini who were predominantly Nordic in nature. The Etruscans followed the Latini and had occupied Italy by the year 800 BC. The origin of these people is a mystery that has not so far been resolved.

Etruscan interplay between their written symbols and inscriptions is unique in that the letters are similar to those of the Greek alphabet, yet its grammatical structure is unlike any other European language. The Etruscans myths were similar to those of the Greeks, in that their gods possessed human attributes and dispositions and they combined Greek influences with stories of their own. Like the Greeks, religion was at the heart of Etruscan culture and the Etruscans followed three books of divination concerned with reading entrails of animals, lightning, and the flight patterns of birds respectively.

If not Greek, the Etruscans were a people who had similarities to the Greek. This tells us that they could have originated in the British Isles where we know that the Druids used letters which were described by Julius Caesar as Greek[97] and whose gods seemed to Caesar to be the same as Roman and Greek gods.

The Etruscans established an advanced society, building cities and settlements more advanced than anything else seen in Italy before that time. In relation to the location of shrines and temples, the Etruscans used surveying techniques and had "a fundamental doctrine of orientation."[98] According to Roman legend, the city of Rome was founded around the year 753 BC by the orphaned twin brothers Romulus and Remus, who were saved from death in their infancy by a she-wolf who had sheltered and suckled them. This may be true but throws little light on the foundation of Rome and its temples. What we do know was that the Etruscans controlled this area at the time and that one of their priorities was to map out and allocate sacred sites. We also know that it was a Roman custom to construct their temples on the sites of existing more ancient temples. We can assume, therefore, that the site of St. Peter's tomb (and eventually of St. Peter's Basilica) was a venerated site originally chosen by the Etruscans.

This is yet further confirmation that any ground pattern that does exist is very ancient and that any coincidence with existing cathedrals, basilicas, and abbeys occurs only because of long held tradition of the Romans and the early Christians to respect ancient traditions and to build their temples and churches on ancient sacred temple/shrine locations.

The ground pattern of Ursa Major and the circle of the poles is a clear indication that, in the earliest of times, the

---

[97] *Julius Caesar, The Conquest of Gaul, Penguin Classics (1983)*
[98] *Paul Devereux, Earth Memory, Llewellyn (1992)*

designers of these monuments were in awe of the heavens. They had knowledge of astronomy over long periods and were able to predict future astronomical events. Astronomer-priests revealed their observations in the form of stories. We will never know whether they believed the stories themselves or whether the pantheon that they introduced and proposed in order to explain their observations became real in the minds of a gullible audience. We do know that the various God stories that have been spun out of their heavenly observations have been fervently and sometimes fanatically believed down the ages and have resulted in more human disagreement and conflict than could ever have been intended.

Chapter Eight

The Hidden Mystery
That is Visible to the World

In the tenth and eleventh centuries in France, it was normal amongst the aristocracy for the eldest son to inherit all lands and titles from his father. Any other sons in the family lived in the benefice of the entitled elder brother. For this reason, the second son of the family often looked to religion and, in particular, to Benedictine monasteries to give him refuge. They did this with the help and assistance of the count, baron, lord, or duke concerned, who, in some instances, founded a new monastery within their own territory to ensure that this younger brother was not too far from their control. No count or duke wanted a rebellious brother to establish a group of fighting men under some rebellious banner in an attempt to take power from him. Second and third brothers in line were more frequently given roles in the army of knights that defended the count or duke, or were given a lesser title (Viscount, Marquis, etc.) and they were delegated management or even ownership of part of their lands since they were no immediate threat to his power and possessions. This philosophy continued down through each level of the aristocracy so that the second son in many families was destined to have a religious life.

The foundation of the Cistercian order was surrounded by mystery and intrigue. In AD 1075, Robert (an untitled son in the house of Tonnerre) was given land by Hughes de Moligny to found an abbey at Molesmes in Burgundy. Eleven years later, he was joined there by Etienne Harding. During the twenty-three years following the founding of Molesmes, the families of Fontaine, Montbard, Tonnerre, and Beaune were drawn together under the influence of Hughes de Champagne, and his brother Phillipe, the Bishop of Chalon-sur-Marne.

Hughes de Champagne married the daughter of the queen in AD 1095, and during the following three years, while his brother was away with the first Crusade, he orchestrated meetings of nobles, barons, and senior clergy, which culminated in the foundation of the Cistercian Order under Robert de Molesmes at Citeaux in AD 1098. In that same year several key figures left the first Crusade and returned to France. They included Etienne Henri, Hughes de Champagne's brother, and Hughes, the brother of the king of France. The following year Jerusalem was taken by the first Crusade.

Politics amongst the clergy meant that Robert returned to Molesmes and both Robert, Count of Flanders, and Robert, Count of Normandy, returned from the Holy Land.

Three years after its construction, the abbey at Citeaux was rebuilt in a location "half a league" from its original position. The new situation created a perfect alignment between Cluny (the founding monastery of the Benedictines), Citeaux, and the sixth point of the Ursa Major ground pattern at Landonvillers (Fig 83). This new alignment is accurate to within ten feet.

In AD 1104, Hughes de Champagne had his marriage annulled, held a succession of meetings with the most high ranking nobles in France, including dukes and counts from every part of the kingdom, and set forth for a four-year stretch with the Crusade in the Holy Land. He was accompanied on his mission by Hughes de Payen, who was later to become the first "leader" of the Knights Templar. On their return in AD 1108, he again convened a series of meetings with France's most prominent noblemen. La Milice du Christ was formed in AD 1111, it being the forerunner of The Military Order of the Temple of the Knights of Solomon or The Knights Templar. The Englishman, Etienne Harding (who is amongst those who might have been responsible for the movement of the abbey) was made Abbot of Citeaux in 1109.

Bernard de Fontaine, the twenty-two-year-old son and nephew of vassals of Hughes de Champagne joined the Cistercians in AD 1112. With him came twenty-five of his relations and friends who were noblemen in the houses of Tonnerre, Montbard, and Burgundy. With the backing of Hughes de Champagne and only three years after joining the order, Bernard had his own Abbey at Clairvaux.

This was beginning of the major expansion of the Cistercian order. By AD 1138 , Clairvaux had created thirty-nine filiates, and by AD 1145, thirty-three years after Bernard joined the Cistercians, there were 359 Cistercian establishments in Europe and thirty gothic cathedrals under construction. All of this happened at a time when transport of stone was by horse and cart and the hewing of the stone was done by hand. This thirty-three-year project probably competes with the construction of the pyramids for first prize in the organization of people (architects, masons, and manual labor) and resources to such a significant outcome.

Bernard was not backwards in coming forwards and even built and sponsored abbeys that had his family name; e.g. Fountains Abbey in Yorkshire and Trois Fontaines in Burgundy.

Two of the magnificent new abbeys that were constructed, La Ferté (AD1113) and Morimond (AD 1115), lie exactly on the line from Cluny, through Citeaux to Landonvillers.

The abbey at Fontenay, which had been constructed in AD 1119, was moved in AD 1131. The new position created an alignment between Cluny, Fontenay, and Notre Dame Reims (Fig 83).

The Abbey at Clairvaux was moved about five hundred meters and the new abbey was consecrated in AD 1136. It had been commenced before the death of Etienne Harding in AD 1134 and before the start of the construction of the new cathedral in Chartres. The new abbey position created an exact and precise alignment between the centers of the abbey at Mont St. Michel, the cathedral in Chartres, and the new abbey at Clairvaux. What is even more incredible is that

Morimond is also on the extended Clairvaux-Chartres-Mont
St. Michel line

With regard to the movement of these abbeys and the accurate alignments they create, there are two possibilities:

1. The abbeys were located on ground that had previously
   been designated as sacred by the Druids in more ancient
   times and which formed part of the ground pattern with
   or without the knowledge of the Cistercians. The fact that
   three abbeys were moved would indicate (at the very least)
   that someone knew that the abbeys should be positioned
   carefully and precisely on such ancient hallowed ground
   and knew how to locate it.
2. Someone involved in choosing/specifying the land and
   the exact position of the abbeys was aware of the pattern
   and had access to surveying techniques (using the stars)
   to help pinpoint the locations.

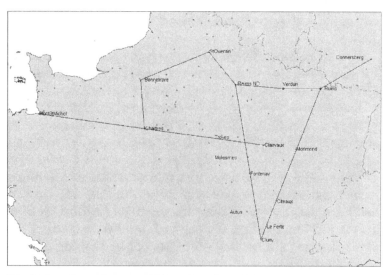

Fig 83 the alignments created by relocation of the Citeaux, Clairvaux,
and Fontenay abbeys

With the exception of Citeaux, the new abbeys were constructed in the gothic style that was just beginning to emerge. This new architecture and all that it implied could account for the desire to reconstruct the abbeys. It does not and cannot explain their relocation to form accurate links and pointers to points in the ground plan of Ursa Major. One thing is certain; these alignments are not some random coincidence. They were designed and executed to a deliberate and precise agenda.

At the Council of Troyes (the seat of the house of Champagne) in AD1128, "The Military Order of the Temple of the Knights of Solomon" was officially recognized as a religious-military order. The rule of the order had been written by Bernard de Clairvaux. The precedent for being both knights and monks had been set AD 1113 when the pope had granted the right to become a religious order to the "The Crusading Order of St. John of Jerusalem" (The Hospitallers).

The order of "The Military Order of the Temple of the Knights of Solomon" (The Knights Templar) had been founded in AD 1118 ten years earlier by nine knights who had taken vows of poverty, chastity, and obedience and had travelled to the Holy Land and presented themselves to King Baudouin of Jerusalem. They claimed that their purpose was to protect the routes to the Holy Land. The fact that they formed a new order rather than join an existing one (The Hospitallers) that had the same stated purpose but which was headquartered in Rome is probably significant. They were joined in Jerusalem by Hughes de Champagne in AD 1124. Hughes is reported to have died in AD 1126 and the Templars returned to France in 1127 in time for the Council of Troyes one year later. Some researchers claim that The Templars brought some ancient parchments back to France that they had discovered whilst tunneling under The Temple of the Mount in Jerusalem in search of "The Ark of the Covenant" or "The Holy Grail" or some other sacred artifact. If it was the objective of The Templars to find "The Ark" or "The Grail," it would be reasonable to ask why Hughes de Payen returned to Jerusalem in AD 1130 with a veritable army. In this scenario, the fact that he did return would be an indication that, at that time, The Knights Templar had not located whatever they was they were looking for.

Bernard de Clairvaux toured extensively in AD 1146 and AD 1147, (sixteen years later) preaching support for the second Crusade. This and the fact that The Knights Templar's presence and influence in the Holy Land was to last 161 years until the fall of Acre in AD 1291 might tell us that the elusive Ark or Grail was never located.

The whole demeanor of The Knights Templar changed after AD 1130 and they were considered to be aggressive and belligerent. They were described by the French Biographer of Philippe Le Bel as "more heroic than efficacious, courageous but undisciplined."[99]

They were eventually prosecuted out of existence by King Phillip of France in the early part of the fourteenth century. The king was jealous of the power and influence of "The Templars" and he acted to eliminate them with the reluctant support of Pope Clement V and a ruthless inquisition. The 127 unproven charges included sacrilege, idolatry, and rejection of Christ, the church, and its practices. Many of The Knights Templar were executed whilst some fled to Scotland and England where, it is suggested, that they became the first Freemasons. "The Military Order of the Temple of the Knights of Solomon" was finally abolished when Jaques de Molay, the Grand Master was burned to death in AD 1314.

Speculation aside, we do know that work on the new gothic design of abbeys and cathedrals started immediately after the first return of The Knights Templar in AD 1127 and that it was promulgated and achieved with the help and cooperation of the Cistercians. Being monks themselves, it is perhaps significant that The Knights Templar had access to the inner sanctums of the abbeys and in particular to the

---

[99] *Edward Burman, The Templars Knights of God, Inner Traditions (1988)*

scriptoria where any sacred documents, translation work, and/or architectural design would have taken place.

These new edifices incorporated sacred geometry[100] and (as we have seen in Chapter six) represented a link between the ancient beliefs of the Druids and the Egyptians. In particular, they acknowledged the hidden belief that the mystery of the fertilization of the Mother Goddess by God is celebrated and that God, his mother, and/or his son are located in the stars that can be seen in the northern constellations.

We can only surmise that the esoteric beliefs, which are inherent in the design, orientation, and location of cathedrals and abbeys was not shared by all The Knights Templar and Cistercian monks. Had it been so, it is unlikely that knowledge of these things would have remained secret. Any arcane secrets held by The Knights Templar were held by a small group of initiates in the inner sanctum of the order. Those lower in the hierarchy who perhaps did work on the various secret elements of the new construction projects were sold only on the magnificence of the new design that paid homage to the then conventional church view of God, the Virgin Mary, and the son of God, Jesus Christ.

Statements by Bernard de Clairvaux that "There is no decoration, only proportion" and that God is "length, width, height and depth" are a clear indication that his view of God closely approached that of the ancient Celtic priest-astronomers who had so assiduously copied the geometric pattern of God and his kingdom onto the ground in Northern France. The four dimensions he referred to (when we know that there are only three) would make sense of "height," which was meant to be height of an object above the ground and the other three the conventional dimensions of the object itself. They do not prove that Bernard himself was an "initiate" but they show, at the very least, that he had been influenced by "initiates" of the highest degree who propounded such philosophies. We can also deduce

---

[100] *Louis Charpentier, The Mysteries of Chartres Cathedral, Avon (1980)*

that the pattern and its implications was known to a select few persons involved in the foundation of The Knights
Templar and The Cistercians at this time.

Chrétien de Troyes was born in AD 1130 and his formative years overlapped, in time and location, the early growth
years and growth hub of both The Cistercians and The
Knights Templar. He was educated under the patronage of
Marie de France or Marie Capet, Countess of Champagne
(AD 1145– March 11, AD 1198), who was the elder daughter of Louis VII of France and of Louis's first wife, Eleanor
of Aquitaine. He is acknowledged to have become the most
prolific writer of medieval romances, which is a claim that
indicates that, at that time, he, like all nobility must have
been taught the art of writing in abbeys by learned monks. In
particular, he would have been schooled in one of the abbeys
that existed under the favor of the House of Champagne.
His earlier works, *Erec and Enide*, *Cligés*, *The Knight of the
Cart* and *The Knight with the Lion* are forerunners for the
stories made famous by other authors. These include Arthur,
Queen Guinevere, Lancelot, and Gawain.

The first Grail story, *Le Conte de Graal*, was written by
Chrétien de Troyes between 1170 and AD 1190. Seven vari-
ations of Grail stories were written by other authors between
1190 and AD 1220. Fifteen years after the emergence of the
unfinished *Conte du Graal*, Wolfram von Eschenbach published *Parzival.* In the epilogue he claimed that Chrétien had
failed to do justice to a tale that already existed. In explanation, he claimed that the original legend came from an Arabic manuscript discovered by a "master" Kyot in Toledo, in
Spain. Kyot in turn spoke of Flegetanis, a "king of old time"
who "could read the Heavens high . . . He read the stars and
strange secrets he saw, and he spake again low with bated
breath and fearful, of the thing that is called the Grail. In a
cluster of stars was it written, the name nor their lore shall
fail."[101]

[101] *Wolfram Von Eschenback; A.T.Hatto (translator), Parzival, Penguin Classics (1980)*

It is probable that any secret quest that had in part prompted the formation of two such powerful organizations as The Knights Templar and The Cistercians was romanticized by young monks who were brothers of the knights involved directly in expeditions to the Holy Land. The escapades and adventures of these knights, along with rumors of any secret quest, were most likely whispered to young aspirants during their many hours of learning. Chrétien would have had his imagination fed by such whisperings. If, simultaneously, he was introduced to the content of the Kyot document or some verbal interpretation of it, the two sources could have provided the inspiration he needed to produce *Le Conte de Graal*.

Jessie Weston tells us, "A prototype, containing the main features of the Grail story; the Waste Land, the Fisher King, the Hidden Castle with its solemn Feast, and mysterious Feeding Vessel, the Bleeding Lance and the Cup, does not, as far as we know, exist."[102] At the same time, along with Roger Sherman Loomis[103] and Alfred Nutt,[104] she proposed that the Grail itself is derived from early Celtic myth and folklore. Loomis traced a number of parallels between medieval Welsh literature and Irish material and the Grail romances, including similarities between the Mabinogion's Bran the Blessed and the Arthurian Fisher King, and between Bran's life-restoring cauldron and the Grail. Weston also makes a strong claim that legends of the wounding of Adonis and Attis (forerunners of Osiris and Jesus) in the thigh bore strong resemblances to the story of the wounding of the Fisher King.

Various authors acknowledge that Arthur is directly related to the bear: "In Cornish folklore, the stellar constellation of the Ursa Major, the Great Bear, is called Arthur's Wain or Cart. Moreover, the initiator of the Arthurian romances in

---

[102] *Jessie L Weston, From Ritual to Romance, Dover Publications (1997)*
[103] *Loomis, Celtic Myth and Arthurian Romance*
[104] *Alfred Nutt, Studies on Legends of the Grail, Kessinger (2003)*

the twelfth century, Geoffry of Monmouth, says that Merlin prophesied the coming of Arthur after seeing a vision of the bear amongst the stars. Both of these legendry references, seemingly coupling Arthur with the Ursa major constellation, clearly demonstrate that he was associated with the bear before the romances became popular throughout Europe".[105]

"The name of King Arthur, which, despite what people would have one think, is not of Latin origin; it is derived from artu or arto meaning bear."[106]

Key symbols in the Grail romances are: the Grail itself, (whether cup or dish) the Lance, the Sword and the Stone. The combination of many of these symbols with other important ingredients of the story – bear, thigh, feeding vessel, cup, and stone – point to a link with the Ursa Major ground pattern. This does not mean that any of the authors were aware of the pattern or of the ancient beliefs that provoked its construction. It does tell us, however, that the authors were influenced by legends, events, and rumors of events to produce romances that mirrored a popular folklore at that time. Interestingly, these same symbols (Cup/dish, Lance, Sword and Stone) are the four suits of the Tarot cards: cup, wand or lance, sword and pentacle (Fig 84).

Much esoteric speculation is given to the origin and meaning of these cards since their emergence in their current form in Italy in the fifteenth century. In actuality, whilst we know that a pentagram and cup would seem to be linked to Ursa Major and the pattern it holds, nothing is known of the origins of the four Tarot symbols and their *raison d'être*. There are encyclopedic assertions that "The Tarot" came to Italy from Egypt but there is no firm evidence for such claims.

It is truly fascinating that each of the Aces of the Tarot is held in a hand and that the seven stars of Ursa Major could easily be viewed as a hand. The cup and the pentacle are (as we have previously shown) contained in the constellation

---

[105] Graham Phillips, The Search for the Grail, Arrow Books, (1996)
[106] Jean Markale, The Druids, Celtic Priests of Nature, Inner Traditions (1999

Fig 84 the four suits of the Tarot as depicted by Rider-Waite-Smith

and could therefore be conjectured to be sitting on a hand. The locations of the sword and the wand/spear/lance are not so obvious and their relation to the constellation (if there is one) is not easily determined. The main clue to the actual situation of each suit of the pack is the picture of the hand. We know that Ursa Major rotates around the pole position and that an observer will view the constellation in different parts of its rotation depending on the time of year and the time of day. The four positions of the hands on the Tarot cards points to the midnight view on the summer solstice (mid-summer's day), the autumn equinox, the winter solstice (mid-winter's day), and the spring equinox, the four most important days in the ancient year. (For definitions of these days, see Appendix 4.)

In Fig 85 we see the constellation as it appears on mid-summer's night, when one is standing, looking north. This

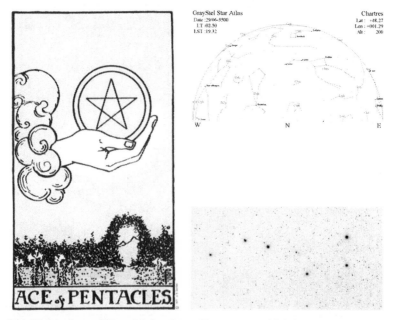

Fig 85 the view of Ursa Major from Chartres at midnight on midsummer's night, 3500 BC (the observer standing looking North)

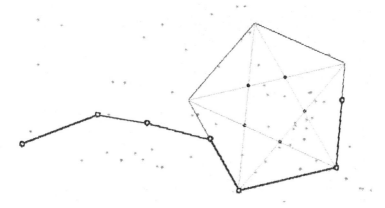

Fig 86 the pentagram in the ground plan of the constellation

corresponds to the picture on the card, which is looking at mountains (north) from fields of flowers (midsummer). The hump of the wrist corresponds to the hump in the tail of Ursa Major. The fact that there are no leaves in the picture might indicate that the pentacle is free standing. The pentagram in the ground reproduction of the constellation is depicted in Fig 86.

To the ground observer, Ursa Major appears to rotate anti-clockwise around the pole position. The view of the Ursa Major constellation at midnight at the Autumn Equinox 3500 BC is shown in Fig 87. In this orientation of the constellation, we can see the tree that was depicted in Fig 37.

It is perhaps significant that Julius Caesar remarked, "The Druids believe that their religion forbids them to commit their teaching to writing, although for most other purposes, such as public and private accounts, the Gauls use the Greek alphabet."[107]

In ancient Greek, there were two words for a tree; δενδρον which meant "tree" and (as far as we know) had no other meaning, and ξυλον, which meant tree, wood, spear, cudgel, cross or staff. This second Greek word gives us the link we

---

[107] *Caesar, The Conquest of Gaul*

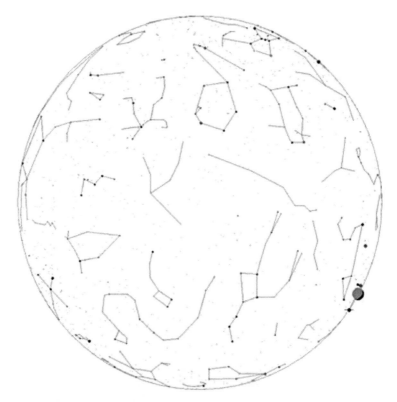

Fig 87 the zenith view of the sky (looking straight up) facing north
from Chartres at midnight on the Autumn Equinox in 3500 BC

need to find the wand or lance hidden in the tree that we already know lies at the heart of the constellation.

In Fig 88, we can see the wand, spear, or lance, which is
the straight line trunk of the tree in the constellation. Several
other stars show us the position of the hand that is holding
the lance. It is even possible to surmise that the leaves on
either side of the wand on the Tarot card are a facsimile of
the key stars of the constellation that sit on either side of the
line.

We have seen, therefore, that the constellation at midsummer and at the autumn equinox represents the first two Aces

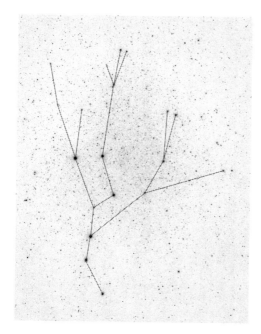

Fig 88a The Tree

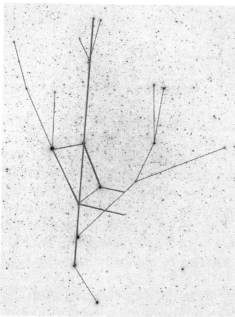

Fig88b The Wand or
Lance

Fig 88c The Constellation
(as a tree), the Wand or
Lance in the tree, and the
Ace of Wands

of The Tarot. In theory, this should indicate that the mid-winter solstice, which is the next of the four key positions, will bring us to the position of The Ace of Cups, the next Ace Tarot card. The orientation of Ursa Major at midnight on midwinter's night is shown in Fig 88. At first look, this orientation seems strange since most people would find it appealing to view "the Cup" as the receptacle we are familiar with that is shown holding the five-sided star in Fig 86.

Once more we are assisted by the picture on the Tarot card.

The Ace of Cups (Fig 90) has the viewer facing south, that being the direction where we might see a pond with water

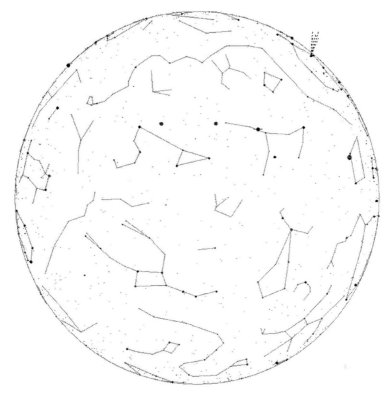

Fig 89 the view from Chartres (looking up at the sky with head facing south) on mid-winter's night, 3500 BC

lilies cupped and no mountains or snow on midwinter's day. The position of the hand is different to that of the hand holding the pentacle (Fig 85).

The thumb is on the near side but is twisted behind the stem of the cup, which can only mean that the cup is in the left hand of the holder.

The key stars of the constellation all lie below the cup (Fig 91). This corresponds with the Tarot picture where the leaves are all shown below the cup. The bearer is left handed, either to hide the base of the cup with the fingers or because a cup held in the left hand has some unknown significance.

Fig 90 the Tarot Ace of
Cups

This picture makes it clear that the persons designing this
Tarot card extracted their pictures from careful studies of the
Ursa Major constellation.

Since there are four aces and four celestial positions, the
last ace, The Ace of Swords, must correspond to the fourth
position of the constellation at Spring Equinox. It differs
from the other three cards in that the thumb of the bearer of
the sword is hidden. However, it is similar to two of the other
cards in that it uses mountains in the background to indicate
that the observer is facing north. Fig 93 depicts the position
and orientation of the constellation in relation to the night

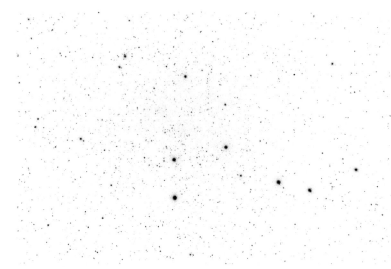

Fig 91 the stars in Ursa Major that form the hand and the cup

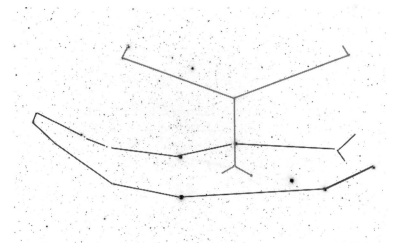

Fig 92 the hand and the cup

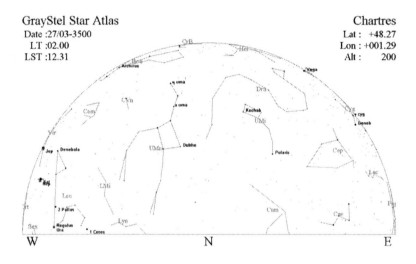

GrayStel Star Atlas

Date :27/03-3500
LT :02.00
LST :12.31

Chartres

Lat : +48.27
Lon : +001.29
Alt :   200

W   N   E

Fig 93 the view of the northern sky from Chartres at midnight of Spring
Equinox in 3500 BC

sky at Spring Equinox. The orientation of the handle of The
Plough (Ursa Major) towards "Corona Borealis" at the top
of the frame (and therefore in the center of the heavens) is
significant.

It triggers the hypothesis that this small constellation is
the crown that sits over the sword and through which the tip
of the sword protrudes (Fig 94).

Once again, the hand is formed by the major stars of the
constellation. The sword itself connects three of the principal
stars of Ursa Major with two in Corona Borealis. The picture
in the Heavens is almost an exact duplicate of the picture of
the Tarot Ace of Swords.

There is no doubt that the four suits of the Tarot and, in
particular, the pictures depicted on the four "Ace" cards represent images created around and by the Ursa major constellation at the summer solstice, the autumn equinox, the winter solstice and the spring equinox. This means that whoever
created these cards was fully aware of the ancient mysteries
and beliefs that surrounded the stars that rotated around the

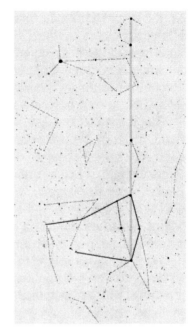

Fig 94 the Ace of Swords   Fig 95 the sword

Northern Pole position and in particular the constellation of Ursa Major.

Arthur Edward Waite was the creator of the Waite-Smith Tarot Published by Rider in1909. He and Pamela Colman Smith, the artist and illustrator lived in London at the turn of the twentieth century and were members of the Hermetic Order of the Golden Dawn. Waite published a series of works on divination, esotericism, Rosicrucianism, Freemasonry, black and ceremonial magic, Cabbalism, and alchemy. The probability is that much of the underlying research for third Tarot deck had taken place before the time of production and that one or both of these two researchers into lost and mysterious knowledge had a precise prescription of what they intended to illustrate.

We cannot know precisely from where the information was gained and/or specified to design the four Ace cards. What we know from our tracking of the links with the Ursa

Major constellation is that Waite or Smith or someone in Hermetic Order of the Golden Dawn or The Freemasons, with whom they associated, was "an initiate" and knew the ancient secrets. This tells us that in the early part of the Twentieth Century, "The Mystery of all the Ages" was still intact and known to a select few.

The Tarot Deck consists of the major arcane of twenty-two cards and the minor arcana four suits of fourteen cards each. Each suit consists of Ace, 2, 3, 4, 5, 6, 7, 8, 9, 10, Page, Knight, Queen, and King. The name Major Arcana is used only in esoteric practice. Game players using Tarot decks for *playing* call them Trumps. In esoteric sets, each Major Arcanum depicts a scene, mostly featuring a person or several people, with many symbolic elements. In many decks, each has a number (usually in Roman numerals) and a name, though not all decks have both, and some have only a picture. The earliest decks bore unnamed and unnumbered pictures on the Majors (probably because a great many of the people using them at the time were illiterate), and the order of cards is not standardized. Nevertheless, one of the most common set of names and numbers is 0 The Fool, I The Magician or Juggler, II The High Priestess, III The Empress, IV The Emperor, V The Hierophant, VI The Lovers, VII The Chariot, VIII Justice, IX the Hermit, X Wheel of Fortune, XI Strength, XII The Hanged Man, XIII Death, XIV Temperance, XV The Devil, XVI The Tower, XVII The Star, XVIII The Moon, XIX The Sun, XX Judgment, and XXI The World.

"The Chariot" and "The Star" are names and titles we have associated with Ursa Major but at first examination neither Waite-Smith Tarot card displays any obvious connection to the constellation. The Star Tarot card features an eight-pointed star compared with the five-pointed star we know to be contained in the cup of the constellation. The number of smaller stars surrounding the main star is seven, the number of the principal stars of The Great Bear, but the pattern on the card is strange, with one of the smaller stars lower than

the other six that appear to surround the central feature sym-
metrically. Despite this, we were not able to locate an eight-
pointed star within the constellation.

The Chariot Tarot card is similarly a challenge to creative
ingenuity. The rider in the chariot has a lance in his right
hand, his sword (if he has one) behind him, an eight-pointed
star is on his head, six-pointed stars decorate his canopy,
wings decorate the front of the carriage and buxom lion-
esses, one black and one white with fixed gazes in the same
direction as the crowned charioteer lie prone in front of a
carriage that must be stationary. We found no obvious direct
link between these aspects of the card and the Ursa Major

Fig 96 the Star

Fig 97 the Chariot

constellation, other that the fact that the card is called "The Chariot."

The most obvious and perhaps interesting link created by the names of the cards is to the Book of Revelation, holder of "the mystery of the Seven Stars." The Cup/Bowl/Vessel, Tree/Spear, Stone and Sword are each featured in this enigmatic text. Perhaps more significantly, fifteen of the twenty-two major arcana of The Tarot are also featured.

In particular, the High Priestess and The Empress are the harlot and the woman or mother, The Emperor is King or Lord and The Lovers are represented by the marriage of the lamb and the woman. The Chariot is depicted as a horse or

Fig 98 Death

chariot, Justice is translated as judgment or righteousness. Strength is a word translated as strength, power or force, or one which means power, strength, influence, or talent, and Death is translated as death, murder, or execution. The Devil is a Greek word meaning Satan or Devil.

The Tower can be a word in Revelation meaning wall or fortress or another word in the text meaning prison or watch-post. The Star, The Moon, and The Sun are all represented directly. Judgment is probably the word translated as judgment, condemnation, or punishment, and The World can be the word meaning earth, land, territory, and sometimes inhabited earth or another word in the text which means civilized world.

As significantly as the names of its protagonists, the Tarot cards of the Major Arcana depict scenes that are stolen directly from the Book of Revelation. At the same time, they give us a direct link to the constellation of Ursa Major and the various aspects of this constellation that we have learned are important.

"And I saw and behold a horse/chariot pale green and the (one) sitting on it, name to him the death."[108]

The Death or execution (in the tree/on the cross in the constellation) is depicted on the horse/chariot (Fig 98) and carries an ornate pentagon/pentagram as his standard.

A link between the Book of Revelation, the Tarot, and the constellation of Ursa Major is clear. The constellation and its aspects can die as the night sky is extinguished by sunlight at daybreak or can die by sinking below the horizon at certain times in the Ecliptic Cycle. On the other hand, death in ancient times was thought to mean that our spirit went to join the stars and, in particular, (if we went to Heaven) the stars that rotate around the North Pole position. The records from Ancient Egypt tell us,

> Here am I; I have come to you that you may drive out all the evil which is on me just as you did for those seven spirits who are in the suite of the Lord of Sepa, whose places ASnibis (Anubis) made ready on that day of "Come thence." Who are they? As for those gods, the Lords of Justice, they are Seth and Isdes, Lord of the West. As for the tribunal which is behind Osiris, Imsety, Hapy, Duamutef and Qebehsenuef, it is these who are behind the Great Bear in the northern sky.[109]

This link between death and a tribunal or judgment is confirmed in the Book of Revelation: "Fear ye the (one) God and give ye to him glory because came the hour/season of the judgment/event of him and give ye worship to the (one) having made the Heaven and the Earth and the Sea and the Fountains of Waters."[110]

---

[108] *Revelation 6,8*
[109] *R O Faulkner, The Ancient Egyptian Book of the Dead, Spell 17*
[110] *Revelation 4,7*

Fig 99 the Magician

The Tarot Magician (Fig 99) has The Sword, The Cup, The Wand/Lance, and The Pentacle in front of him ("he is holding all the aces") and he performs his magic over them to create the annual drama of the seasons. The sword, cup lance, and pentacle are known to represent aspects of the constellation. The magician is therefore the universal architect known as Thoth to the Egyptians. He is the God that is responsible for *The Mystery of the Seven Stars.*

The Tarot card depicting The World (Fig 100) is the clearest example of a direct connection between the Tarot and the Book of Revelation. The card has a naked woman at its center and at its four corners the head of an eagle, lion, calf, and

Fig 100 the World

a man. These links will be investigated more fully in a later
chapter and it will be shown that these, too, are aspects of
the constellation. They are "the four living creatures" mentioned in the Book of Revelation, ". . . and in the middle of
the throne and around the throne, four living creatures fill-
ing/full of eyes before and behind. And the living creature
the first like to a lion and the second living creature like to a
calf and the third living creature having the face as of a man
and the fourth living creature like to an eagle flying."[111]

"[A]nd the woman whom thou sawest in the city the (one)
great, the (one) having kingdom over the kings of the earth"[112]

---

[111] *Revelation 4,7; 4,8*
[112] *Revelation 17,18*

Fig 101 the Empress

The Empress Tarot card (Fig 101) contains a combination of Egyptian and Christian iconography mixed with elements of the constellation. She is surrounded by seven pomegranates that represent the seven stars of Ursa Major. The crown is Egyptian, the pillars are from the Old Testament, and the moon underneath the feet is a direct take from the Book of Revelation:

"[A]nd a sign great was seen in the Heaven, a woman wearing the sun and the moon underneath the feet of her."[113]

---

[113] *Revelation 12,1*

The picture is very similar to classical pictures of Isis and of the Virgin Mary (Fig 102). The only difference is that the child in the Egyptian and Christian portrayals is replaced by a book or scroll on the Tarot card.

A series of connections and discoveries have therefore been made:

- The ground pattern of Ursa Major was known to a small number of initiates in the hierarchy of The Templars and/or Cistercians in the twelfth century
- The Grail stories came into existence simultaneous with the formation of The Templars and the Cistercians. The first Grail narrative was written close to and under the protection of the House of Champagne, the House that sponsored the creation of the Templars and the Cistercians, and it contains allusions to the ancient and annual parodies that are played out in, with, by, and around the constellation of Ursa Major.
- The Tarot, which may have emanated out of Egypt, contains all the iconography of the Grail romances. This

Fig 102 Isis (left) suckling Horus and the Virgin Mary (below)

iconography is a representation of the characters and stories contained in the Book of Revelation.

- This discovery provokes the belief that there is a direct link between the sacred text of the Book of Revelation and the ancient Celtic and Egyptian beliefs that saw the birth and were the feeding ground for the original grail stories.

Is it possible that the 302.4-mile long ground pattern of Ursa Major can be explained through/by study of the last and most mysterious book of the New Testament? Were we given clues to the origins of the current Judeo-Christian belief system inconveniently wrapped in the intimidating words of *The Apocalypse?*

Chapter Nine

A Connection to the Book of Revelation

During the first two centuries AD there were two centers of Christianity, one in the Mediterranean port of Alexandria in Egypt and the other in Rome. The Alexandrian based Church was noted for its Gnostic teachings under the influence of Origen and Clement. The Roman center vied for power and influence over the early Christians seeking to establish itself as the single location for the headquarters of the Christian movement.

Alexandrian philosophy was akin to and leant heavily on the Greek philosophies that had been taught by Pythagoras and Plato, where the soul comes from Heaven and returns there at death. Origin (AD 185–254) in particular studied astronomy and sought to explain early Church teachings in the context of a heaven full of stars. He included Hellenistic (ancient Greek) theories on the life and nature of stars into his cosmology. For this he was eventually condemned as a heretic by Rome but he was successful in incorporating traditional theories about the stars into biblical theology.

The ethos of the Roman school is best exemplified by "The Refutation of all Heresies," a treatise published in ten parts by Hippolytus in the early third century (contemporary with Origen). It catalogues both pagan beliefs and thirty-three Gnostic Christian systems deemed heretical, making it a major source of information on early opponents of Catholic orthodoxy and/or philosophies that the Roman Church believed were threatening. Some of these philosophies/theologies had existed for many centuries prior to the time of Hippolytus, and *The Refutation of all Heresies* was the first move by the Church to condemn any and all teachings or

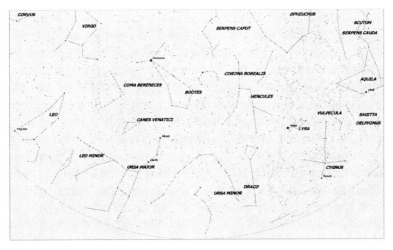

Fig 103 the Galaxies mentioned by Hippolytus

beliefs that were different to its own. It might also be argued that one immediate purpose was to eliminate the influence of Alexandria. The value to us of this treatise is that it explains clearly and unambiguously the popular beliefs of the time.

Amongst its compendious pages it mentions two subjects that are of interest. In particular, it outlines the belief that "The Beast" and "The Dragon" and even Jesus (the logos) are amongst the northern polar constellation of Aratus, Lyre, Canis, Corona, Ursa Minor, and Ursa Major, and gives guidance as to where exactly they were thought to be found (Fig 103). In particular, it describes Ursa Major as the Greek symbol of Heaven, the one by which we are regenerated and which fights against "The Beast" on our behalf. (see the quotation from Book 4, Chapter 48 of The Refutation of all Heresies in Appendix 5). This is the most direct and unambiguous link between the key players in the Book of Revelation and the northern constellations. It tells us that this belief was prominent at the time and that Hippolytus found it necessary to include it amongst those things it was necessary to condemn.

The other topic criticized in *The Refutation of all Heresies* that is of interest to us in the context of our understanding of the Book of Revelation is Numerology or Gematria (appendix 6). This arcane science involved the allocation of a numerical value to each letter of the alphabet and a numerical value to each word, it being the sum of the letters in the word. A (alpha) had the value 1, β (beta) had the value 2, γ (gamma) had the value 3 and this continued through the Greek alphabet to the final letter ω (omega) which had a value 800. If there was a Greek word spelled ωγβα (which there is not) the value of this word would be the sum of the value of the letters. i.e. $800+3+2+1$ which equals 806. The table of Greek and Hebrew values for each letter of the alphabet is included in the appendix.

The Greeks system (called in Greek Isopsephia) was sophisticated and by the fifth century BC every Greek god's name was formulated according to isopsephic principles. It was in common Greek usage by the time of the Hellenisation of Palestine in the second century BC at which time it was introduced (in its final form) into Hebrew, probably simultaneous with the introduction of Square Hebrew.

A system of numerology had existed since antiquity and had been in wide use in Babylon in the eighth century BC It was thought to have been in existence in 2300 BC when numbers were used to write words and syllables in cuneiform. Robert Graves speculates that a similar science existed in early Celtic Britain.[114]

We have uncovered two pieces of information that make us reasonably sure that Gematria was used in the formulation of the Book of Revelation.

David Parker, professor of New Testament Textual Criticism and Palaeography at the University of Birmingham in England, has been using modern technology to scour some four hundred thousand bits of papyri, which were originally

---

[114] *Graves, The White Goddess*

Fig 104 the ancient Greek papyrus

discovered in 1895 at a dump outside the ancient Egyptian city of Oxyrhynchus.

Many of the sections have been damaged and discolored, but a modern imaging process is shedding new light on the sacred text of the Book of Revelation and it now seems that 616 was the original number of the beast. The papyrus in the spotlight (Fig 104) is believed to originate circa 300 AD and is probably about one hundred years before any other version known. The find is significant because the previously common version of the Book of Revelation created an interesting play on the numbers associated with the words (translated from the Greek) making up Revelation 13,18: "Here the wisdom is The (one) having mind/ insight/intention let him count the number of the (of a) beast a number for/in fact of man it is And the number of it six hundred sixty six"

Below is the numerical value of each of the final five words of this verse where numerical values have been attributed to the letters in the original Greek word and thus to the word itself. When this is done the phrase and the numerical value of each word become;

Word	And	the	number	of it/him	six hundred, sixty six
Numerical value	31	70	430	1171	666

The sum of these five numbers is 2368 and this number (2368) is the Gematria (numerical value) of the words "of Jesus Christ." If the phrase "and the number of it/him six hundred, sixty six" is replace by "of Jesus Christ" Rev 13, 18 would then read (in equivalent terms): *Here the wisdom/ knowledge is. The (one) having mind/insight/intention let him count the number of the beast. The actual number of man is of Jesus Christ.*

The newly located original version "And the number of it/ him 616" would mean that this play on the words no longer exists and that the numerical total of the words in the phrase would be 2318. This number (2318) using Gematria, is equal in value to three other phrases (from Revelation), "and he shall be to me a son," "and he cried (out) from the glory/ splendor of him," and "because of the word/computation/assertion/proportion of the witness/evidence/proof."

With 616 inserted (instead of 666), Rev 13,18 would read (in equivalent terms): *Here the wisdom/knowledge is. The (one) having mind/insight/intention let him count; the number of the beast a number in fact (of) man is, because of the computation of the evidence/proof.*

It would appear, therefore, that whoever changed the number of The Beast from 616 to 666 did so to hide this embedded message from the scrutiny of anyone versed in the science of numerology and to lead them falsely to the name of Jesus Christ. The change itself is evidence of the very thing that the perpetrators were trying to hide, that the document was compiled using Gematria or numerology to incorporate hidden and perhaps sacred messages.

There is a second piece of evidence suggesting that the Book of Revelation is built on a sophisticated and detailed application of Gematria or numerology.

One of the most significant astronomical numbers is the length of the precessional year. As discussed in Chapter Seven, the earth wobbles and creates an imaginary circle in the heavens. What we see as the North Pole (the point in the heavens around which everything appears to rotate) moves slowly around this circle, taking 25,920 years to complete one precessional year. Since, in ancient times, the Pole position denoted the ascendancy of God, this number was thought to have great significance. It was known to the Ancient Egyptians[115] and was quoted accurately by Hipparchus[116] in the second century BC. In view of the number's importance, the Book of Revelation was examined to see whether (using Gematria) the sum of any one phrase in the text added to 25,920. Interestingly, there is only one phrase with this total value. We met it previously when we looked at The World Tarot card (Fig 100), and, as we might expect, the phrase infers a rotation.

"Four living creatures full of eyes before and behind. And the living creature the first like (to) a lion, and the second living creature like (to) a calf, and the third living creature having the face as of a man, and the fourth living creature like (to) an eagle flying."[117]

In the Book of Revelation, the Greek word for lion has a numerical value of 885. This is also the numerical value of the Greek words meaning (image, likeness, picture, simile, phantom, or notion) of the Greek word meaning Sardonyx and of the Greek phrases meaning 'thou art the Lord' and the Greek phrase meaning 'he/it receives a mark/bite/stamp'. These other words and phrases with the same value as the word "lion" prompted us to look closely at the Ursa Major constellation in the same place that Sennedjem indicated to us that the likeness or face of "The Lord" is to be located (Chapter 5).

The facsimile of a lion that is contained within the Ursa Major constellation is shown in Fig 105. It is the view as seen at the Summer Solstice orientation of the constellation in 3500 BC (identified as the "pentacle" position in Chapter Eight.)

---

[115] *Herodotus The Histories,*
[116] *G. J. Toomer, Hipparchus and Babylonian Astronomy; Erle A Scientific Humanist: Studies in Memory of Abraham Sachs (1988), pp. 353–362;*
[117] *Revelation; 4,6 and 4,7*

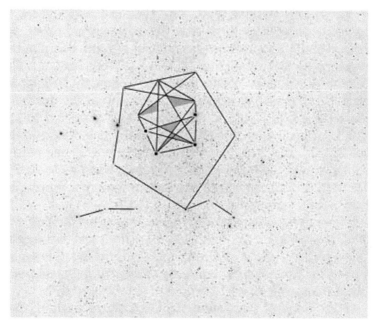

Fig 105 the lion within the constellation of Ursa major

The creation of this picture involved:

- drawing the pentagram within the cup of the constellation
- drawing a larger, inverted pentagram by extending three sides of the cup to find four of the points and by using two of the major stars of the constellation
- joining the internal points of the two pentagrams to locate the exact positions of the mouth, nose, and eyes.

The picture so produced is spectacular and the lion is very visible. One can even see how the protrusions of the constellation (seen in other contexts as horns or antlers) create the paws of the reclined beast. This picture also shows/explains in part:

- The previously unexplained difference between the inverted pentagrams of the Tutankhamen mask (Fig 70)

Fig 106 the two lions Shu and Tefnut with the horizon hieroglyph between them

and the face of Osiris (Fig 64), i.e. one pentagram pointed upwards and the other pointed down.

- One reason for the distinctive shape of the headwear of Egyptian Pharaohs (Fig 70), which is significantly different to the animal heads, crowns, and other headwear of the Egyptian Gods.
- Why *The Book of the Dead* tells us, "I am he who crosses the sky, I am the lion of Ra."[118] Ra is the self-engendered Eternal Spirit. The magic used by Ra in his creation of the world and everything in it was "The Word" [119]
- The Egyptian Gods Shu and Tefnut (aspects of Horus) who were "The Lion of the Western Horizon" and "the Lion of the Eastern Horizon" respectively (Fig 106). Ursa Major (the barque that carried Osiris) traversed the sky, carrying the sun (Amun-Ra) on its journey and then re-crossed the sky after sunset to be there to allow Osiris bring about sunrise again the following day (Fig 107).
- The Sphinx at Gaza was originally carved as a lion. Later the head was altered to resemble that of Khafre,[120] a

[118] Faulkner, Book of the Dead, Spell 62
[119] Manfred Lurker, The Gods and Symbols of Ancient Egypt, Thames & Hudson (1980)
[120] Robert Bauval, Graham Hancock, Keeper of Genesis, Arrow Books (1997)

Fig 107 Ra in/with the sun in the day and (below) taken by Osiris at sunset to the following day's sunrise

Pharaoh who saw himself as God. Despite this desecration, since Thutmosis IV, it has been known as Harmakhis, Horus-on-the-Horizon (Fig 108).

The Book of Revelation tells us that the second living creature is "like to a calf/young bull." The Greek word for calf is included in the text of the Book of Revelation only once and has a numerical value of 1710. It is in the dative form and therefore means "to/with a calf." The nominative version of the Greek word for calf has a numerical value of 1180.

The most meaningful phrase with a value of 1180 is "the (one) (who) is and the (one) (who) was and the (one)." Incredibly, this phrase can only represent Ra, the god who is self created and who created all the other gods to be but aspects of him.[121]

If this implies that if the calf is to be found in the constellation of Ursa Major, then the four living beings must

---
[121] Faulkner, Book of the Dead, Spell 17

Fig 108 the Sphinx at Gaza, where the head of Khafra can be seen clearly to be too small in proportion to the rest of the body

in turn represent the position and shape of the constellation at the same time and day of the year, 6,480 years apart (1/4 of the precessional year). Interestingly, when we select the summer solstice position in 3500 BC (the position chosen for the lion) as the starting position, the appearance of the constellation from the ground 6,480 years later will be similar to that of the Tarot wand/lance position (Fig 70), albeit it will be in a different quadrant of the heavens.

A picture of a calf was not difficult to find. In one of the rooms of the burial chambers of Set at Thebes, Nut is symbolized by the animal we are looking for (Fig 108). A search for this calf in the Ursa Major constellation with its orientation as outlined produces a representation that is strikingly similar to the picture in the Temple at Thebes. The head of the calf sits around the four principal stars of Ursa Major and body of the calf incorporates the constellations of Ursa Minor and Draco, which, as has been previously discussed, are major players in the ancient drama (Fig 110).

Fig 109 the calf displayed at Thebes

The next "living creature" in the quadruplet is the one "having the face as of a man." The value of the phrase "the face as of a man" (in Gematria) where "the face" is nominative has the same value as if "the face" were accusative, i.e. 4330. Two other phrases in the Book of Revelation with this same value are;

> "and an almighty shrine of it/him (it) is and the Lamb"
>
> and
>
> "the (one) old the (one) called Devil and the Satan the (one) deceiving/going astray."

The face of a man on the Tarot card is side-on and one stage further clockwise around The World Tarot card. A face similar to that on the Tarot card of The World is locatable within the constellation (Fig 111), but the stars that make this picture do *not* give the view of the Ursa Major constella-

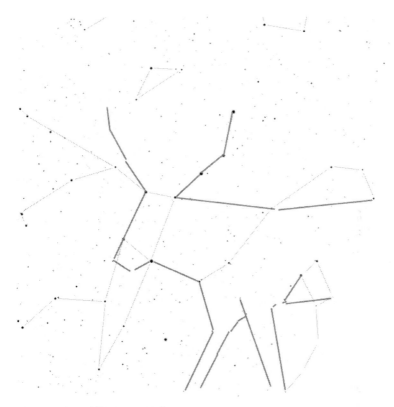

Fig 110 the calf in Ursa Major

tion at midnight on the summer solstice 6,480 years later (or 19,440 years earlier) than the position found for The Calf.

This implies that whilst the "face of a man" found on The World Tarot card can be located in the constellation, its Tarot position is associated with the four seasons (the solstices and the equinoxes) and therefore the annual cycle of the earth rather than the earth's position relative to the 25,920-year precessional cycle. "The face of a man" at midnight on the third quarter of the precessional cycle is to be found elsewhere.

Assuming that we started our precession sequence with Ursa Major in the center of the midnight field of view, the

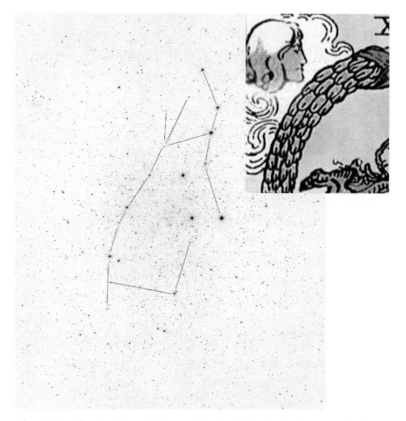

Fig 111 the face in Ursa Major, which is similar to the face on the Tarot
card of The World (inset)

constellation is higher in the sky 12,960 years earlier or
12,960 years later but is not dissimilar to the shape that produced the picture of The Lion (Fig 105). To prove that these
stars are connected to the Book of Revelation, therefore, we
must discount the Tarot picture and assume the stars that
produced The Lion will also produce "the face of a man."

A link to "the face of a man" (with the constellation in
"the lion" position) has already been established when the
faces of Osiris (Fig 64) and Tutenkhamun (Fig 70) were
found to be linked to the shape of the pentagram and to the

Fig 112 *basalt* carving of Set, his wife Nephthys by his side. A picture of Satan is inset

pentagram contained in Ursa Major, in particular (Chapter Five). The Gematria link to the image of Satan (above) would therefore be conclusive proof of a causal link between the *Revelation* text and the constellation of Ursa Major but leaves us looking for Satan.

An obvious candidate for the Devil or Satan role in the Egyptian pantheon is Seth, who, late in Egyptian history, became generally regarded as the personification of evil-doing. Interestingly, the basalt carving of Set (Fig 112) is similar to the conventional view of Satan (inset), a picture that is readily discernable in the Ursa Major constellation (Fig 113).

The stars making up the constellation were examined in their correct orientation, giving their appearance to the

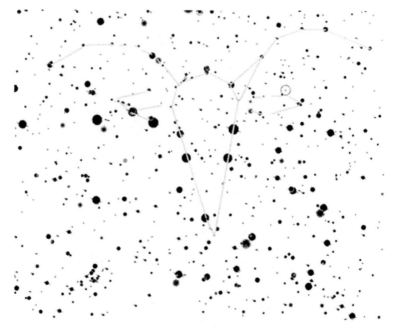

Fig 113 the head of Satan found within the constellation of Ursa Major

viewer on midsummer's night at this stage of the precessional cycle. Various combinations of head and horns were
located in and around the four principal stars of the constellation of Ursa Major (Figs 113 and 114). They are dramatic
and compelling but they do invite the question, would it be
possible to find this same shape in many other constellations
and groups of stars?

The advantages that Ursa Major has over any of the possible other constellations and groups of stars (where similar
images might be created) are:

- It utilizes the same set of stars that have formed the bas-
  es of all the other mythical and theosophical shapes so
  far located.
- The pentagram (so often associated with Satan) contained within the cup of the constellation can superimposed on/over the head of Satan (Fig 114).

Fig 114 an alternative head of Satan (in the same location as Fig 113), which matches The Devil tarot card

As much as this discovery may be distasteful, its existence means that the previous hypothesis that "The Seven Stars mentioned in the Book of Revelation[122] relates directly to the seven principal stars of the constellation of Ursa Major" is proven. Similarly, the location of the face of Satan with the constellation shows clearly that Gematria or Isopsephia was used in the compilation of the original text. The author of the Book of Revelation was someone of great learning. To complete the text, as now being uncovered, he would need to have been conversant in mathematics, astronomy, and the mysteries of the ancients.

The fourth and final "living creature" mentioned in Revelation 4,7 is an eagle, "*the fourth living creature like to an eagle flying*". The nominative value of the Greek word for (eagle) is 576, which is the same value as that for the Greek word meaning spirit, wind, air, breath, life, mind, inspiration, imagination, ghost, spiritual being, holy ghost, soul, essence, angel, demon, or evil spirit. The numerical value of the phrase "an eagle flying" is 1396, the number of the phrase "second angel."

The orientation of the constellation could be found at midsummer's night in 9980 BC or AD 15940 A.D. (These dates represent the third quartile of the 25,920-year precessional cycle, assuming that the starting lion position is in 3500 BC.) It is similar to The Calf orientation but the constellation is higher in the sky and further north from the position that gave us The Calf (Fig 115). For that reason, The Eagle was probably viewed looking northwards. Any connections to an angel that may exist are not obvious but when regarded this way, The Eagle in Ursa Major is evident (Fig 116).

The "four living creatures" can be seen in and around the constellation of Ursa Major and in the positions and orientations of these same stars viewed from the ground at each of the four quarters of the 25,920-year precessional cycle.

---

[122] *Revelation; 1,20*

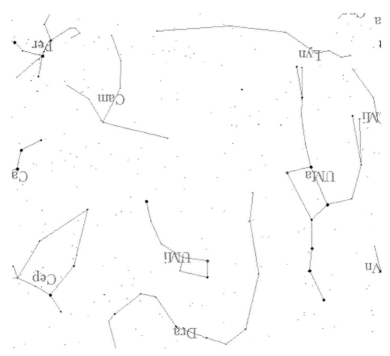

Fig 115 the view of Ursa Major looking North at midnight on 9980 BC or 15940 AD

Alteration of the number of the beast from 616 to 666 and the now proven link to the number 25,920 shows conclusively that Isopsephia or Gematria (numerology) was used in the compilation of the Book of Revelation and that whoever made the changes to Revelation 13,18 was as conversant with the numerical key to the text as had been the author. Additionally, the identification of the locations of "the four living creatures" is conclusive evidence that "the seven stars" mentioned in this erstwhile sacred document are the seven stars of Ursa Major and not the seven stars of the Pleiades as other researchers have speculated.

In Ancient Egypt and Ancient Greece, "The Mysteries" were celebrated with exhaustive and elaborate rituals and ceremonies. One of these ceremonies restaged the Isis, Osiris,

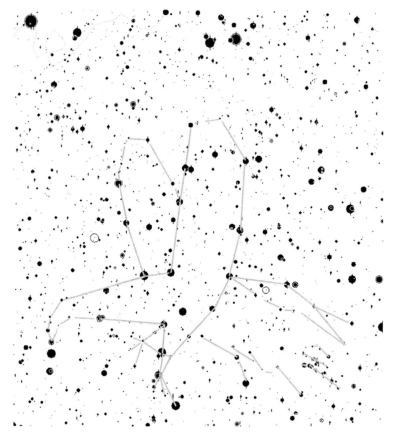

Fig 116 the eagle flying in Ursa Major

Set drama and concluded with the opening of the mouth ceremony detailed in Chapter four. This story was shown to be related to the movement of the pole position through the constellations of Draco and Ursa Major and whilst we can now speculate what "the mystery" actually is, its link to the stars that stay above the northern horizon and appear to rotate around the North Pole position is clear.

The Book of Revelation includes the word "mystery" four times: "the mystery of the seven stars,"[123] "the mystery of the

---

(one) God,"[124] "a written mystery,"[125]and "the mystery of the woman."[126] Many of the characters and artifacts in the Book of Revelation have been shown to exist in and around the constellation of Ursa Major including the tree/spear/lance, cup, bowl, sword, face, eagle, calf, and the head of Satan. The text makes reference to "the seven stars" and mentions a bear, a thigh, and a horse/chariot, which are known designations of the same constellation. There can be no doubt on the basis of this evidence that this document encodes pictures and stories captured and elaborated out of the patterns and movements of the circumpolar constellations in the earliest of times.

We suspect that the oldest and most sacred of the ancient mysteries is closely associated with the group of seven stars that are the principal stars of the constellation of Ursa Major and also with the stars that seem to surround them. There is compelling evidence to suggest that, by deciphering the mysteries in the Book of Revelation (perhaps with the help of Isopsephia/Gematria), the ancient secret beliefs concerning the origins of God and the human race will finally be revealed.

---

[124] *Revelation 10,7*
[125] *Revelation 17.5*
[126] *Revelation 17,7*

Chapter Ten

Names and Aspects of God

There are an abundance of names of Egyptian and Greek gods and goddesses. Since we cannot attempt to find all of their names in the region of Ursa Major, we have limited our search to some prominent names from the Greek and Egyptian pantheon.

The origins of Osiris (the Egyptian god mentioned in chapter five) are unknown. He was a member of the Great Ennead and the earliest references to him are found in the pyramid texts. How he was worshipped in prehistoric times or where his cult center originated is unclear. We can deduce that he was as important to the Egyptians as Christ is (and has been) to the Christians and interestingly, like Christ, he was murdered and then raised from the dead.

Hieroglyphic symbols in which the Osiris name is written are a seat/throne ⏜ and an eye ⬿. These are phonetic signs, being translated as *ws* and *ir* making *Wsir*, which the Greeks pronounced as Osiris. We already know the location of the left eye as it is defined in the painting in the tomb of Sennedjem (Chapter five). A reasonable facsimile of a seat and eye together, with the eye in this same general location, is shown in Fig 117. All of the seven major stars of the Ursa Major constellation are included in this selection.

As if to confirm that the name of Osiris is in Heaven, one of the most significant claims made in the Book of Revelation is that the name of God is "written" in the theater where all the other drama of the Apocalypse is taking

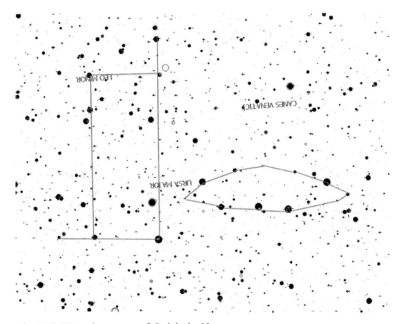

Fig 117 *Wsir,* the name of Osiris in Heaven

place. Extracts from the Book of Revelation that make this claim are:

- "I know where thou dwellest where (is) the throne of the Satan and thou holdest the name of me and not thou didst deny the faith of me even in the days of Antipas" Rev 2,13
- "and on/over the stone a name new written which no man knows except the (one) receiving (it)" Rev 2,17
- "They have over them a king the angel of the abyss name to him in Hebrew Abaddon and in the Greek name he has Apollyon" Rev 9,11
- "the (ones) but eyes of him a flame of fire and on/over the head/top of him diadems many having a name written which no one knows except he" Rev 19,12

- "and on/over the thigh of him a name written king of kings and lord of lords" Rev 19,16

The name of the Greek god Apollo (rev 9.11) was written two ways in ancient Greek, Ἀπολλων meaning *Apóllõn* or Ἀπελλων meaning *Apellõn*. This latter appellation is readily identifiable amongst, in, and around the Ursa Major constellation (Fig 118). In this configuration, stars in Ursa Major help form the last five letters of the name whilst the first two letters fall in "Bootes" and "Corona Borealis." The stars that have been utilized to form *epsilon* could (almost as easily) form *omicron* so that the name stays intact whatever the original appellation.

The same verse in Revelation (9,11) mentions Abaddon as well as Apollyon. This Hebrew name is written in the same section of the constellation as Apollo and is depicted in figure 119.

The son of Zeus and Leto, and the twin brother of Artemis, Apollo was the god of music and also of prophecy, colonization, medicine, archery, poetry, dance, intellectual inquiry, and the protector of herds and flocks. He was also a god of light, known as "Phoebus," and was sometimes identified with Helios the sun god. He was at the same time "The God of Plague" and was worshiped as Smintheus (from *sminthos*, rat) and as Parnopius (from *parnops*, grasshop-

Fig 118 the name of Apollo written in the heavens

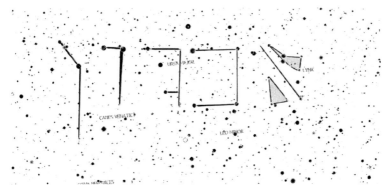

Fig 119 the name Abaddon (in Hebrew) written in the stars

per) and was known as the destroyer of rats and locust. According to Homer's *Iliad*, Apollo shot arrows of plague into the Greek camp. Apollo being the god of religious healing would give those guilty of murder and other immoral deeds a ritual purification.

Sacred to Apollo are the swan (one legend says that Apollo flew on the back of a swan to the land of the Hyperboreans, the people of the Great Britain, and would spend the winter months among them), the wolf, and the dolphin. On his head he wears a laurel crown and his attributes are the bow and arrows and the cithara (or lyre) and plectrum. His most famous attribute is the tripod, the symbol of his prophetic powers.

Abaddon, on the other hand, has become associated with Satan and means "destruction." In Biblical references (*Job* 26:6; *Proverbs* 15,11) the name implies "place of destruction" or "the realm of the dead" and is associated with Sheol. It implies an underworld abode of lost souls, or perhaps Hell. In some Jewish legends, it is identified as a realm where the damned lie in fire and snow, one of the places in Hell that Moses visited. For that reason, Abaddon has traditionally been associated with Satan.

It seems bizarre that two names for the same being can have such disparate meanings, particularly when these names can be located in the same area of the heavens (Fig 119). Strangely, the clue that is needed to point us to the solution of this conundrum may be that all of these beings and appellations are in the same place. The only difference between them is their individual orientation or the particular selection of stars that they utilize.

Anyone looking north from Egypt at midnight in mid-winter would have seen the northern stars in Fig 120. This is a picture of the stars in which the Egyptians saw Osiris with his lateral horns and a crown above his head. It is the same picture used to construct the painting in the tomb of Sennedjem that was discussed in chapter five. The picture of Satan, on the other hand (Fig 121), has the constellation totally inverted from the "God position" and could only have been seen in this position if the observer lay on the ground with his head facing north. Of course, if the observer could have seen the stars during daylight, he would have seen the constellation in the "Satan position" as it rotated to the other side of the circle that it appeared to make around the pole.

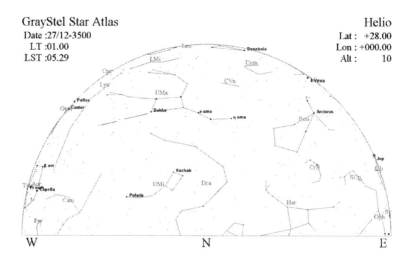

Fig 120 the picture of the night sky from Egypt on 27 December

Despite this apparent contradiction, there was recognition in ancient times that the area in which all the aspects and manifestations of God operated was the land of the dead.

> With the Greek, Dionysus the good Demiurge is identified with Hades. In Egypt, Osiris was Lord of death; with the Scandinavians, Odin the God beneficent, was, at the same time, king of the infernal regions.[127]

For this specific reason, and because all stars are visible in all their aspects simultaneously, we are of the view that the conventional view of the "fallen one" as evil and in conflict with the rest of the occupants of Heaven has come about because of the difference in orientation. Some researchers claim that the basis for all the ancient religions was brought to the Middle East by the Hyperboreans, Celts, and Druids.[128] If this hypothesis is true, then depending on their latitudes, the originators of the God stories would have been able to see the constellation in its "Satan position" during the dark days of winter as the constellation rotated around the pole position and they would probably have connoted evil with what they saw as the removal of the sun.

The names of Apollo and Abaddon (Figs 118 and 119) can be seen when the orientation of the sky is 180° on from that in Fig 120, i.e. where the constellation presents the head of Satan. In other words, they exist in profile, looking north, during the day when the stars (and therefore any pictures that they make) cannot be seen. Can this be the reason why the name of God has been described as "hidden?"

The name of God appears in Hebrew Scriptures as the four Hebrew letters yed, he, vav, he (YHVH), which format is known as the Tetragrammaton. From these letter derives Jehovah and Yahweh and in Jewish tradition, this name of God is "not to be uttered" in order that it is not profaned.

---

[127] Godfrey Higgins, Celtic Druids, Kessinger (1993)
[128] Higgins, Celtic Druids; Graves, The White Goddess; Knight and Lomas, The Book of Hiram;

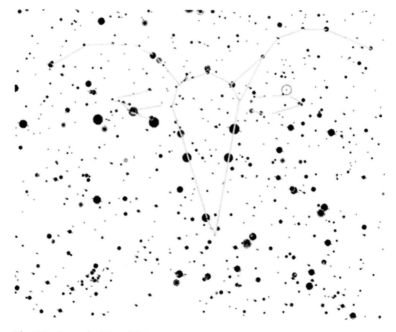

Fig 121 Satan in Ursa Major

The first two letters of this designation represent the name (of himself), which the Old Testament tells us that God gave to Moses when he said, "I am that I am." This form appears in the formation of many of the sacred Hebrew names such as Eli-Yahu (Elijah), Jehu-dah, Yeshi-Yahu (Isaiah), and the messianic name Yahu'shuah.

"The name Iahu is far older than the sixteenth century BC and of wide distribution. It occurs in Egypt during the sixth dynasty (middle of the third millennium BC) as a title of the God Set; and is recorded in Deimel's Akkadian-Sumerian Glossary as a name of Isis. It also seems to be the origin of the Greek name Iacchus, a title of the shape shifting Diony-sus Lusios in the Cretan mysteries."[134]

---

[134] *The White Goddess; Robert Graves*

"Iahu as a title of Jehova similarly marks him out as a ruler of the solar year, probably a transcendental combination of Set, Osiris and Horus (alias Egli-Iahu, the calf bull)"[134]

We know that Egyptians located their gods in a very particular part of the heavens and we are told that Moses had been steeped in the teachings of the Egyptians. Since Moses' vocation was to usurp the Egyptian pantheon and replace it by a single all powerful deity, it seems obvious that the name of God in the language of "the chosen race" should appear in this same place as the Egyptian deities, albeit hidden. If this is so, it may even explain why Moses and those who followed him believed themselves to be the "Chosen People."

Revelation 19,16 tells us that the written name is or means "king of kings and lord of lords." The title "lord" was used by the Hebrews in order to prevent themselves using the name of God irreverently. They adopted a term used by Heathens referring to the God Sol in Greek "Ηλιος," in Latin "Dominus," in ancient Celtic "Adon," which converted into Semitic languages as Adni or Adonis or Tammuz.[129] This fact implies that the phrase "king of kings and lord of lords" must mean "God of gods" and in the Hebrew must therefore equate with the sacred God of gods, YHVH.

The name of God was sacred and we apologize if our examination creates any offence to Jewish people. The subject is not new and there is evidence from eminent Jewish authors that God or his name existed in the stars.[130]

Use of the name YHVH, first disclosed to Moses, was discontinued around 520 BC, the time of the restoration of the Temple of Jerusalem. This occurred because the Hebrews wished to distinguish their God from the ram-headed God of the Egyptians whose name(s) was used indiscriminately. The alternative they used brought with it an additional difficulty. Documents from this period show that YHVH was designated as "The God of Heaven." When translated into

[129] Higgins, Celtic Druids
[130] Elias J Bickerman, The Jews in the Greek Age, Harvard University Press (1990)

Greek or Latin, this title implied "the God of the firmament" and appeared to refer to the cosmic deity of the Egyptian and Chaldean astronomers. Since astrology was a growing force at this time, there was even a danger that "The God of Heaven" was involved in and sanctioned the philosophy that was claimed for this new "science."

In reality, the formation of these four Hebrew letters exists in the same locality as Apollo and uses many of the stars that were used to form the name Abaddon. As can be seen in Fig 122, they form an accurate representation of the Tetragrammaton. Other than the obvious fact that one has to locate the name amongst the northern stars, the name is hidden in the sense that this view of the constellation could only be had in the Middle East by an observer by lying on the ground at night, face up, head facing north.

Again, however, it is important to address the reasonable skeptic who will ask again, "surely with all the stars in the sky, it would be possible to select these shapes and words in many places?"

Of course this is true! What would be impossible to do (anywhere else) would be to reproduce these names (and the shapes we have seen in previous chapters) in a single area of the sky and centered on one particular constellation. Perhaps

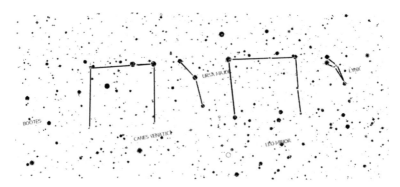

Fig 122 a representation of YHVH, the Hebrew name of God found in and around Ursa Major

this is why the Book of Revelation talks about "the mystery of the seven stars."

To add to the weight of evidence that has been generated here, other shapes, names, and images mentioned in the Book of Revelation have been located in and around the constellation of Ursa Major and several of them that show the link between The Book of Revelation and their various religious traditions are illustrated below. For example, one of the Christian epithets for Jesus is "the lamb of God."

A lamb is mentioned in the Book of Revelation several times, one example being: "and I saw and behold the Lamb standing on/over the Mount Sion and with him/it a hundred (and) forty four thousands having/holding the name of him/it and the name of the father of him/it written on/over the foreheads of them."[131]

The image of a lamb located in the northern stars is clear, its head being in the four stars that make the cup of Ursa Major (Fig 123). The fact that the lamb is described as standing on "the mount Sion" gives us a significant clue to the location of this image of a mountain in the stars of Leo Minor and Leo Major.

The attribution of divine status to "the lamb" seems to be a Christian phenomenon. To the Egyptians, Greeks, and Hebrews, the lamb was a "clean" meat and formed part of the staple diet of the area. There is no recorded information of a lamb being part of the heavenly pantheon in any of the three traditions. That said, it is true that gods depicted as horned rams (the lamb's older brother) were extremely popular in pre-dynastic Egypt and retained their influence through the entire Egyptian history as a symbol of strength and virility. Many pictures of the gods depicted them to be wearing ram's horns (Fig 26). The best known Egyptian Ram God was the Ram of Mendes that represented the soul of Osiris. It is no coincidence, therefore, that the head of the lamb in figure 123 is within the four principal stars of Ursa Major.

---

[131] *Revelation 14,1*

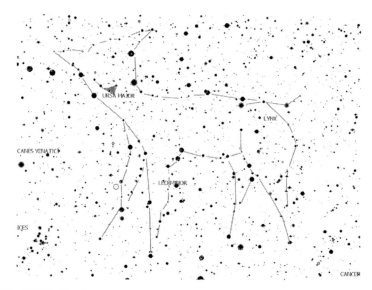

Fig 123 the lamb

Perhaps the most powerful claim made in the Book of Revelation is in Rev 2,5 where Lord the (one) God says;"I am the Alpha and the Omega, the beginning and the end." This self-appropriated attribute invites careful study of the northern stars since its location there would be extremely persuasive evidence of the hypothesis that all the God stories emanated from this part of the heavens and from the constellation of Ursa Major in particular. A search produces a number of different possibilities.

"Ω" (omega) is relatively easy to locate as there are only a small number of stars in the vicinity of the seven principal stars of Ursa Major that contrive the shape of this Greek letter. The A (alpha) that combines with it is more difficult to identify.

The most visually attractive possibility is the design in figure 124, which uses six of the seven principal Ursa Major stars. Its esoteric pattern is compelling and its symmetry beguiling. Despite this, the stars do not provide a compelling cross piece for the "alpha."

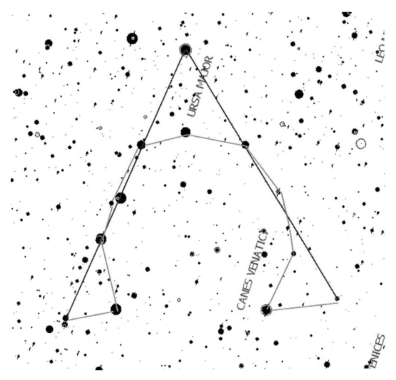

Fig 124 one possible location of "The Alpha and the Omega"

It is therefore rejected in favor of the pattern in figure 125. This second shape uses five of the seven principal stars of Ursa Major, surrounds the other two, and is symmetrical about a line extended from the base of the cup. The orientation of the sky that allows a view of A (alpha) upright occurs at midnight on Spring Equinox (Fig 93), which is the time of the earth's awakening or beginning. The orientation of the sky that produces Ω(omega) occurs at midnight (Fig 87) on the autumn equinox, the end the productive season. This is one possible meaning of "the beginning and the end."

The Greek word used for "beginning" in the Book of Revelation meant beginning, origin, the person or thing that commences, the first person or thing in a series, the leader,

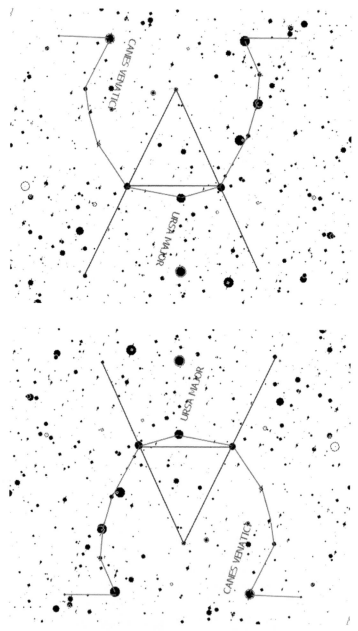

Fig 125 the Alpha and the Omega, the beginning and the end

the extremity of a thing and the first place, principality, rule, magistracy of angels and demons.

The Greek word used for "end" in Greek meant end, termination, the limit at which a thing ceases to be (always of the end of some act or state, but not of the end of a period of time), the last in any succession or series, eternal, that by which a thing is finished, its close, issue, and the end to which all things relate, the aim or purpose. It can be seen from these two definitions that (apart from the fact that Greek letters are used) the claim in the Book of Revelation that I am "the beginning and the end" could equally be read as I am "where you come from and where you return." This corresponds well with what we know of Osiris (for example) being both the god of creation and the god of the netherworld.

There are several other significant items that are to be found in the Book of Revelation and which are easily discernable in and around the constellation of Ursa Major. A complete and comprehensive compilation of all the personalities and objects mentioned in the Book of Revelation will

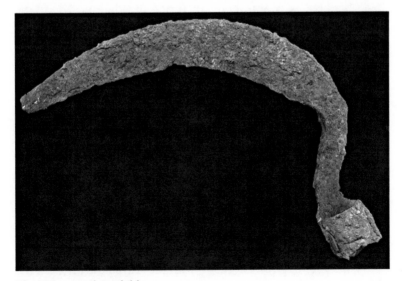

Fig 126 an ancient sickle

Fig 127 a painting in the tomb of Sennedjem

be detailed in *Revelation Decoded*. Two of these items are described below.

A "sickle" is mentioned six times in Chapter 14 of the Book of Revelation and the Greek word has a numerical value of 360. The words meaning"A sickle sharp" have a numerical value of 890. Interestingly, in Greek, the phrase "things which (are)" is represented by the Greek letter alpha, which has a numerical value of 1. Thus, "Things which (are) a sickle sharp" has a value of 891, which has the same value as the word "Heaven" and the words "the stars." The phrases that include the word "sickle" in the Book of Revelation are:

". . .in the hand of him a sickle sharp" (Heaven/the stars) Rev 14,14:

". . .Send/thrust (thou) the sickle of thee" Rev 14,15:

". . .thrust the (one) sitting on the cloud the sickle of him over the earth" Rev 14,16:

". . .another angel went forth from the shrine the (one) in the Heaven having also he a sickle sharp" (the stars) Rev 14,17:

"and another angel went forth from the altar the (one) having authority over the fire and (he) spoke (with) a voice great to the (one) having the sickle the (one) sharp saying; send/thrust of thee the sickle the (one) sharp." Rev 14,18:

"And thrust the angel the sickle of him into the earth." Rev 14,19:

Archeological finds have shown us that the sickle of ancient times is not totally dissimilar to its present day descendent (Fig 126). An accurate representation of the same shape is found in and immediately around five of the principal stars of the constellation of Ursa Major (Fig 128). Some readers may have drawn the handle a little differently, but, all in all, this is likely to be the location of the pattern referred to as "the sickle sharp." Egyptian tomb paintings of such tools (Fig 127) confirm their shape and show the way this implement was held. They also provide another link between the religions and practices of Ancient Egypt and the last book of the New Testament.

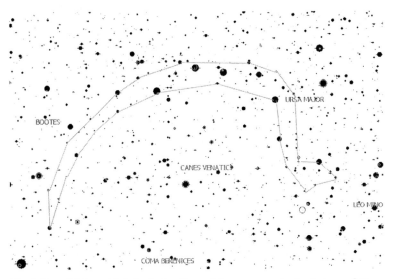

Fig 128 a sickle, which includes five of the seven principal stars of Ursa Major

The Book of Revelation uses two words that imply a temple. The first Greek word is ναος which is translated as "shrine." In ancient times it was used of the temple at Jerusalem, but only of the sacred edifice (or sanctuary) itself, consisting of the Holy place and the Holy of Holies. In classical Greek it was used of the sanctuary or cell of the temple, where the image of gold was placed which is distinguished from the whole enclosure. It was also used for any heathen temple or shrine. The second Greek word σκηνη is translated as tabernacle, temple, house, theater, or arbor. This word was used in reference to "that well-known movable temple of God after the pattern of which the temple at Jerusalem was built."[132]

Modern day thinking would put a tabernacle inside a shrine. In ancient Greek, we believe that it is likely that the shrine is contained inside the tabernacle.

"and after these things I saw and was opened the shrine/ temple of the tabernacle of the testimony/proof in the heaven" [133]

"the (one) actual Lord the (one) God the almighty shrine of it (the city) is and the Lamb."[134]

The Greek word most commonly translated as "temple" in the New Testament is not used or included in the Book of Revelation. Its replacement by the word translated as tabernacle leads us to presume that "the tabernacle" does not have the conventional shape of a temple, Greek, Egyptian, or otherwise. If we assume "the shrine" to be the cup of Ursa Major, which holds the pentagram and the pentagon, then "the tabernacle" would therefore be some recognizable shape that envelops it.

The only distinctive shape associated with Egypt, other than the shape of the temples, is the pyramid. The most notable example of this shape is the Great Pyramid on the Giza

---

[132] *The online Greek Bible, www.greekbible.com*
[133] *Revelation 15,5*
[134] *Revelation 21,22*

Fig 129 the Great Pyramid at Giza

plateau outside Cairo, (Fig 129), one of the seven ancient wonders of the world. It is the largest of three pyramids, which are adjacent to the Sphinx. Its existence means that it was thought by its constructors to have been a shape of some significance even though it was a different shape to anything constructed on Earth before it.

On examination, one discovers that this pyramid is spectacular in the extreme:

- Its dimensions incorporate the sacred mathematical ratios of π (pi, the ratio of the circumference of a circle to its diameter) and φ (phi, the golden ratio discussed in chapter five and explained in Appendix 2).
- Its unit of measurement was chosen so that each side of the edifice is equal (in cubits) to the number of days in a year.

- Its various dimensions include indicators of the earth's radius, the diameter of the earth's orbit around the sun, and the number of years in a complete processional cycle.[135]
- Perhaps more interestingly, the position of the north facing shafts of the construction envelops the constellation of Ursa Major in the Heavens.[136]

The design of this pyramid required a deep understanding of mathematics, astronomy, and architecture and the underlying reason for its construction implies an even deeper knowledge of the mysteries that upheld Egyptian religious tradition.

Herodotus visited Egypt in 443 BC and recounted how Pharaoh Cheops (the Greek name for Khufu) built the Great Pyramid during his reign with one hundred thousand men in twenty years. This would have dated the construction to circa 2500 BC.

He is known to have been an initiate in the Egyptian Mystery Schools and would have been sworn to secrecy regarding the true nature of the Great Pyramid. Because of this, it is possible that he reproduced the tale about the origins of the monument that was then in circulation. In addition, the Greek historian's account stands in sharp contrast to most other Egyptian, Hebrew, Greek, Roman, Hermetic, Coptic, and medieval Arabic scholarly sources, which agree that the Great Pyramid was not constructed during the time frame of Pharaoh Khufu or Dynastic Egypt, but was the product of the "Age of the Gods" thousands of years earlier. The most conclusive indication of Herodotus' error is the testament of the Pharaoh Khufu that he only did repair work on the Great Pyramid.

The Inventory Stele, found in 1857 AD by Auguste Mariette just to the east of the Pyramid, dates to about 1500 BC,

---

[135] Peter Lemesurier, *The Great Pyramid decoded,*
[136] Bauval and Hancock, *Keeper of Genesis;*

but according to Maspero and other experts, shows evidence of having been copied from a far older stele contemporaneous with the Fourth Dynasty. In the Stele, Khufu himself tells of his discoveries made while clearing away the sands from the Pyramid and Sphinx. He dedicated the account to Isis, who he called the "Mistress of the Western Mountain" and "Mistress of the Pyramid" and identified the Pyramid itself as the "House of Isis."

The Stele describes how Pharaoh Khufu "gave to her (Isis) an offering anew, and he built again (to restore, renovate, reconstruct) her temple of stone." From there, the Pharaoh inspected the Sphinx, according to the text, and related the story of how, in his time, both the monument and a nearby sycamore tree had been struck by lightning. The bolt had knocked off part of the headdress of the Sphinx, which Khufu carefully restored. The Stele then ends with the story of how Khufu built small pyramids for himself and his daughters, wife, and family next to the Great Pyramid. Today, the ruins of three small pyramids are indeed situated on the east side of the monument.

Archaeologists have found independent evidence that the southernmost of the three small pyramids flanking the Great Pyramid was in fact dedicated to Henutsen, a wife of Khufu. Everything in the inscription thus matches the known facts. If this information is accurate and true, then the additional information that Khufu was only a restorer of the Great Pyramid and not its builder may also be historically true.[137] Whatever the actual date, the Great Pyramid was an extraordinary and totally unique construction.

Remarkably, an accurate representation of this distinctive shape can be found in the heavens holding the seven stars of Ursa Major inside it (Fig 130). For the first time, we can see a shape that is meant to be three-dimensional, which is perhaps an indication that some of the other shapes mentioned

---

[137] *Joseph Jochmans, How Old are the Pyramids?; http://www.world-mysteries.com/ mpl_2_4.htm*

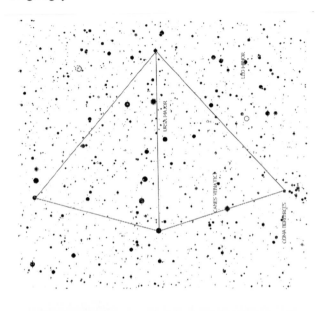

Fig 130 the pyramid that surrounds the seven principal stars of Ursa Major and its image on the American dollar bill

in the Book of Revelation are meant to be perceived as three-dimensional. The shrine, which is the cup of Ursa Major is also the home of God in Heaven. This shrine is held inside a tabernacle that is shaped like a pyramid. It is small wonder that Pharaohs wanted to be entombed in a grand facsimile of the place where they believed themselves to be headed and that the pyramid itself incorporated everything that the ancients believed to be sacred.

These representations (the various names of God, the lamb, the alpha and the omega, the sickle and the tabernacle) show that there is a visible and profound link between Ancient Egyptian, the Hebrew, and the Christian philosophies. This link is maintained indefinitely through the stars of Ursa Major that the Egyptians called *ikhemu-set*, which is a name that means "the Imperishable ones" or "The indestructible Ones."[138]

We are told that the Pentateuch, the first five books of The Old Testament, is attributed to Moses, who spent all of his formative years in the Royal House of Egypt. Did he and his followers take out of Egypt remnants of ancient beliefs that have been protected and kept hidden for 3,000 years? Was this information rediscovered by The Knights Templar when they excavated under the Dome of the Rock in Jerusalem?

Was it passed on in myths such as the Grail legends, presented in pseudo arcana such as Tarot Cards, and misrepresented to us through the oppressive scenarios presented in the Book of Revelation, which so many seem to want to take literally? Has this information been kept from us because of its significant and profound implications? Why is it useful to those in the know that we maintain our faith in God? Is the picture of a pyramid and the all-seeing eye on the humble American dollar our indication that there are among us those who are aware of the origins of our belief systems and who are dedicated to maintaining forever the Secret of the Ages?

---

[138] Robert Bauval, *The Egypt Code*, Century Hutchinson (2006)

Chapter Eleven

The Book of the Dead

During the Egyptian Old Kingdom (up to 2134 BC), the afterlife was only available to the king. After the Old Kingdom collapsed, the people became more self-reliant, and with this new development came a process by which the common people received the promise of the afterlife. Egyptologists refer to this evolution of thought as the "democratization of the afterlife."

Once the common people had a chance at "life after death," they had spells carved on their coffins or sarcophagi that contained instructions and protections for their continued existence after their death. These spells were descended from the Pyramid Texts and formed the basis of *The Book of the Dead*. Over one thousand spells have been recorded. Collectively, these spells are known as the "Coffins Texts."

The Book of the Dead is a New Kingdom collection of texts composed primarily from earlier funerary works such as the Pyramid and Coffin Texts. An individual text was usually written on papyrus, however many individual chapters of the Book or spells have been found on tomb walls, scarabs, statuettes, and on at least one royal mortuary temple (Rameses III).

They vary in quality and date from between 1500 BC and 200 BC and vary in content. Some, bound in leather, include almost the entire *Book of the Dead.* Others, from tombs of the less wealthy, "had to make do with a ready written text in which spaces had been left for the insertion of the name of buyer."[139]

---

[139] *Faulkner, The Book of the Dead, Introduction*

These scrolls have incantations engraved on them, which indicate a commonality of thought regarding the afterlife and theosophical conviction from one grave to another and over a long period of time.

In 1999, the British Museum published a compilation of these scrolls under the title "Book of the Dead" that had been translated into English by R O Faulkner for the Limited Editions Club of New York. The preface of this book tells us that Dr R O Faulkner was "the leading modern British authority on the progressive stages of funerary texts" and that "his translations of the 'Pyramid Texts" appeared in 1969 and of the 'Coffin Texts' between 1972 and 1978." It claimed that Dr Faulkner omitted a few spells/incantations at the request of the original publisher because "they duplicate or virtually duplicate spells which are included and a few others which are too corrupt or obscure to yield intelligible translation."[140]

The introduction to *The Book of the Dead* includes the affirmation that, "The *Pyramid Texts* also reflect a belief in the astral afterlife among the circumpolar stars." It does not say but rather infers that the afterlife was supposed to be in the presence of the gods and specifically in the company of the god Osiris. In reference to the evolution of Egyptian traditions over a long period of time, the introduction also tells us, "In Egyptian religion old beliefs were rarely discarded, new ideas and concepts were merely tacked on, even when in direct contradiction to existing views. That is why the Egyptians could believe in an afterlife in which the deceased could spend eternity in the company of the circumpolar stars as an *akh*, at the same time as being restricted to the burial chamber and offering chapel of the tomb as a *ka*, but also visiting the world of the living, inhabiting the Elysian Fields and travelling through the Underworld with the sun-God as *ba*."

---

[140] Faulkner, *The Book of the Dead, Introduction*

Thought provoking in its implications, it also claims,

> During the Old Kingdom (about 2686-2181 BC) when only the great nobility, apart from the king, were assured of an afterlife, living one's earthly life according to a strict moral code was considered sufficient to secure eternal bliss. But the breakdown of order during the political troubles of the First Intermediary Period, which led to tomb robbery and the desecration of cemeteries, shattered this belief. So, in an attempt to deter such wrong doing, the idea was encouraged that judgment would be passed on the dead for the actions they had committed on earth.

The later Christian philosophy seems to have mirrored this old Egyptian means of control and it parallels, from the applicant's point of view, the threats and pronouncements of the Christian God of Judgment contained in the Book of Revelation. In fact, the personalities, places, and objects in the two texts show a remarkable similarity (see Appendix 7), particularly when we know that the many different of names of the Egyptian gods reflect aspects of the same God. Surprisingly (within the limitations of accurate translation), there are over three hundred words representing places, things, or events that are common to the two texts. One of the most intriguing examples of these is the reference in both texts to the winged female that resides in Heaven.

When discussing winged beings in Chapter 2, we showed a picture of Isis with wings (Fig 29). She was often depicted on coffins with wings outstretched (Fig 130), and *The Book of the Dead* tells us;

"Beneficent in command and word was Isis, the woman of magical spells, the advocate of her brother. She sought him (Osiris) untiringly, she wandered round and round about this earth in sorrow, and she alighted not without finding him. She made light with her feathers, she created air with her wings, and she uttered the death wail for her brother" (whom had been killed and been dismembered by Seth).[141]

---

[141] *E A Wallis Budge, The Papyrus of Ani. Book of the Dead;*

Fig 131 the winged figure of Isis

"As for the plumes on his head, it means that Isis and Ne-phthys (another version of Isis) went and put themselves on his head when they were the Two Kites, and they were firm on his head. Otherwise said: They are the two great and mighty uraei (winged serpents), which are on the brow of his father Atum. Otherwise said: The Plumes on his head are his eyes."[142]

These extracts correspond well with one of the most pro-vocative statements in the Book of Revelation: "And were given to the woman the two wings of the eagle the (one) great in order that she might (fly) to the desert to the place of her where she is nourished there a right place/time and right places/times and half of right place/time/proportion/circum-stance from a face of the serpent."[143]

The Book of the Dead quotations tell us that the plumes, which are the wings of Isis, are the eyes of God. In Chap-ter five, we found the location of the eyes of God to be the extensions on either side of the four principal stars of Ursa Major (Fig 49). This means that the wings of Isis should be similarly positioned (Fig 132), thus placing the head and torso of Isis over the four central stars of the constellation.

In this coincidence of shapes, one aspect of Isis (and therefore God) overlays the location of the eyes of God. By

[142] Faulkner, *The Book of the Dead*, Spell 17
[143] Revelation 12,14

Fig 132 the wings of Isis in the same location as the Eyes of God (inset)

implication, therefore, it overlays the face of God. The location of Isis here is one of the clearest visual insights into the concept of differing names and aspects of one and the same God, a view that is confirmed in spell 17:

> I have made use of my feet for I am Atum, I am my city. Get back, O Lion bright of mouth and shining of head; retreat because of my strength, take care, O you who are invisible, do not await me for I am Isis. You found me when I had disarranged the hair of my face and my scalp was disordered . . . I am Wadjet, Lady of the Devouring Flame.
>
> Otherwise said . . . As for me having disarranged the hair of my face and disordered my scalp, it means that Isis was in the shrine of Sokar and she rubbed the hair. As for Wadjet, Lady of the Devouring Flame, she is the Eye of Re.[144]

---

[144] *Faulkner, Book of the Dead; Spell 17*

Other than the twenty-year period when the Pharaoh Akhenaton attempted to replace the god Amen by the god Aten/Aton (1352–1332 BC), Amen or Amun was the Egyptian God of Gods in his aspect of Amen-Re or Amun-Ra, Ra being the essence of God hidden in the sun. The worship of Amun-Ra represented one of ancient Egypt's most important theologies. Amen/Amun was originally a local god from Thebes and was regarded in Thebes to be among the gods who created of the world. In the Ptolemaic Period, he was regarded as the Egyptian equivalent of Zeus. Surprisingly, the Book of Revelation uses "Amen," the Egyptian name of God, throughout:

- The glory and the might unto the ages of the ages Amen 1.6
- Behold he comes with the clouds and will see him every eye and (those) who him pierced and will wail over him all the tribes of the land/earth yes Amen Rev 1,7
- Write though these things says the Amen Rev 3,14
- The four living creatures/creations said, Amen Rev 5,14
- . . . they (all the angels) gave worship to the (one) God saying Amen Rev 7,11&12
- The strength to the God of us unto the ages of the ages, Amen Rev 7,12
- They gave worship to the (one) God to the (one) sitting on the throne saying, Amen halleluiah Rev19,4
- Says the (one) witnessing these things, yes I am coming quickly, Amen Rev22,20

This use of "Amen" by the author of the Book of Revelation is perhaps significant when making any comparison with the content of the papyri making up *The Book of the Dead*. The funereal papyri tend to focus on Re/Ra, Osiris, and the other gods of the Ennead for their entreaties while occasionally invoking the usurper Aten, the God of the sun and creator of man. Amun or Amen is mentioned only rarely.

Tomb paintings, carvings, and hieroglyph symbols that go back to the beginnings of Egyptian civilization are much more prone to depict and mention Amun/Amen despite Akhenaton's later attempts to have all of these references to Amen removed.

The Book of Revelation and *The Book of the Dead* are both based on scrolls or papyri that were created after 1500 BC, albeit that the former was created many years after the latter. The use of Amen so liberally in the Book of Revelation could therefore be an important indication of the author's intention to link this document with the old (pre Aten) religion of Egypt. (A hypothesis that would explain this phenomenon is contained in the final chapter of this book.)

Despite this major difference, both books indicate:

- That a Heaven exists where God sits on his throne surrounded by angels giving him acclaim and praise/worship.[145]
- The idea that there are "Elders" in Heaven.[146]
- That the testimony or proof of God existed in a "shrine" in a tabernacle that also held the seven angels/stars.[147]
- The dragon, a beast, and their followers are attacked by the angels and driven out of Heaven to a place where they blaspheme God and the name of God. The beast continues to pursue the woman and they tempt and torment humanity until vanquished and condemned to eternal torment.[148] The pictures illustrating the vanquishing of the serpent in both books show a remarkable similarity (Fig 118).
- The idea that we (human beings) will go before God for "judgment" based on our life on Earth, to be judged as worthy of Heaven or condemned to the worst unpleasantness.[149]

---

[145] *Revelation 7,1: Book of the Dead, spells 15 & 42*
[146] *Revelation 11,16: Book of the Dead, spell 57*
[147] *Revelation 15,5&15,6: Book of the Dead, spells16 & 180*
[148] *Revelation 12,19 & 20,10: Book of the Dead, spells 39 & introductory hymn.*
[149] *Revelation 20,9&20,12: Book of the Dead, spells 65, 125 & 137A*

- There are in their theosophy a series of mysteries.[150]
- That God is accompanied and Heaven occupied by a woman who manifests various different aspects.[151]
- The idea of seven spirits.[152]
- The idea of a great star.[153]

In all but the replacement of Aten by Amen, the Book of Revelation infers the same scenario as *The Book of the Dead,* the only difference being one of orientation. Instead of a cringing applicant who is voicing entreaties in the form of supplicating compliments in *The Book of the Dead,* the Book of Revelation presents a vengeful and unforgiving God voicing intimidating threats. Even the illustrations in the two texts depict remarkably similar events (Fig 133).

The Book of the Dead seems to be more positive to the reader because the spells and entreaties of the applicants acclaim the wonder of God's existence that they believe is their destiny. Only occasionally do they revert to entreaties regarding their wish to avoid the painful alternative. The Book of Revelation, on the other hand, focuses on the dreadful alternative to infinity with God in Heaven and seems to have been written to allow earthly religious leaders to gain control of their flocks by wielding (on God's behalf) the threat of eternal damnation in perpetual fire.

The Book of the Dead and the Book of Revelation both acknowledge that the inherent mystery of God and his domain are associated with "The Great Bear" or "the seven stars." *The Book of the Dead* is more specific and states that the tribunal of Osiris (the one that will judge the dead) is located "behind the Great Bear in the Northern sky."

Perhaps more interestingly, both texts imply that a special shape is associated with this same place. *The Book of the*

---

[150] *Revelation 1,20, 10,7, 17,5 & 17,7: Book of the Dead, spell 78*
[151] *Revelation 2,20; 12,1;4,6,13,14,15,16 &17; 17,3,4,6,9 & 18: Book of the Dead, spells 17,110,*
[152] *Revelation 1,4; Book of the Dead, spell 17*
[153] *Revelation 8,10; Book of the Dead, spell 180*

Fig 133 the vanquishing of the serpent/dragon in *The Book of the Dead* (left) and in the introductory illustration to St. Etienne Harding's Book of Revelation (right)

Dead is explicit and indicates that this "shape" is seen as the shape of Osiris.

> N will be restored to his true shape, his true god-like form. . . It is a great secret of the West, a secret image of the Netherworld, since the gods, spirits and dead see it as the shape of the Foremost of the Westerners (Osiris).[154]

Since the face of Osiris is, or is enclosed by, the pentagram shape (see chapter five), we examined the words used for "face" in the Book of Revelation. In ancient Greek there are two words meaning, "face," προσωπον, which is used throughout the Book of Revelation, and οψις, which is used only once. The latter word is defined as "the outward appearance or look" and is used in Rev 1,16:

---

[154] *Faulkner, Book of the Dead, spell 137A*

"And having in the right hand of him stars seven and from the mouth of him a sword two edged sharp proceeding and the face/appearance/look/shape of him as the sun shines/becomes evident/seems to the mind, with/in/by the power/inherent power, of it/him."

The locations of "the stars seven" and "the sword sharp" have been identified and are known to be at the core of the constellation of Ursa Major. It would therefore seem that this verse from the Book of Revelation is pointing us directly to the space inside the four stars of Ursa Major that make the cup and thus to the pentagon it contains. The face or shape referred to must be the pentagon, and the face must be in the same location as the face of Osiris (Fig 67). The pentagon shape, or the five-pointed star that it creates within itself, is the shape that "the sun seems to the mind by the inherent power of it."

It is no coincidence that the stars depicted in Egyptian tomb paintings are five-pointed. Egyptian temples were complex models of the cosmos; paintings of stellar deities and constellations appeared on the ceilings and tombs.

Egyptians believed that the *ba* or soul of the dead person might ascend into the heavens to a region in space called the *Duat* where the souls of dead pharaohs and others went as one of the myriad of stars. The symbol of this was the five-pointed star. As followers of Osiris, these stars could also represent souls in the underworld and evidence of this is to be found in tombs of pharaohs.

The pattern of the ceiling of the tomb of the pharaoh Thutmosis III is shown in figure 134. In spell 177, Nut confirms to the applicant, "You have opened up your place among the stars of the sky, for you are the lone star of the sky."

The deceased person is meant to be a departed soul that has gone to his new heavenly abode (in the *Duat*) and has assumed an image of God. Since Osiris was the god that occupied the Netherworld and he in turn was an aspect of the God of Gods, Amun-Ra, this great god (by definition) must have had the same five-pointed shape.

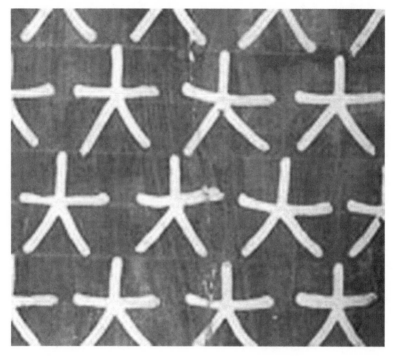

Fig 134 ceiling pattern

Another word used in the Book of Revelation that could be related to shape is σημειον, defined as "a sign, mark, token" or "that by which a person or a thing is distinguished from others and is known." Revelation 12,1 tells us, "And a sign/shape great was seen in the heaven, a woman clothed in/thrown around the sun and the moon underneath the feet of her and on/over the head of her a crown of stars twelve."

An examination of the picture of Isis in figure 117 shows that her crown is made by joining twelve stars, implying once more that the sun or its essence is contained at the center of the Ursa Major constellation. This is another confirmation of the link between the Book of Revelation and

The Book of the Dead and a clear indication that all the gods and goddesses are aspects of, or particular groupings from, the many stars and galaxies that are can be seen in this area of the sky.

This is nowhere better corroborated than in spell 17:

Here I am; I have come to you that you may drive out all the evil which is on me just as you did for those seven spirits who are in the suite of the Lord of Sepa, whose places Anubis made ready on the day of "Come thence."

"*Who are they?* As for those gods the Lords of Justice, they are Seth and Isdes, Lord of the West. As for the tribunal which is behind Osiris, Imsety, Hapy, Duamutef, and Qebehsenuef, ir is these who are behind the Great Bear in the Northern sky . . .

"O Re . . . may you save me from that god whose shape is secret, whose eyebrows are the arms of the balance, on the night of the reckoning of the robbers.

"*Who is he?* He is Sheshmu, he is the mutilator of Osiris.

"*Otherwise said:* He is Apep, he has only one head which bears righteousness.

"*Otherwise said*: He is Horus, he has two heads, one bearing right and one bearing wrong; he gives wrong to whoever does it and right to whoever comes with it.

"*Otherwise said:* He is Horus the Great pre-eminent in Letopolis.

"*Otherwise said*: He is Thoth.

"*Otherwise said*: He is Nefertum, son of Bastet. These are the tribunal who take action against the enemies of the Lord of All.

The Book of the Dead is telling the same story as the Book of Revelation but from a different perspective. The story in both texts is enacted in the heavens in the region of the constellation Ursa Major. The only significant differences between the two previously unfathomable texts involve the names and aspects of God and his female companion(s) along with the female gods in their many aspects that all get merged into a much smaller cast of players. From this we can deduce that whatever mystery has been kept so guarded down the ages, it is as old as and perhaps older than the written records that have emerged from ancient Egypt. It also indicates that Christian theology is somehow linked to the earliest Egyptian religious beliefs.

This link did not die with the demise of the Egyptian culture. It was carried into the Book of Revelation and seems to have been known to key persons involved in the formation of the Knights Templar and of the Cistercians (see chapter four) in the eleventh and twelfth centuries. More intriguingly, if the Freemasons are offspring of the Knights Templar,[155] the hidden secret that this more modern but enigmatic organization is thought to possess (or keep hidden) might well relate to this connection between "The Creator" and the constellation of Ursa Major in the Northern circumpolar stars.

---

[155] *Knight & Lomas, The Hiram Key*

Chapter Twelve

Adam and Eve

In chapter four, we encountered a strange series of conjunctions that occurred in 6750 BC, which led us to the deduction that this year might have been the year of the birth of the Egyptian pantheon.

One other interesting astronomical phenomenon occurred on or very close to that same year. An analysis of the 25,920-year circle of the poles made by the precessional wobble of the earth (see Chapter Seven) indicates that the pole moved into the Bootes constellation at that same time (Fig 135).

The principal star in the Bootes constellation is the star Arcturus (Fig 136). This star is mentioned in the Old Testament: "Canst thou bind the sweet influences of Pleiades, or loose the bands of Orion? Canst thou bring forth Mazzaroth in his season? or canst thou guide Arcturus with his sons?"[156]

There has been much speculation about the phrase "Arcturus with his sons." Traditionally, Bootes has been the constellation of the "herdsman" and the conventional view is that Arcturus refers to Adam and that the "sons" refer to the "bears" in the constellations of Ursa Major and Ursa Minor.

The concept of Adam being within this constellation fits well with the new birth in 6750 BC However, it is much more likely that the "sons" refer to the stars other than Arcturus that make up the constellation. An examination of the northern stars was undertaken to see if a male figure could be located associated with the constellation Bootes and be

---

[156] *The Old Testament; Job 38, 31-32*

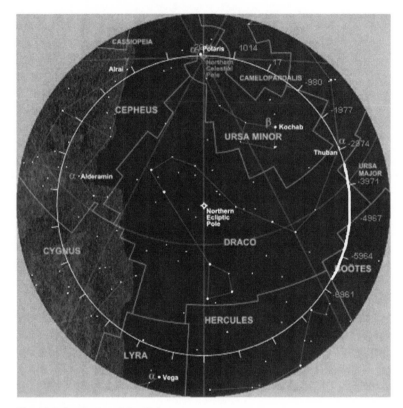

Fig 135 the circle of the Poles

linked to its main star Arcturus. After much research, an interesting figure of a man was indeed created by utilizing the
principal stars in the two constellations, Bootes and Ursa
Major (Fig 137).

This man shape does not itself incorporate the star Arcturus (one of the brightest stars in the heavens), which may
explain why the Book of Job speaks of "Arcturus' sons." Instead, Arcturus is perfectly positioned to represent the position of the *uraei* or serpents seen to ornament the foreheads
of the Egyptian God-Kings (Fig 137).

Given the position of Bootes relative to Ursa Major (the
Chariot), Arcturus could also represent the star that we see

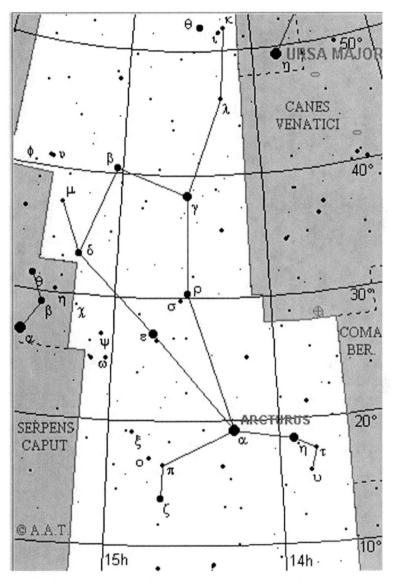

Fig 136 the constellation of Bootes adjacent to Ursa Major

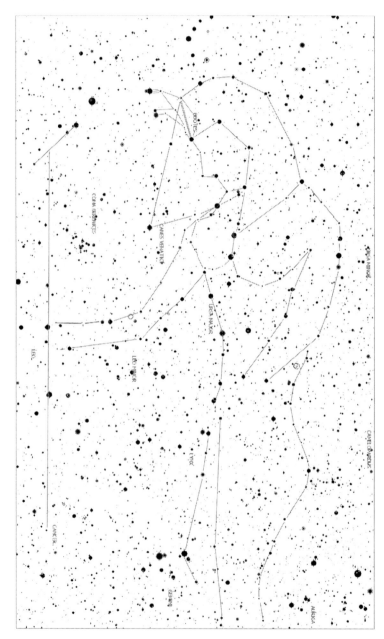

Fig 137 the picture of Adam in Bootes and Ursa Major

on the forehead of the charioteer on the chariot Tarot card (Fig 97).

The evidence suggests, therefore, that the picture of a man that has been created in Bootes and Ursa Major (Fig 137) represents Adam. Since Adam was the first man and was the first link between God and mankind, he was the first God-King. This fits with him wearing a version of the Egyptian head-dress. Three stars, including Arcturus, are in the correct place to create the *uraei* of the Egyptian God Kings (Fig 138); the seventh star of Ursa Major helps create the conventional beard of the Egyptian God Kings. The ribs of the man are formed by the four principal stars of Ursa Major

The right hand of the figure would seem to be holding something and there are sufficient prominent stars in an area

Fig 138 the uraei on the forehead of Tutankhamen

to suggest that it could be the staff of a herdsman or the rod of office held in so many of the paintings of the Egyptian God Kings (Fig 139).

His left hand is either hiding or holding the man's phallus and the two stars below the position of the left hand are perfectly positioned to represent the man's testicles. If this man is meant to be Adam, it behooves us to look closely at the story of this first man to see what coincidences might be determined between the man in the story and the image in the heavens.

Chapter 1 of The Book of Genesis tell us,

God said, "Let the earth produce every kind of living creature in its own species: cattle, creeping things and wild animals of all kinds.' And so it was. God made wild animals in their own species, and cattle in theirs, and every creature that crawls along the earth in its own species. God saw that it was good. God said, 'Let us make man in our own image, in the likeness of ourselves, and let them be masters of the fish of the sea, the birds of heaven, the cattle, all the wild animals and all the creatures that creep along the ground.' God created man in the image of himself, in the image of God he created him, male and female he created them. God blessed them, saying to them, 'Be fruitful, multiply, fill the earth and subdue it. Be masters of the fish of the sea, the birds of heaven and all the living creatures that move on earth.' God also said, 'Look, to you I give all the seed-bearing plants everywhere on the surface of the earth, and all the trees with seed-bearing fruit; this will be your food. And to all the wild animals, all the birds of heaven and all the living creatures that creep along the ground, I give all the foliage of the plants as their food.' And so it was. God saw all he had made, and indeed it was very good. Evening came and morning came: the sixth day."

These eight verses tell us that God created man and woman on the sixth of seven days. The verse following this tells us that God rested on the seventh day, implying that the creation process (including the day's rest) took a total of seven days.

Fig 139 Osiris holding his staff

The complete precessional cycle takes 25,920 years. If this time period is divided into seven equal periods (great days), each of them would last 3,703 years. This time period coincides very accurately with the length of time between the pole position (on the precessional circle) moving into the constellation *Bootes* and it leaving the constellation of *Ursa Major* (marked in white in figure 135).

If this is the "great day" during which man and woman were created, then it is important that the creation story fits the picture in the heavens. In other words, the picture which contains all the elements of the Adam and Eve story must lie within the *Bootes* and *Ursa Major* constellations.

Genesis gives us more detail about the creation of man and woman:

> God took the man and settled him in the Garden of Eden to cultivate and take care of it. The God gave the man this command, "You are free to eat of all the trees in the garden. But of the tree of the knowledge of good and evil you are not to eat; for, the day you eat of that, you are doomed to die." God said, "It is not right that the man should be alone. I shall make him a helper." So from the soil God fashioned all the wild animals and all the birds of heaven. These he brought to the man to see what he would call them; each one was to bear the name the man would give it. The man gave names to all the cattle, all the birds of heaven and all the wild animals. But no helper suitable for the man was found for him. Then, God made the man fall into a deep sleep. And, while he was asleep, he took one of his ribs and closed the flesh up again forthwith. God fashioned the rib he had taken from the man into a woman, and brought her to the man. And the man said: This one at last is bone of my bones and flesh of my flesh! She is to be called Woman, because she was taken from Man. This is why a man leaves his father and mother and becomes attached to his wife, and they become one flesh. Now, both of them were naked, the man and his wife, but they felt no shame before each other.

Eve was created from the rib of the man and she was brought to the man. This means that a rib of man must be integral in the formation of the woman. "They become one flesh" can only mean that each of their flesh occupies the same space in the heavens.

In chapter eleven, we identified the location of Isis (Fig 132). To see how the images of the man and women fit together, the two illustrations (Fig 132 and Fig 137) were superimposed without Isis' wings (Fig 140). Remarkably, when this is done, the body of Isis lies over the ribs of the man figure. In addition, her left hand lies close to the mouth of the male and her right hand is hiding or holding the male phallus. The right hand position may be another aspect of the mystery of Isis and Osiris outlined in Chapter Four where Isis is the one who finds and reinvigorates the lost phallus of her dismembered husband.

The story of Adam and Eve does not end with their creation. Genesis Chapter 3 tells us, "Now, the serpent was the most subtle of all the wild animals God had made. It asked the woman, 'Did God really say you were not to eat from any of the trees in the garden?' The woman answered the snake, 'We may eat the fruit of the trees in the garden. But

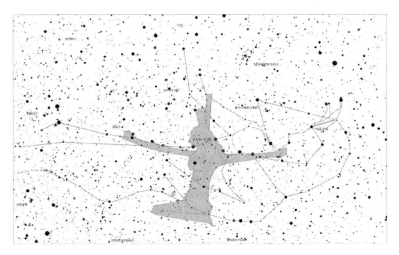

Fig 140 the figure of Isis overlaying the image of the first man

of the fruit of the tree in the middle of the garden God said, 'You must not eat it, nor touch it, under pain of death.'"

For pictorial image of this story to be valid, there needs to be a "tree in the middle of the garden." Chapter three discussed in detail the question of a tree or trees forming an integral part of ancient theological thinking in a wide variety of ideologies. A depiction of the tree that lies in Bootes (the base) and Ursa Major (the trunk and foliage) was illustrated in Fig 37. This tree lies directly over the figures of the man and Isis and a representation of the superimposition is given in Fig 141. Genesis Chapter 3 continues, "Then the serpent said to the woman, 'No! You will not die! God knows in fact that the day you eat it your eyes will be opened and you will be like gods, knowing good from evil.' The woman saw that the tree was good to eat and pleasing to the eye and that it was enticing for the wisdom that it could give. So she took some of its fruit and ate it. She also gave some to her husband who was with her, and he ate it."

If we assume that the brighter stars in the constellation are fruit on the tree, the image created in Fig 124 satisfies these aspects of the Adam and Eve allegory very precisely. One of the four principal stars of Ursa Major is in her mouth. There is fruit in the woman's right hand (she took some of its fruit) and fruit in her mouth (and ate it) and fruit in her left hand, which lies close to the mouth of the man (she gave some to her husband who was with her and he ate it).

The serpent has not been positioned on the same image since his/its identity is open to question. If, however, he/it is Satan (as illustrated in Fig 113), then his face is located over the four main stars of Ursa Major and he/it would overlay the figure of Isis so that his face is upside down to and facing hers with his mouth close to her ear (Fig 142). In this position, he/it is ideally placed to tempt and even overpower her. This interpretation would seem to be confirmed by the Book of Revelation where there are a variety of interpretations of the "serpent."

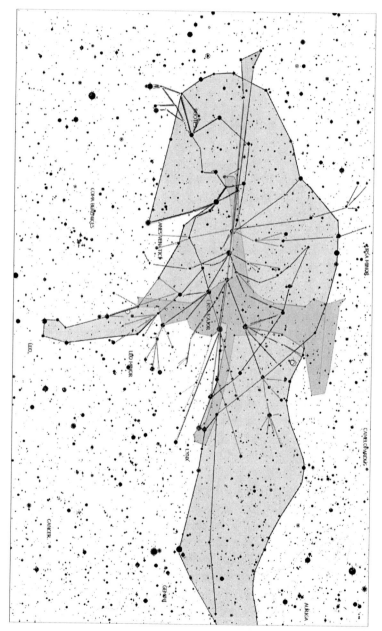

Fig 141 the man, the woman and the tree

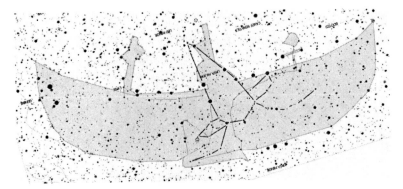

Fig 142 Isis with the head of Satan overlaid

Rev 12,9 states; "and was cast/let fall the dragon the (one) great the serpent the (one) old the (one) called Devil and the Satan the (one) deceiving the inhabited (earth) whole was cast/let fall to the earth and the angels of him with him were cast/let fall". In this part of the Book of Revelation, the dragon named Devil may be a different character to that of Satan whereas in Rev 20,2 (below) the Devil and Satan seem to be the same serpent personality and are different to that of the Dragon. ". . . and laid hold of the dragon the serpent the (one) old who is Devil and the Satan and (he) bound him a thousand years". Rev 20,2

Everything points to there being two serpents, one who is the dragon and therefore (in all probability) linked to the constellation Draconis, and a second called Satan, both from time to time being called Devil, which also means (in Greek) slanderer or fiend. We have already seen that the concept of "evil" may relate to the Satan figure being faced in the opposite direction to the other gods (and their aspects) than can be represented in the constellation of Ursa Major. It is perhaps significant, therefore, that Satan, being in the "evil" mode, is introducing Eve to "evil" which is his nature and to the fruit of a tree which is 90° to both these positions and therefore contains "knowledge of both good and evil."

The story of Adam and Eve does not end with the eating of the fruit. Genesis Chapter 3 continues,

Then the eyes of both of them were opened and they realized that they were naked. So they sewed fig leaves together to make themselves loincloths. The man and his wife heard the sound God walking in the garden in the cool of the day, and they hid from God among the trees of the garden. But God called to the man. "Where are you?" he asked. "I heard the sound of you in the garden," he replied. "I was afraid because I was naked, so I hid." "Who told you that you were naked?" he asked. "Have you been eating from the tree I forbade you to eat?" The man replied, "It was the woman you put with me; she gave me some fruit from the tree, and I ate it." Then Yahweh God said to the woman, "Why did you do that?" The woman replied, "The snake tempted me and I ate." Then God said to the snake, "Because you have done this, accursed be you of all animals wild and tame! On your belly you will go and on dust you will feed as long as you live. I shall put enmity between you and the woman, and between your offspring and hers; it will bruise your head and you will strike its heel." To the woman he said: "I shall give you intense pain in childbearing, you will give birth to your children in pain. Your yearning will be for your husband, and he will dominate you." To the man he said, "Because you listened to the voice of your wife and ate from the tree of which I had forbidden you to eat, accursed be the soil because of you! Painfully will you get your food from it as long as you live. It will yield you brambles and thistles, as you eat the produce of the land. By the sweat of your face will you earn your food, until you return to the ground, as you were taken from it. For dust you are and to dust you shall return." The man named his wife "Eve" because she was the mother of all those who live. God made tunics of skins for the man and his wife and clothed them. Then Yahweh God said, "Now that the man has become like one of us in knowing good from evil, he must not be allowed to reach out his hand and pick from the tree of life too, and eat and live forever!" So Yahweh God expelled him from the Garden of Eden, to till the soil from which he had been taken. 24 He banished the man, and in front of the Garden of Eden he posted the great winged creatures and the fiery flashing sword, to guard the way to the tree of life.

The winged creatures and the sword are hidden in the constellation of Ursa Major and have been identified in previous chapters. The concept of God expelling the man from the Garden of Eden still needs to be explained.

Chapter 3, verse 22 of Genesis tells us that "the man has become like one of us." The "us" confirms the early Egyptian view of God and implies that there is more than one God or more than one aspect of God and that Adam became like them because he ate "the fruit" in disobedience of a direct instruction. It goes on to say, "he must not be allowed to reach out his hand and pick from the tree of life too and to live and eat forever." In other words, the eating of the fruit gave knowledge of good and evil and the picking of the fruit by Eve meant that because of her actions she was able to "live forever" and that this privilege was to be kept from her partner.

In the Egyptian pantheon the full figure of the man (Osiris) is not contained in the constellation Ursa Major and his presence became camouflaged by the unseen pentagon at the center of the four principal stars.

The face of Adam also fell outside the constellation and in his case was found in the constellation of Bootes. If "Heaven" was (or came to be) within the boundaries of Ursa Major, this could explain Adam's expulsion once the pole position had moved out of Bootes and into the Ursa Major constellation.

The woman, in whatever aspect is assigned to her, stayed and can be located in Heaven at the center of the Northern stars. She is Eve and Nut, the first mother, the goddess of the heavens and the sky, depicted covered in stars, the female counterpart of the many aspects of God.

Now it is possible to see how Nut can form three of the sides of a regular pentagon in which the virgin birth takes place (Fig 143). In the aspect of earthly wife and child bearer, she was "expelled," which could explain her appearance as she nurses the baby Horus, who is the constellation of Ursa Minor.

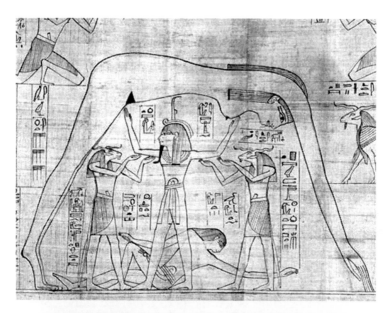

Fig 143 Nut as mother of Heaven and as the Heavenly Cow (inset)

This analysis of the Adam and Eve myth completes an incredible investigation into the origins of the God story and into the basis for the many elements it contains.

God's creation of man and woman who (as they were the rulers of all things human) were (by definition) the first God-Kings, the location of God in all his aspects, the endurance of the Mother Goddess and the final judgment and destiny of each human being are all explained by allegories woven by ancient astronomer priests. In particular, these allegories seemed to have been based on a period between 6750 and 1000 BC when the pole position passed from Bootes through Ursa Major and Draco into Ursa Minor.

These same priests even allocated controlling status to the supposed master of each particular constellation as it assumed the "pole" position. Whether these allegories were created during this 5750 period or were devised in a period 25,920 years earlier, when the pole traversed same constellations is unknown. The only obvious fact is that the complete story could only have been concocted before it was fully enacted out in the sky. This could have occurred if the observers had the intelligence to forecast the future from extrapolation of their observations or (alternatively) if they had records of previous precessional cycles.

Chapter four told us that Greek and Roman historians recorded the claim that the Egyptian priests (or their predecessors) had kept records for many more than 25,920 years. This claim can never be proven, but if it is true, it would fit with the proposition that the Egyptian God stories were created during an earlier precessional rotation through the same constellations.

Astronomer priests were thought to be wise men but they hid information from the people by declaring that their knowledge and conclusions constituted "Mysteries." At the same time, they imposed their own controls and claimed protected status by declaring themselves to be the intermediaries between the people and the gods above and by suggesting rules of behavior that would belay the wrath of the same gods. At the same time, they gained the confidence of temporal rulers by confirming to them their God King status and by promising the reward of eternity in the presence and company of the gods of Heaven.

It is most likely that the priests believed their interpretations of the stars in the heavens and, because of that, they proclaimed "The Mysteries" with extreme passion, a passion that was able to invigorate the populace and which became basis of "faith" and "belief" amongst the bulk of ordinary people. The effect was a slave-like belief in the teachings and pronouncements of the priests and God-Kings, which brought the welcome benefit of a subdued population and social order.

Postscript

On the seventeenth May 2008, the author met with Callum Jenson to carry out an alignment check on Lincoln Cathedral. During conversation, Callum told the author that his wife and son were both autistic. The following day, the author sent a copy of the star chart that he had been using to create the various images that are included in this book and he asked Callum to show the star chart to his wife and son. Callum sent two emails in reply that are duplicated below:

"Mrs J took one look—and without any prior info from me said that she saw; A man and a woman . . . Adam and Eve . . . getting married . . . and the pairing of chromosomes . . . CJ"

"and then 'binary streaming' . . . and then . . . 'time to stop' . . . scary . . . nearing God. CJ"

Chapter Thirteen

A Summary of the Evidence

In these chapters we have shown a wealth of evidence to show that the ancient god stories were created from illusions relating to the stars in and around the constellation of Ursa Major in the northern sky.

- A copy of the seven principal stars of Ursa Major can be found duplicated on the ground across 302.4 miles of Northern Europe and its existence was known to a select few amongst The Knights Templar and The Cistercians.
- The cup of Ursa Major has been shown to have contained a regular pentagon (and the pentagram it in turn holds), which is the figure/shape at the heart of all sacred geometry, is a self reproducing shape, and was thought by the ancient Egyptians to hold the face of God (chapter five). From the most ancient of times, the five-pointed star has been at the heart of all things arcane.
- The constellation has a series of protrusions from the four stars at its heart and these protrusions can readily be seen and interpreted as horns and/or wings, giving rise to a direct link with the horned and winged gods that dominated the religions of Europe and the Middle East from the most ancient of times.
- The common designations of the constellation as chariot, plough, throne, thigh, cup, and bear are all linked to the mysteries, myths, and magic that interconnect the ancient stories of wise men, prophets, kings, and (more recently) wizards.

- The tree has been at the heart of all sacred stories through the ages and it is no coincidence that the constellation can be depicted as a tree.
- The normal depiction of Nut, the mother of creation, is in the shape of the four principal stars of the constellation.
- The *adze*, a sacred implement used by the Egyptians in *The Opening of the Mouth* ceremony, was shaped in the same shape as the seven principal stars of the constellation
- The ancient Isis-Osiris mystery can be shown to be a re-enactment of the movement of the pole position in the sky through the constellation and its neighbors.
- Egyptian temples were constructed to be aligned with the constellation.
- Chartres Cathedral represents *Dubhe*, which is the star α *(alpha)* Ursa Major (Fig 144) in the ground copy of the constellation. The cathedral points directly at the constellation in the heavens on three of the four principal days in the astronomical calendar.
- Stonehenge is thought to represent the star λ (lamda)Ursa Major (Fig 144) in the ground copy of the constellation (Fig 150). Like Chartres Cathedral, it points directly at the constellation in the heavens on three of the four principal days of the astronomical calendar.
- The ground pattern provides a link to the circle made by the precession of the pole position in the heavens and this circle is linked with the ground position of the key abbeys of France and the location of St. Peter's Basilica in Rome.
- There is a version of The Tarot that is most closely associated with the most esoteric aspects of theosophy, the occult, and the ancient mysteries. The pictures of the four suits (the sword, the staff, the pentacle, and the cup) are all duplicates of pictures that are readily found within the constellation at the four principal days of the annual astronomical calendar. The authors had access

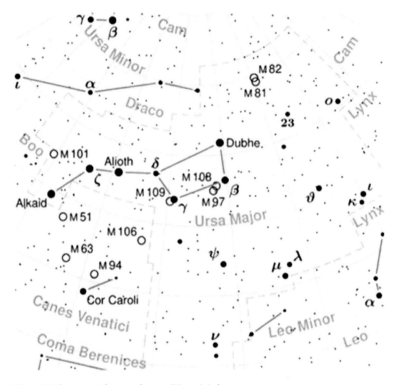

Fig 144 the stars that make up Ursa Major

to the secrets of The Masons who are thought to have inherited information from The Templars.

- A direct link exists between "The World" Tarot Card, the length of the precessional circle made by the apparent position of the North Pole, the Book of Revelation, and the Ursa Major constellation.

- The four living creatures of the Book of Revelation (a lion, a calf, the face of a man, and an eagle) are readily identifiable within the constellation at each of the four corners of the precessional circle made by the apparent sequential position of the North Pole.

- A representation of Satan or The Devil is easily locatable within the constellation and its evil connotation is explained.

- The actual written names of Osiris, Apollo, Abaddon, and YHVH are readily traceable at the heart of the constellation.
- Characters/entities from the Book of Revelation such as the bride, the Lamb of God, the Alpha and the Omega, the sickle, and a pyramid (the tabernacle) are visible. Other items such as the sword, the staff, and the cup are similarly evident.
- The winged figure of Isis is centered in the four principal stars of the constellation.
- The existence, temptation, and eating of the forbidden fruit by Adam and Eve are visible to anyone knowing the route of the precessional pole through Bootes and Ursa Major.

A skeptic will say that the abundance of stars in the sky allows us to make pictures anywhere. Of course this is true! What is incredible in this instance is that the particular pictures that are central and important to the Celtic, Egyptian, and Judeo/Christian religions are all locatable within and around the same constellation and the majority of them incorporate the four stars at its very center. More importantly, the pictures and stories that are central to the mysteries of these great religions can be seen and understood when we plot the position of the pole though Ursa Major and its neighboring constellations. There can be no doubt that this is not just some random coincidence. It is the greatest mystery of all time, written in stone for us to now uncover.

The human tendency to allocate divine characteristics and offer occult explanations to those things that we do not understand led our ancestors to create gods and god stories from their observations of the heavens. Those recounting the stories were the sages, the learned people of the age. They were respected as priests and magicians and were therefore not to be argued with by their audience. Common folk were told to believe and they did believe. "Faith" became so strong that the leaders of organized religions were able to incite their followers to defend and prosecute this "faith" with their lives. It even led to the development of an excuse for the slaughter of our fellow man under labels such as "Holy War."

The concept of tribes was understandable in the context of extended families on an under populated planet. The emergence of the idea of Nation States was allied in part to natural geographical boundaries that confined the various tribes but also to the emergence of Organized Religions and the beliefs that underpinned them. Until very recently, church and state were intertwined and religion was used by kings and other self appointed State administrators as a means of controlling its citizens. At the same time, a small but privileged few knew the secrets that underscored the prevailing religion but they were unable or unwilling to give more than occasional signs of their secret knowledge. An example of this might be seen in the actions of the Duke of Normandy when he invaded England.

The original coat of arms of Normandy was instituted by Rollo, who took control of the province in the tenth century. It consisted of a single lion, sometime passant, sometimes guardant (Figs 145 and 146).

There is argument about the origins of the three lions of England. Some claim that the three lion emblem was introduced by King Richard the Lionheart at the time of the Third Crusade. However, there are contemporaneous pictures that show William the Conqueror wearing the English crown and sporting a shield and other excessive ornamentation that bears three lions (Fig 147).

Fig 145 the lion passant of Normandy

Fig 146 the lion on the Norman shield

It can be deduced, therefore, that one of the first tasks of William, after assuming the English throne, was to alter the coat of arms so that it portrayed three lions. Why did he do this? What was so important about three lions?

We know from our examination of the locations of "the four living creatures" found in the Book of Revelation that Ursa Major can be represented as a lion passant. To the initiated

Fig 147 William the Conqueror with his three lions

that would mean that the ground duplication of the constellation in Northern France was a duplication of the same lion.

What is not so obvious is the concept that proximate to the ground location of the seven stars of Ursa Major would lay similarly prescribed and sized ground representations of Leo Minor and Leo Major, which would lie over the British Isles.

Leo Minor would lie over the English South Midlands and the alpha and beta stars (Fig 148) may lie over Cambridge

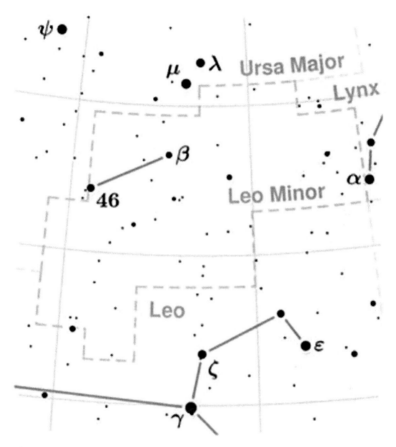

Fig 148 the constellation of Leo Minor

and Oxford. (Fig 150). The more northerly line of stars in Leo
Minor would make an interesting contour from South Wales
in the west, up through the Midlands to the most Northerly
star of the constellation at Louth in the east (149).

Leo Major (Fig 149) would have been constructed with
the alpha star Regulus lying close to Edinburgh (Fig 150)
and it may fall on the chapel made famous for its Templar
inheritance at Rosslyn. Such a coincidence of location may
account for the fact that the area around Edinburgh is called

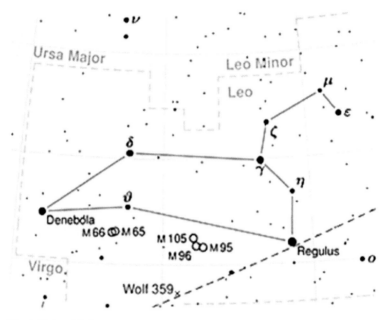

Fig 149 Leo Major

"The Lothians." The Lothians have been inhabited by various peoples since the last Ice Age but the name itself may be the link to the Leo Major constellation.

The name Lothian's earliest written form *Lleudinyawn* occurred in a twelfth century Welsh poem but is probably much older. The meaning of the name is debated but may mean "the land of Lleu's fortress." In Welsh, Llew meant "lion" and it is likely that Lleu was a local variant. In other words, the ground position of *Regulus*, the alpha star in the Leo Major constellation, lies at the heart of "the land of the lion's fortress."

William the Conqueror's alteration of the Coat of Arms from two lions to three is in itself strong evidence that he believed the move to be significant. If so, it is also an indication that William and/or his advisors were aware that Ursa Major had been copied on the ground in Northern France and that Ursa Major could be seen and represented as a lion.

William (*Guillaume le Conquérant*) was born in 1027 and was therefore thirty-six years old when he led his forces into England. He was two years older than Robert of Molesmes who, may years later (1098), was to drive the foundation of the Cistercian order. The first Crusade left France at about the same time this new order was established and twenty years before the formation of the Knights Templar.

From the time of his marriage in 1053 until his death, William did form a close relationship with the Clunic Abott of Bec, Lanfranc. Lanfranc was born in 1005 at Pavia, where later tradition held that his father, Hanbald, held a rank broadly equivalent to magistrate. He was trained in

Fig 150 The UK with the approximate positions of μ, λ (mu, lamda) Ursa Major, Leo Minor and $\alpha \, \eta, \gamma, \zeta, \mu, \epsilon$ (alpha, eta, gamma, zeta, mu, epsilon) Leo Major

the liberal arts, a field in which northern Italy was famous. About 1039 he became the master of the cathedral school at Avranches, but in 1042 he entered the newly founded Bec Abbey where, until 1045, he lived in absolute seclusion. He was then persuaded by Abbot Herluin to open a school in the monastery. From the first he was celebrated (*totius Latinitatis magister*). His pupils were drawn not only from France and Normandy, but also from Gascony, Flanders, Germany, and Italy.

Many of them afterwards attained high positions in the Church and it is possible that one, Anselm of Badagio, became pope under the title of Alexander II. The favorite subjects of his lectures were logic and dogmatic theology.

He opposed the uncanonical marriage of William with Matilda of Flanders (1053) and for his reward he was exiled.

The quarrel was settled when he was on the point of departure and he undertook the difficult task of obtaining the pope's approval of the marriage. Lanfranc successfully interceded at the same council, which witnessed William's third victory over Berengar (1059), and he thus acquired a lasting claim on William's gratitude. In 1066 Lanfranc became the first abbot of St. Stephen's at Caen and was appointed archbishop of Canterbury. From then on, Lanfranc exercised a perceptible influence on his master's policy. William adopted the Clunic program of ecclesiastical reform, and obtained the support of Rome for his English expedition by assuming the attitude of a crusader against schism and corruption. It was Alexander II, a pupil of Lanfranc's and a close friend, who gave the Norman Conquest the papal benediction.

As a Benedictine Abbot, Lanfranc would have been a confidant of Robert of Molesmes. He may therefore have been party to knowledge that Robert subsequently used in the positioning of the fist abbey at Citeaux. At the very least he would have shared the same Clunic philosophies. Whatever the origins of their beliefs, we can deduce on the basis of the evidence we know that someone within the group that was advising William knew something of the relevance of the three lions encompassing France and its neighbor across the English Channel.

Just another coincidence! There are those who will say that there is nothing to link such a change in coats of arms to the patterns on the ground and certainly nothing to link them to ancient god myths. Again we must say that this may be true. However, when the wealth of circumstantial evidence is overwhelming and it all points in the same direction, and there is little or no bulk of actual evidence pointing to a single alternative explanation, the deduction is irrefutable. "When it looks like a duck, walks like a duck, and quacks like a duck, it must be a duck."

Chapter Fourteen

A Hypothesis

Before the Ice Age that began about thirty-five thousand years ago, there had been about ninety-five thousand years when the climate had been relatively mild. From this period, artifacts, especially art, can be found in caves all over the world. Such a wide distribution of cave paintings suggests that human culture had developed intellectual capability to a high level. Material technology other than basic tools came later.

During the ninety-five-thousand-year period, the Earth was not continuously warm. There were several cold intervals such as one about seventy-five thousand years ago caused by a large volcanic eruption at Toba, Sumatra. Generally, the climate got cooler as time progressed. As the climate deteriorated, most of the humans migrated from the cold areas to the remaining warmer areas. Some of the more highly cultivated people did not relocate to the warmer areas, but stayed on in spiritual communities, and adapted their way of life to the cold weather.

During the Ice Age from about thirty-five thousand years ago until about eleven thousand six hundred years ago, sea levels were lower due to the water in the glaciers. At the peak of Earth's glaciations, about eighteen thousand years ago, sea level was about eight-five meters lower than it is now and land masses that are now separated by water were connected and more easily traversed. Eighteen thousand years ago, the earth looked like the map from Earth and Life through Time, by Steven Stanley (Freeman, 2nd edition, 1989) (Fig 151).[157]

---

[157] *Gary D. Thompson, Quotation and illustration from "Ice-age Bear Constellation?"*

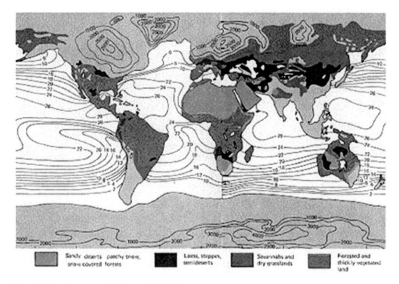

Sandy deserts patchy snow;   Loess, steppes,   Savannahs and   Forested and
snow covered forests   semideserts   dry grasslands   thickly vegetated
                                                                    land

Fig 151 glaciers of about 20,000 years ago

The archaeological evidence of man's existence tells us that evidence of star patterns and star movements could have been collected for more than 25,920 years. Giant star observatories and edifices that align to sun, moon, and star conjunctions such as those at Stonehenge and Newgrange in Ireland could not have been put together as accurately as they were if the architects had only had data accumulated over a short time. The probability is that thinking human beings from these ancient times played "join the dots" with the stars in the sky in the same automatic way that today's civilized world population read books and watch TV. There was little ground light and the stars would have seemed very bright to the ground observer. The patterns they formed would have been intense and real, particularly if they pointed out by wise men and priests.

The Ursa Major constellation was anciently identified as a bear constellation throughout many parts of the world. There is also archaeological evidence that the seven stars were anciently recognized as a constellation. In her 1954 article on

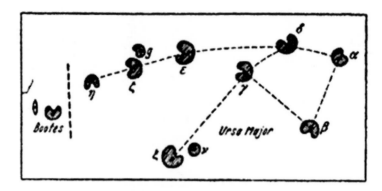

Fig. a. Representation of stars in Ursa Major and Bootes on an amulet from the stone-age. The different size of Mizar and Alcor is noteworthy. The form of the Big Dipper suggests a rather high age for the amulet.

Fig 152 the Maud Makemson Amulet

"Astronomy in Primitive Religion,"[158] the noted astronomer Maud Makemson reproduced what she believed was a representation of the stars in Ursa Major and Bootes on an amulet from stone-age northern Europe (Fig 152). Her further interpretation of the amulet included the fact that:

1. The engraver had taken care to indicate the differences in brightness of the stars by varying the sizes of the cavities.
2. The depicted configuration of the stars indicated a high age for the origin of the amulet.

The amulet's significance could be challenged. However, as if to confirm its significance, a prehistoric map of the night sky has been discovered on the walls of the famous painted caves at Lascaux in central France, known as the Shaft of the Dead Man. The map, which is thought to date back over sixteen thousand years, has fifteen hundred paint-

---

[158] Maud Makemson, The Journal of Bible and Religion, Volume 22, Number 3, July, Pages 163-171

Fig 153 the Summer Triangle

ings of various animals, many of which are said to represent
the stars. As well as dots that represent actual stars, it shows
three bright stars as the eyes of a bull (Fig 154), birdman,
and bird, representing the three stars Vega, Deneb, and Al-
tair, three of the brightest stars in the northern sky, known
today as the Summer Triangle (Fig 153).[159] Dr Michael Rap-
penglueck of the University of Munich has also identified a
fourteen-thousand-year-old star map on the walls of a cave
at Cueva di Castillo in Spain, which he claims includes a
clear illustration of Corona Borealis (Fig 155).

This evidence suggests that early observation of the cosmos
is confirmed by the later construction of astronomical observatories that may, at the same time, have been temples.

The earliest known such location is the Goseck Circle in
the Burgenlandkreis district in Saxony-Anhalt, Germany. It

[159] *Gary D. Thompson, Paleolithic European Constellations - star maps in Lascaux cave in France 16,500-13,000 BC.*

Fig 154 a bull painting in the cave at Lascaux

consisted of a set of concentric ditches 246 feet across, and two palisade rings containing gates in defined places. The Goseck ring is one of the best preserved and extensively investigated of the many similar structures built at around the

Fig 155 Corona Borealis at Cueva di Castillo

same time. Its preservation and investigation have led to the
belief that it was a solar observatory. The palisades had three
sets of gates facing southeast, southwest and north. At the
winter solstice, observers at the center would have seen the
sun rise and set through the southeast and southwest gates
(Fig 156). Potsherds at the site suggest that the observatory
was built *ca* 4900 BC because they have linear designs compared to standard chronologies of pottery styles. The culture
that produced the Circle is called the Stroke-Ornamented
Pottery Culture.

Archaeologists tell us that Goseck Circle was used for astronomical observation. They tell us that it was used to make
calendar calculations and was set up to coordinate an easily
judged lunar calendar with the more demanding measurements of a solar calendar, embodied in a spiritual religious
context.

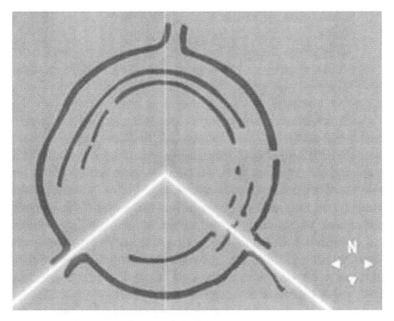

Fig 156 a plan of the Goseck Circle

The most famous temple-observatory is the one at Stone-henge in Southern England (Fig 54). A massive stone construction, it was commenced around 3500 BC and it is estimated that it would have taken three million man hours to complete. Accurate alignments of the sun's rays and key stones occurred on key days in the annual earth-sun-moon astronomical calendar, and recently, eminent archaeologists have shown that it had been a special burial location since its inception. Fig 157 shows a plan of Stonehenge and its geographical alignment. Incredibly, the feeder channel at Stonehenge has the same orientation as Chartres Cathedral. For that reason, the alignments detailed in appendix three that apply to Chartres also apply to Stonehenge:

- A line from the center of Stonehenge past the heel stone is pointed directly at the cup of the constellation of Ursa Major at sunset on the spring equinox.
- A line from the center of Stonehenge past the heel stone points directly at the cup of the constellation of Ursa Major at midday on the summer solstice.
- A line from the center of Stonehenge past the heel stone points directly at the cup of the constellation of Ursa Major at sunrise on the autumn equinox.

Such an accurate alignment is absolute proof of the significance placed by our ancestors on this northern group of stars. It is not difficult for us to imagine that the interpretations of the stars and the resultant stories related to some power which the observers believed was omnipotent. The origins of mankind, the creator, the relationship between humankind and this creator, and where we go when we die are the fundamental philosophical questions that human beings have asked themselves from the beginning of time. The early astronomer priests found their answers in the stars and, because of this, it could be argued that God, in his many aspects, was created by man.

There is little doubt that the dogmatic assertions of the priest astronomers were taken to Mesopotamia and the vari-

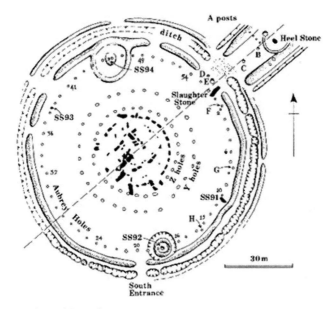

Fig 157 a plan of Stonehenge

ous Middle Eastern areas of civilization in the earliest of times as migration from the cold took people into warmer climates.[160] In places such as Sumeria, Assyria, Akkadia, Chaldea, and Egypt, their wisdom evolved and was interpreted into a variety of ideologies and God stories.

In this regard, Egypt is a treasure trove. It is the one country where accurate records exist in the form of temples, tombs, and pyramids, which contained wall paintings and engravings going back to 3500 BC.

Ancient stories about the origins of the God-King, the creation of Heaven and the Earth, the evil one, horned gods, death and resurrection of the savior, a miraculous child, and the Mother Goddess depicted sometimes as the sacred cow were all promoted and used by the pharaohs to consolidate their power. During the middle kingdom (2055-1650 BC),

---

[160] *Knight & Lomas, The Book of Hiram*

the religious teachings became more refined and more con-trolling. They included the threat of the judgment of the dead by Osiris, whose mysteries were promoted. Some say that these mysteries were based on the ancient religion of Thoth, the supposed original architect planner God and this view is perhaps confirmed by the claims of a Ptolemaic papyrus:

> Thoth wrote the Book with his own hand and in it was all the magic of the world. If you read the first page, you will enchant the sky, the earth, the abyss, the mountain, and the sea; you will understand the language of the birds in the air, and you will know what the creep-ing things in the earth are saying, and you will see the fishes in the darkest depths of the sea. And if you read the other page, even though you are dead and in the world of the ghosts, you will come back to earth in the form you once had. And besides this, you will see the sun shining in the sky with the full moon and stars, and you will behold the shape of the Gods.[161]

The pharaohs were believers and their efforts to ensure their own afterlife would seem to confirm this. Their sub-jects, who were not given access to the same privileged education as their spiritual leaders, were taught through the annual festivals and the stories and the implied threats that were propounded and celebrated to be obedient citizens.

In those times, Egypt was largely cut off from its neigh-bors by mountains to the south, The Red Sea, and the Medi-terranean Sea to the east and north and by the desert to the west. This relative isolation facilitated uninterrupted devel-opment until Northern Egypt was overrun by the Hyksos around 1750 BC

The Hyksos blended into the culture and religion of the Egyptians during their period in power and, for that reason, the temples and other artifacts remained intact. Soon after 1560 BC, however, the Hyksos were removed from power by Ahmose 1 (1550-1525), and the so-called New Kingdom period of Egyptian history was inaugurated (the eighteenth dynasty) (see chart of eighteenth dynasty pharaohs below).

---

[161] Bojana Mojsov, Osiris, Death and afterlife of a God, Wiley-Blachwell (2005)

During that time, a concerted effort was mounted to rid Egypt of any trace of Hyksos influence. One illustration of that is found in the historical records of Thutmosis III (1479-1425 BC). This sovereign appears to have launched at least twenty-one military campaigns against the Hyksos and their Asiatic allies (Amorites, Hurrians), and in a few of those he boasted that he even crossed the Euphrates River to rout the enemy and to free Egypt from its influence. The ravages and destructions caused by intrusion and war came later when Egypt was conquered by the Romans. The library at Alexandria, which housed many of history's most precious documents, was first burned by Julius Caesar in 48 BC and later overrun during a series of religious based insurgencies.

There has been prolonged discussion amongst researchers about the similarity between the expulsion of the Hyksos and the biblical story of a Jewish exodus.

Eighteenth Dynasty Egyptian Pharaohs

Name	Approximate Dates	
Ahmose I, Ahmosis I	1550–1525	
Amenhotep I	1525–1504	
Thutmose I	1504–1492	
Thutmose II	1479–1425	
Hatshepsut	1473–1458	
Amenhotep	1425–1400	
Thutmose IV	1400–1390	
Amenhotep III	1390–1352	
Akhenaton	1352–1334	
Smenkhkare	1334–1333	possibly co-regent with Akhenaton
Neferneferuaten	1335–1333	possibly Akhenaton's daughter
Tutenkhamun	1333–1324	believed to be the son of Akhenaton
Kheperkheprure Ay	1324–1320	
Horenheb	1320–1292	

The bible states clearly that Joseph and Moses were both prominent in the ruling houses of Egypt. This has led many to speculate that Joseph was first minister serving one of the Hyksos kings.

The Hyksos coming to power about 1750 BC would fit in right nicely with the phrase in the bible, "Now there arose a new king over Egypt, who did not know Joseph" (Exodus 1:8). This bible text refers to a "new king," not a "new pharaoh." This implies a "non-Egyptian King." If this were not the case, it could only refer to the new pharaohs who revolted against the Hyksos and drove them out of Egypt.

If a later date of the Exodus is used, then the four hundred and thirty years added to the date of Seti I, Rameses II, and an Exodus date of 1290-1275 BC would bring us to 1730 BC This would be the time of Joseph arriving in Egypt and taking his authoritative position about twenty years after the Hyksos arrival.

Moses, on the other hand, is a much more elusive personage than Joseph. The Old Testament and the Koran speak of Moses being born in Egypt, brought up in the royal palace, and (later) leading the Israelites in their Exodus.

In a new book titled *The Seventy Great Mysteries of Ancient Egypt*, it is stated (p 273): "Since antiquity, many writers have tried to associate Moses with Akhenaton (Fig 158) Manetho, who claimed that the founder of monotheism, whom he called Osarsiph, assumed the name Moses, and led his followers out of Egypt in Akhenaton's reign. The specter of Akhenaton was also transformed into Moses by writers such as Lysimachus, Tacitus and Strabo." [162]

Agreeing with this school of thought was Sigmund Freud. In his book *Moses and Monotheism* (New York: Knopf, 1939), Freud described himself as thinking the unthinkable. Moses, the liberator of the Israelites, who gave them their religion and laws, was, Freud speculated, an Egyptian who had formerly been a priest and aide to Akhenaton.

---

[162] *Bill Manley, The Seventy Great Mysteries of Egypt, Thames & Hudson (2003)*

Fig 158 stone statue of Akhenaton illustrating his elongated features

The Old Testament tells us that Moses was brought up in the royal household as the son of the monarch and it is not difficult to imagine that a foundling adopted by the royal household would be called Mose, which meant son.

Ahmed Osman, the most prolific modern researcher and writer on this subject, agrees with Manetho and claims that Moses was in fact Akhenaten.[163] He tells us that, during his reign, Akhenaton took moves to abolish the complex pantheon of the ancient Egyptian religion and replace it with a single god, Aten, who was hidden in the essence of the sun.

Osman points out the Egyptian elements of the monotheism preached by Moses as well as his use of phrases and expressions that betray his deep-seated familiarity with Egyptian spiritual practice. He even shows that the Ten Commandments betray the direct influence of Spell 125 in *The Egyptian Book of the Dead*. More importantly, he provides a radical challenge to the long-standing beliefs concerning the origin of Semitic religion and offers a solution to the puzzle of Akhenaton's rebellion against his upbringing and everything he had been taught.

Whether Moses was Akhenaton or someone else brought up in the royal household (as the Bible tells us), he would have been familiar with the intricacies of the Egyptian religion that he encouraged his followers to reject.

The bible tells us that the Semitic peoples that formed the body of the Exodus were devout followers of the ancient Egyptian religious tradition. Even Moses's number one man, Aaron, was of similar inclination. Moses found it very difficult to suppress these beliefs and needed to resort to extreme measures (and some would say trickery) to bring the people in line.

When the people saw that Moses delayed to come down from the mountain, the people gathered themselves together to Aaron, and said to him, "Up, make us gods, who shall go before us; as for this

---

[163] *Ahmed Osman, Moses and Akhenaton, Bear & Company (2002)*

Moses, the man who brought us up out of the land of Egypt, we do not know what has become of him." And Aaron said to them, "Take off the rings of gold which are in the ears of your wives, your sons, and your daughters, and bring them to me." So all the people took off the rings of gold that were in their ears and brought them to Aaron. And he received the gold at their hand, and fashioned it with a graving tool, and made a molten calf; and they said, "These are your gods, O Israel, who brought you up out of the land of Egypt!" When Aaron saw this, he built an altar before it; and Aaron made proclamation and said, "Tomorrow shall be a feast to the Lord." And they rose up early on the morrow, and offered burnt offerings and brought peace offerings; and the people sat down to eat and drink, and rose up to play.[164]

The Bible goes on to tell us of the first slaughter of innocent people. Murder was the prerogative of the initiated and was obviously the prime motivator used by the instigators of the Judeo-Christian-Islamic God that we have today:

And when Moses saw that the people had broken loose (for Aaron had let them break loose, to their shame among their enemies), then Moses stood in the gate of the camp, and said, "Who is on the Lord's side? Come to me." And all the sons of Levi gathered themselves together to him. And he said to them, "Thus says the Lord God of Israel, 'Put every man his sword on his side, and go to and fro from gate to gate throughout the camp, and slay every man his brother, and every man his companion, and every man his neighbor.'" And the sons of Levi did according to the word of Moses; and there fell of the people that day about three thousand men. And Moses said, "Today you have ordained yourselves for the service of the Lord, each one at the cost of his son and of his brother, that he may bestow a blessing upon you this day."[165]

Without deadly force and the killing of nonbelievers, religions that claim to be based on love, peace, and goodwill

---

[164] *The Old Testament, Exodus 32, 1–6*
[165] *The Old Testament, Exodus 32, 25–29*

would not have been born and would not have grown to their current level of influence.

A little more than a millennium after the Exodus, Israel Palestine and Lebanon had been overrun by the Romans. The Hebrew authorities that had suppressed any re-emergence of the old religions were now answerable to a regime whose policy was one of religious freedom. It is possible to imagine, therefore, that in these circumstances, the intellectual underground that clung to the old and secret religions and traditions that had been passed by word of mouth through one hundred and fifty generations brought its deeply held beliefs into the open. The believers in the old religion then were as ardent in their faith as many orthodox Christians, Jews, or Moslems might be today.

The missionaries of the old truth could not use the old god names or tell the old stories in exactly the same way and because of that it invented a new, more modern god story that was constructed around the key elements of the old Egyptian Mysteries.

Imitators of this old religion and those who prosecuted it were clever. They spread a story based on supposed happenings to a real person, a man-god, a superman, someone of the then modern genre.

There were no written records. The stories were spread by word of mouth and it is probable that they were aggrandized with each successive telling. They appealed to the instincts of many people in the lands that surround the Eastern Mediterranean and they echoed legends and myths that people had been told by their parents and grandparents.

It is no coincidence that one of the earliest centers of Christianity was in Alexandria in Egypt. There, philosophers and Gnostics gathered to ponder over the implications of the new faith. The bishops there maintained an ongoing debate with Rome as the doctrine of the early church was formed.

Some 140 years after the Christ person was supposed to have existed, writings on Jesus Christ appeared. Many were not subsequently retained as being worthy of authenticity and the emerging Church ordered them to be hidden, hence their name "Apocrypha." "Perhaps a hundred Gospels were suppressed."[166] Some of the texts of these works have been well-preserved because they "benefited from the fact that they were generally valued."[167] Works such as the Gospels of the Nazarenes, the Gospels of the Hebrews, and the Gospels of the Egyptians, known through quotations taken from the Fathers of the Church, were kept. The same was true of Thomas's Gospel and Barnabas's Gospel.

Some of these apocryphal writings contain imaginary details, the product of popular fantasy. Authors of works on the Apocrypha often quote paragraphs that are literally incredible. Segments such as these are, however, to be found in *all* the Gospels. "One has only to think of the imaginary description of events that Matthew claims took place at Jesus' death."[167]

The Gospels, as we know them, were not mentioned until long after the works of Paul. Before AD 140 there was no witness to the knowledge that a collection of Gospel writings existed. The earliest mention of collective writings was St. Justin's reference to "memoirs of the apostles" in AD 150. It was not until circa AD 170 that the four selected gospels acquired the status of canonical literature.

One can only surmise on the criteria that drove those who made the selection to choose the writings they did. At a time when Rome and Alexandria were competing to be the center of the Christianity, it is perhaps no coincidence that the four "gospels" selected by the Roman contingent included text that indicated that Christ had selected Rome to be the headquarters of the new religion. Three of these four written texts were so similar to one another that their very similarity brings their authenticity into question. If four people in the year 2000 (say) had written commentaries of the life of

[166] M. E. Boismard, Synopsis of the Four Gospels The United Bible Societies (1972)
[167] Introduction to the New Ecumenical Translation of the Bible, New Testament (Introduction à la Traduction oecuménique de la Bible, Nouveau Testament) edited 1972[23]

Madame Tussaud or William Wordsworth, who both died in 1850, and all they had to rely on was the oral tradition of enthusiasts, it is highly unlikely that the four stories would have been similar.

As if to confirm this ambiguity, "the grouping of Jesus' sayings and the sequence of narratives is made by the use of fairly vague linking phrases such as 'after this' and 'when he had' etc. In other words, the framework of the Synoptic Gospels is of a purely literary order and is not based on history."[168]

No record of Christ (or anyone like him) occurred in Roman records. Nothing of anyone who might have been the Christ is found in the Hebrew Talmud. In the end, belief in Jesus Christ really is "a matter of faith!"

The basis on which the Book of Revelation was selected to be part of "the canon" and take its place as the final book of The New Testament is not known. We have seen in the earlier chapters that, coupled with the evidence of the ancient Celtic duplication of Ursa Major in Northern Europe by our Celtic ancestors, it is the one document that provides the link between the Celtic tradition, ancient Egyptian Mysteries, Christianity, the Grail tradition, and the secrets of the Theosophists.

We do know that there was resistance to the authenticity of "the Apocalypse" (as it was described). Circa AD 200, a group designated "the Alogi" claimed that the author of the document was Cerinthus, an intellectual from the first century. The most formidable of these was Dionysius, Bishop of Alexandria, disciple of Origen. The Alogi were condemned as heretics and the authenticity of the St. John Gospel and The Apocalypse was defended by St. Hippolytus, the same Roman Bishop who was responsible for *The Refutation of all Heresies* (Extraction seen in Appendix 5).

During the fourth and fifth centuries there was a tendency to exclude the Apocalypse from the list of sacred books. St.

---

[168] *O Culmann, The New Testament (Le Nouveau Testament);*

Cyril of Jerusalem does not name it among the canonical books (Catech. IV, 33-36), nor does it occur on the list of the Synod of Laodicea, or on that of Gregory of Nazianzus (AD 325-389).

The text of The Apocalypse seems to present a God who pronounces (for himself) the complete opposite philosophy to the "love thy neighbor as thyself" philosophy proposed by Jesus Christ. It mirrors the oppressive and dictatorial tradition of the Egyptian pharaohs and those that established the Jewish tradition. For these reasons, the Apocalypse was only fully included in the canon of the Roman church to coincide with Charlemagne's aggressive repression of the pagans. In the name of Jesus Christ he repressed all who were seen as a threat to Christianity and to the establishment of what grew into the Holy Roman Empire.

Summary

There is evidence that the ancient religions were based on stories concocted from long term observations of the Northern stars. This evidence tells us that the ancients believed that God (in his many aspects) and all his creations were based in and emanated from the area in and around the constellation of Ursa Major. The Celtic priests, who may have been the originators of the story, planned and constructed a copy of the constellation across 302.4 miles of Northern France and West Germany, the area settled by the Arcadians.

In the oldest of times, these God stories travelled to Egypt where, over 2,500 years and continued study and extrapolation of the patterns and personalities produced by "joining the dots" in the sky, they developed into a sophisticated theosophy.

The Ancient Egyptian religions were largely eliminated in the latter half of the final millennium BC Remnants of their underlying theosophy were carried out of Egypt by some of the Semitic followers of Moses and remained suppressed until it was safe for them to resurface. Peoples holding the same philosophical orientation are likely to have reached Israel by more protracted routes during the same period.

The Christ story was an updated version of the ancient Egyptian mysteries introduced when religious freedom allowed a re-emergence of an updated version of the old (Egyptian) religion.

Some intellectuals amongst the evangelists of the new religion knew of its true origins and hid them in the Book of Revelation, which they promoted until it became part of the canon of the New Testament. Some scrolls acknowledging this deception and referencing the ancient mysteries were hidden under the Dome of the Rock in Jerusalem where many believe that they were rediscovered by French knights in the eleventh century.

These scrolls led to a new gothic style of the "palace of worship" in Europe, which appeared at the same time that the Grail myths appeared. They, in turn, were precursors to the re-emergence of the Egyptian Tarot and the theosophical tradition.

The Tarot, the Grail myths, the secrets of the Masons and the Knights Templar, the mysteries of Christian tradition, the ancient mysteries of Greece and Egypt, the God cults of Mesopotamia and the ancient Celtic traditions all came from the same place. The earliest stories of God all related to the stars in and around the constellation of Ursa Major and knowingly or unknowingly have continued to be so.

The stories were all born out of ignorance. Innocent minds studied the stars with the ardor of astronomers and they wondered at their magnificence. In wonderment they tracked the sunrise and sunset over the year and at night they looked up and "joined the dots." Over a long period of time they recorded the 29,520-year circular movement of the North Pole.

Because they did not know that they were scientists and had nothing other than their observations to rely on, they concluded mistakenly that they were observing the home of God. They even identified his secret and divine shape. These first philosophers decided that the Heaven they concocted was where we each came from and it was to this place that they decided we would return.

Today the myths live independently of the stars that helped create them. The human race was misled by scientists, who were confused by observations that they could not explain. As with all things unexplainable, they dubbed their findings supernatural. It is a parody of the human condition that the only proof offered for the continuing God stories is "it's a matter of faith!"

God, as created by these scientist-astronomers, is unlikely to exist. The early stories that helped embed this God into the human consciousness are probably fictions. The incredibly high number of pictures relating to these stories then can be attributed to patterns in the stars around the Ursa Major constellation are too numerous to just be a coincidence.

Key people throughout the ages knew of the fiction yet suppressed the facts from us. The power of faith was and is so strong that anyone questioning the basis for it was and is thought to be deluded. Believers conclude that if other people have a different ideology to them, it is permitted (by God) to follow the Moses example and to revile and even injure these other people in the name of their God. The words attributed to Jesus in Matthew Chapter 10 verse 34 have been prophetic: "Do not suppose that I have come to bring peace to the earth. I did not come to bring peace, but a sword."

Scientists now have their attention focused elsewhere and quantum physicists tell us that there is no God and there is no "time." They believe that *we* create our own reality and that we exist simultaneously alongside other dimensions.

What will we be being told in another 5,000 years? Do we have a continuing cycle that takes us from interpretations of scientific observations to gobbledegook?

Appendix 1
The Self Reproducing Pentagram

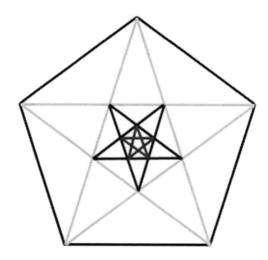

The outer blue shape above is a pentagon. The pentagon is a regular five-sided shape with each side the same length and having each interior angle the same (108°). When the five corners of the pentagram are joined (the green star inside the blue pentagon), a new, but smaller, pentagon is created in the center.

This process can be continued indefinitely, producing a never ending series of small pentagons–blue, green, blue, purple, etc . . . Alternatively, one can produce an indefinite series of ever larger pentagons by extending each of the sides until it meets one of the other extended sides. For example, the blue pentagon in the center produces the green pentagon outside it, if the sides of the blue pentagon are extended to create the blue star and the green pentagon that encases it.

The regular five-pointed star is called a pentagram or pentacle.

Appendix 2
The Golden Ratio in the Pentagram

In mathematics and the arts, there are parts included in the golden ratio. The golden ratio is achieved when the ratio between the sum of these two parts and the larger part is the same as the ration between the larger part and the smaller. The golden ratio is approximately 1.618. It is a mathematical constant, usually denoted by the Greek letter φ (*phi). In other words, the Golden Section or Golden Ratio divides a line at a point such that the smaller part (b) relates to the longer (a) as the longer part (a) relates to the entire length (a+b): the ratio of the lengths of the two sides is equal to the ratio of the longer side to the sum of the two sides

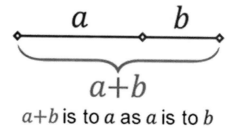

$a+b$ is to a as a is to b

The Egyptians and the Greeks incorporated this "divine" ratio or divine proportion into the design of their pyramids and temples. This process has continued since that time so that many artists and architects have proportioned their works to approximate the golden ratio, especially in the form of the golden rectangle, in which the ratio of the longer side to the shorter is the golden ratio, believing this proportion to be aesthetically pleasing. To the Renaissance artists and designers of Gothic Cathedrals, this "divine" proportion was an essential ingredient that produced harmony.

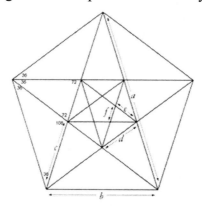

In the pentagram a/b = phi

$$b = c + d$$
$$(c + d)/c = b/c = phi$$
$$c/d = phi$$
$$d/e = phi$$
$$e/f = phi$$

This analysis also tells us that if the side of an isosceles triangle with a base angle of 72° is divided by the base, the result is phi.

Production of the Golden Ratio

In ancient times, designers and architects could reproduce the divine proportion with a length of cord, a piece of stick, and a straight edge

- First they drew their line AB.
- At point B, they drew a perpendicular line BC, BC being half the height of AB. This is relatively easy using the piece of cord and straight edge.

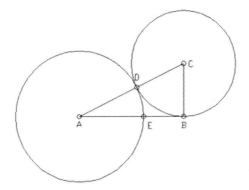

- Using the cord tied to the stick they drew a circle around B with radius AB.
- Using the straight edge they extended the line AB.
- From A and from the point where extended AB meets the larger circle, they drew arcs, which would have intersected above and below point B.
- Half the length of AB was obtained by folding a piece of cord (length AB) in two.
- Next they drew a line joining points A and C.
- They then drew a circle at point C with radius CB. Circle C intersected AC at point D.
- Finally centered at point A, they drew a circle with radius AD. This circle intersected AB at E.
- The Golden Section or Divine Ratio is AE/EB= Phi=1.618. . .

Appendix 3
Star Charts

Star chart at sunset on the Spring Equinox 1200 AD–
Chartres is at the center of the picture and its orientation is
indicated by the line on the chart.

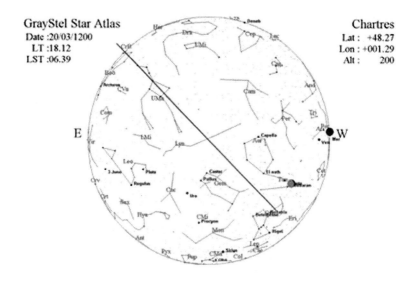

Star chart at midday on Summer Solstice 1200 AD–Chartres is at the center of the picture and its orientation is indicated by the line on the chart.

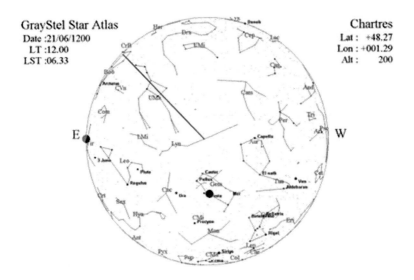

Star chart at sunrise on Autumn Equinox 1200 AD–Chartres is at the center of the picture and its orientation is indicated by the line on the chart.

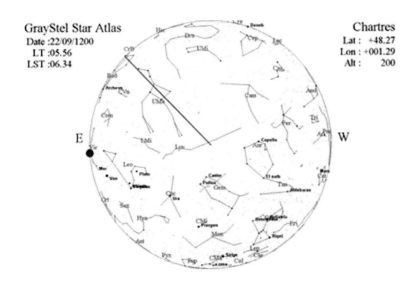

Appendix 4
The Four Key Days
in the Annual Celestial Cycle

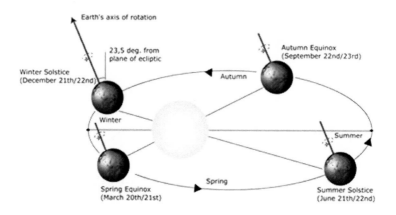

The earth is tilted relative to its plane of rotation around the sun. In the summer, the northern hemisphere is tilted towards the sun and in the winter, it is tilted away from the sun.

As the earth rotates around the sun, there is a day when in the northern hemisphere the tilt of the earth is directly towards the sun and the northern hemisphere experiences the longest daylight of the year. This day is known as Summer Solstice or midsummer's day.

Six months later, the tilt of the earth is directly away from the sun and the northern hemisphere experiences its shortest day, known as Winter Solstice or midwinter's day.

In spring there will be a day when the plane of the tilt of the earth is at right angles with the plane of Earth's rotation around the sun. On that day, the northern hemisphere experiences a day when there is as much daylight in the twenty-four hours as there is night time. This day is known as Spring Equinox.

The converse will be true in autumn. Again, the plane of the tilt of the earth will be 90° to the plane of the rotation of the earth around the sun. This time, it will be a transition from long days to long nights and at the point of transition, there will be a day when the length of the day equals the length of the night. This day is called Autumn Equinox.

APPENDIX 5
The Refutation of All Heresies

Chapter 48. Invention of the Lyre; Allegorizing the Appearance and Position of the Stars; Origin of the Phoenicians; The Logos Identified by Aratus with the Constellation Canis; Influence of Canis on Fertility and Life Generally (translation by the rev J H MacMahon M.A).

And Aratus says that (the constellations) Lyra and Corona have been placed on both sides near him—now I mean Engonasis—but that he bends the knee, and stretches forth both hands, as if making a confession of sin. And that the lyre is a musical instrument fashioned by Logos while still altogether an infant, and that Logos is the same as he who is denominated Mercury among the Greeks. And Aratus, with regard to the construction of the lyre, observes: 'Then, further, also near the cradle, Hermes pierced it through, and said, Call it Lyre.' It consists of seven strings, signifying by these seven strings the entire harmony and construction of the world as it is melodiously constituted. For in six days the world was made, and the Creator rested on the seventh. If, then, says (Aratus), Adam, acknowledging his guilt and guarding the head of the Beast, according to the commandment of the Deity, will imitate Lyra, that is, obey the Logos of God, that is, submit to the law, he will receive Corona that is situated near him. If, however, he neglects his duty, he shall be hurled downwards in company with the Beast that lies underneath, and shall have, he says, his portion with the Beast. And Engonasis seems on both sides to extend his hands, and on one to touch Lyra, and on the other Corona—and this is his confession—so that it is possible to distinguish him by means of this (sidereal) configuration itself. But Corona neverthe-

288

less is plotted against and forcibly drawn away by another beast, a smaller Dragon, which is the offspring of him who is guarded by the foot of Engonasis. A man also stands firmly grasping with both hands, and dragging towards the space behind the Serpent from Corona; and he does not permit the Beast to touch Corona, though making a violent effort to do so. And Aratus styles him Anguitenens, because he restrains the impetuosity of the Serpent in his attempt to reach Corona. But Logos, he says, is he who, in the shape of a man, hinders the Beast from reaching Corona, commiserating him who is being plotted against by the Dragon and his offspring simultaneously.

These constellations, "The Bears," however, he says, are two hebdomads, composed of seven stars, images of two creations. For the first creation, he affirms, is that, according to Adam in labors, this is he who is seen "on his knees" (Engonasis). The second creation, however, is that according to Christ, by which we are regenerated; and this is Anguitenens, who struggles against the Beast, and hinders him from reaching Corona, which is reserved for the man. But "The Great Bear" is, he says, Helice, symbol of a mighty world towards which the Greeks steer their course, that is, for which they are being disciplined. And, wafted by the waves of life, they follow onwards, having in prospect some such revolving world or discipline or wisdom that conducts those back that follow in pursuit of such a world. For the term Helice seems to signify a certain circling and revolution towards the same points. There is likewise a certain other "Small Bear" (Cynosuris), as it were some image of the second creation that formed according to God. For few, he says, there are that journey by the narrow path.[15] But they assert that Cynosuris is narrow, towards which Aratus[15] says that the Sidonians navigate. But Aratus has spoken partly of the Sidonians, but means the Phoenicians, on account of the existence of the admirable wisdom of the Phoenicians. The Greeks, however, assert that they are Phoenicians, who have migrated from (the shores of) the Red Sea into this country where they even at present dwell, for this is the opinion of Herodotus. Now Cynosura, he says, is this lesser Bear, the second creation; the one of limited dimensions, the narrow way, and not Helice. For he does not lead them back, but guides forward by a straight path, those that follow him being the tail of Canis. For Canis is the Logos, partly guarding and preserving the flock, that is plotted against by the wolves; and partly like a dog, hunting the beasts from the creation, and destroying them; and partly producing all things, and being what they express by the name "Cyon" (Canis), that is, generator. Hence it is said, Aratus has spoken of the rising of Canis, expressing himself thus: "When, however, Canis has risen, no longer do the crops miss." This is what he says: Plants that have been put into the earth up to the period of Canis' rising, frequently, though not having struck root, are yet covered with a profusion of leaves, and afford indications to spectators that they will be productive, and that they appear full of life, though in reality not having vitality in themselves from the root. But when the rising of Canis takes place, the living are separated from the dead by Canis; for whatsoever plants have not taken root, really undergo putrefaction. This Canis, therefore, he says, as being a certain divine Logos, has been appointed judge of quick and dead. And as the influence of Canis is observable in the vegetable productions of this world, so in plants of celestial growth — in men — is beheld the power of the Logos. From some such cause, then, Cynosura, the second creation, is set in the firmament as an image of a creation by the Logos. The Dragon, however, in the center reclines between the two creations, preventing a transition of whatever things are from the great creation to the small creation; and in guarding those that are fixed in the great creation, as for instance Engonasis, observing at the same time how and in what manner each is constituted in the small creation. And the Dragon himself is watched at the head, he says, by Anguitenens. This image, he affirms, is fixed in heaven, being a certain wisdom to those capable of discerning it. If, however, this is obscure, by means of some other image, he says the creation teaches men to philosophize, in regard to which Aratus has expressed himself thus: "Neither of Cepheus Iasidas are we the wretched brood."

Appendix 6
Gematria/Isopsephia

Number	Greek	Hebrew
1	α	א
2	β	ב
3	γ	ג
4	δ	ד
5	ε	ה
7	ζ	ז
8	η	ח
9	θ	ט
10	ι	י
20	κ	כ
30	λ	ל
40	μ	מ
50	ν	נ
60	ξ	ס
70	ο	ע
80	π	פ
100	ρ	ק
200	ς	ר
200	σ	
300	τ	ש
400	υ	ת
500	φ	ך
600	χ	ם
700	ψ	ן
800	ω	ף

The practice of giving each letter of the alphabet a numerical value was first practiced in the wider Mesopotamian area[a]. Each letter had a value and therefore each word had the value that was the sum of the values of the letters in the word. At that time all the gods had numbers, which Simo Parpola[b] has shown to be numerically related by the Assyrian Tree of Life. For example, Sargon (d.705 BC) states that the perimeter of his palace at Khorsabad (16,283 cubits) was equal to his name.

This practice was in common use in Babylon in the Eighth Century BCE. and was further developed in Greece under the influence of Pythagoras (circa 500 BC) where it was known as Isopsephia (equal to the calculation/count). So, for example, Zeus is the Geometric Mean of Hermes and Apollo.[c] This common use is an indication that the science was developed earlier than this and may have been a key to the development of alphabets in the Middle East.

The Hebrew Gematria came from the Greeks. It is claimed that textual specialists, Soferim (counters), were specialists in Gematria and that they used their skill to ensure that the scriptures and torah were replicated without error.

The numbers of the letters in both Gematria and Isopsephia are shown in the table opposite.

---

[a] *Everyday life in Babylon and Assyria; Georges Contenau*
[b] *The Assyrian Tree of Life; Simo Parpola*
[c] *Jesus Christ, Sun of God; David Fidler*

Appendix 7
Words (nouns) Appearing in the Book of Revelation and in *The Book of the Dead*

The Book of the Dead The Book
   of Revelations
King of Eternity king
King of the gods king
King of the kings king
Lord of Bakhu lord
Lord of All lord
Lord of business lord
Lord of Everlasting lord
Lord of Lords lord
Lord of the Sky lord
Lord of the Wereret Crown lord
Lord of the West lord
Lord of truth lord
the (one) blue of head
the (one) golden of body
The Great God the (one) God
Unique One
(the) dead
abomination
abundance authority/abundance–
   wealth/abundance
abyss
accuser
affliction
air
arms
arms of the balance balance/beam
   of the balance

ass
associates
awe fear/awe
balance
barley corn/wheat/grain
battlements wall/fortification/for-
   tress–city/citadel
bear
beauty grace/loveliness
belly stomach
birds
blood
board of offerings altar
body
book scroll/book
boundary mount/boundary
bow-warp
bowl bowl
bread corn/wheat/bread
breadth breadth
breast (of Shu) breasts
breath soul/breath–life breath
brightness glory
brother
brow forehead
bulti-fish
calf calf
canoe
cauldron cup–bowl

cavern cave
chaos gods demons
characters (in the presence of
    Wennefer) crowd
chief
children (of uraei) child/children
city
clothing (of the dismembered
    one) robe
cloak garment/cloak
coffin ark/box
combatants army
coming forth creation/founding
common folk nation/people–peo-
    ple
cone censer
cord chain?
corpse corpse
crocodile beast?
crook staff?
Crown (white) crown
cubit cubit
daily birth
darkness cloud/darkness
day
day of reckoning judgment
day when the god ferries across
Day-bark bowl/cup
the dead the dead
death
deeds righteous deed–word/deed
desert
desire life/desire–lust/desire -
luxury/desire-pain/intense
desire–will/desire–wrath
devastation destruction/ruin/loss
destruction destruction/ruin/loss
dignity burden/dignity
divine words words of God
door

door-bolt key/bolt
double son
dragoman of the two lands de-
    mon–devil–dragon
dust
earth
east
emmer
enemies enemies
Enneads
entourage (who make men)
    crowd–apostles
eternity age/eternity
evil misdeed/evil doing
eye (of sobk) eye
eye (sacred eye) eye
eyes (fiery) appearance/(the)
    eyes–vision/(the) eyes
Face to whom men are ushered
    face
falcon eagle/vulture
falsehood lie
father
feet
ferryman steersman
field of offerings earth/field
field of rushes earth/field–work/
    cornfield
fields lands/fields
fine linen
fire
firmament Heaven/firmament
flame
flesh
flower (of Hathor) hyacinth?
Followers of Horus apostle
food corn–grass/food–supper/
    food–wheat/food
food of the spirits fruit
food offerings supper

foot
forms/shapes appearance
fowl bird/fowl
fruit fruit
garment garment
gates
gifts
god (great) god
gods
gold gold
goodly shape right proportion
guardians of the deserts demons/
    guardian spirits
hair hair
hall of justice court
hand balance balance
hand(s) hand
happy place Heaven?
harpoon sting/deadly weapon
head
heart
helmsman Sailors?–steersman
heron
him who is hidden mystery/hid-
    den thing
hinder parts tail/after part
horns
horned bull
hounds dogs
house tabernacle/house–dwelling
    place
house of cool water tabernacle/
    house
illuminator (great) light/luminary
ills (which are on my flesh)
    plagues–sores
image (secret image) idol?–im-
    age–likeness
intelligence wisdom/intelligence
island

island of fire
incense
inventory cargo?
iron
island
jackals dogs
jasper jasper
joy grace/joy
jug bowl/vessel
justice righteousness–judgment/
    justice
ka
knife (sharp) dagger
knot
labor in excess labor
lake
lake of fire lake of fire
land of Manu Heaven?
land of the dead Hades?
Land of Vindication Hades?–Har-
    magedon?
lands land(s)
laws ordinances
length of eternity age/eternity–
    length
lies lie(s)
likeness
linen
lion-God lion
living one the (one) living
living soul life/living being/soul
loaves
loaves of the gods manna
magic sorcery
magician sorcerer
majesty glory?
male
mankind man/human being
Mansion of the Prince Heaven?–
    shrine/temple -

tabernacle?–door/palace?
Manu-mountain mountain
meal supper/meal
meat flesh
members
men man/men
messenger (of any god) angel/
    messenger
(the) midst
might authority/might–might
milk
mistress wife/mistress
moment of being critical moment/
    right proportion
moon
morning star star bright of morn-
    ing
mother
mountains mountains
mouth
mouths of children
myriad
myrrh spice
name
Names
net (in the river) linen/fishing net
netherworld abyss/netherworld
night
Night-bark ship/vessel
noise sound
north
nose (of the lord of the wind)
obstacle stumbling block
offerings
office (of his forefathers) begin-
    ning/office
offices
ornaments vessels/ornaments
orphan
oura

ox (of Geb) ark/chest/ox
pace speed
pain pain
path way/path
palace door/palace–court/palace
peace
phoenix
pillar (of faince) pillar
pillar (of Myriads) pillar
place
place of truth corpse/ruin/fall
power authority/power–power
praise blessing/praise
presence of Osiris
prison
produce fruit/harvest/produce
property life/property–beast of
    burden/property
prosperity wealth–peace/prosper-
    ity
protector
provisions corn/provisions
ram sheep
rays sun/rays of sunshine
realm of the dead Hades?
rebel-serpent serpent–devil/Satan
rest
right side right side/hand
righteousness righteousness
rising (of Atum) rising (of sun or
    stars)
road street
robber thief
ropes vessels/sail ropes
rule kingdom/rule
ruler
Ruler of Rulers almighty/ruler
    of all
Sacred Land Hades?–Heaven?
sand

scale pan (which weighs truth)
    balance
scorpion
script scroll/written document
seasons
seat throne
secret mystery/secret
secret place Harmagedon?
serpent serpent
serpent of evil Satan
serpent-foe dragon–serpent–
    beast–Satan
servant slave
servant of the master slave/ser-
    vant–woman/wife/servant
seven knots seven stars?
seven spirits
shaft
sharp knife sharp sword
shape work/construction–creature/
    creation–likeness
ship
shouting clamor–railing
shrine
silence
silent land Hades?
silver
sin misdeed–sin
sky heaven/firmament
slaughter murder/slaughter
son (firstborn) child/son
songstresses musicians/poets
soul anger/soul/life/desire–soul
Soul-mansion paradise?–shrine/
    temple
Sovereign king
spirit
spirit shape spirit–image
staff
standing scales balance

star (great) Star (bright)
stars
stern-warp
stick tree/stick
strength
stone (pointed) stone/marble
storm wind/storm
south
speech word/speech
stroke
suffering pain
suite tabernacle
sun-disc sun
sweat water/sweat
sword
table of offerings altar
tablet(s) stone(s)
tail
teeth
temples churches
testament covenant/testament
the Great Place Hades?–Heaven?–
    paradise?
the Presence
the Sovereign king
thick cloth sackcloth/course cloth
thigh
Thinite nome
those who control slaves chill-
    iarchs
three portions three parts
throne
toes
tomb
tongue
tree (moringa) tree (fig) -(palm)–
    tree
tribunal throne/tribunal
truth
turquoise beryl

Two Lands
vindication judgment–fulfillment
visage face/appearance
voice
wall
war
waters water–sea
waterway river
weariness labor/weariness
well fountain/well
west west
wife
will will–anger/will–authority/
    will–grace/free
will–love/will
wind wind
windings fine linen

wine
witness
womb (of Nut) stomach/womb?–
    Womb
woman
women
word
word (of very truth) sound/word–
    word
wounds plagues/wounds
(the) writings scroll
wrath
wrong misdeed–sin
wrong doing misdeed–sin
years (millions of) age/space of
    time/eternity

INDEX

Lightning Source UK Ltd.
Milton Keynes UK
29 September 2010

160552UK00001B/59/P